EAST EUROPEAN MONOGRAPHS

III

WILLIAM O. McCAGG, JR.

JEWISH NOBLES AND GENIUSES IN MODERN HUNGARY

1972

EAST EUROPEAN QUARTERLY, BOULDER
DISTRIBUTED BY COLUMBIA UNIVERSITY PRESS, NEW YORK

FOR
LOUISE,
XANDA,
AND
TORY

TABLE OF CONTENTS

LIST OF TABLES

PREFACE

This study results from research done in Budapest during the winter fo 1966—1967, and during the summer of 1969. I must express my great thanks to the Inter-University Committee on Travel Grants, and to the Hungarian Institute for Cultural Relations, which financed my project during 1966—1967; to the directors and members of the Historical Institute of the Hungarian Academy of Sciences, the Museum of the History of Budapest, the Hungarian National Archive, the National Széchenyi Library, the Ervin Szabó Library, and the Jewish Community in Budapest who have regularly and liberally given me help and advice; and to the Department of History at Michigan State University, which has given me leaves of absence to write up my research.

* * *

My personal gratitude is due in particular to Dr. Péter Hanák of the Historical Institute in Budapest who with his deep knowledge of the Dualistic Era guided me in my project and continuously advised and assisted me in finding my way around Budapest; and to Dr. Károly Vörös of the Budapest Historical Museum who was not only always available for consultation, but also let me use his own research data on the families and individuals here studied. Dr. Sándor Scheiber of the Budapest Rabbinical Seminary also gave generously of his time. Dr. Tibor Kolossa of the Historical Institute and Dr. Károly Jenei of the Hungarian National Archive both read the manuscript critically at an earlier stage. Mr. Samuel Goldberger of Hartford Community College, Professor Gábor Vermes of Rutgers University (Newark), Professor Paul R. Duggan of Michigan State University, and Mrs. Firth Fabend of New York have read and criticized the final manuscript.

I am most indebted to them all for their help, but must stress that they are in no way responsible for any flaws in the final product. Acknowledgement belongs here also to the Misses Edit Mirlay and Márta Tömöry of Budapest who assisted me in the summer of 1969; and to Mrs. Ann Brown who supervised the typing of the manuscript. Fnally, I would like to express my deep obligation to my wife, Louise, who both read and edited the manuscript, and tolerated my foibles all through the years of research and composition.

PART I

INTRODUCTION

CHAPTER I

PROLOGUE

A never-named yet famous physicist is supposed to have been speaking once about a professional congress in Buenos Aires where he exchanged information with colleagues from all over the world; and when asked how men from so many different lands communicated with one another, he is supposed to have replied: "Why, of course, we all spoke Magyar." The anecdote contains a grain of truth. Certain it is that in the international scientific community in recent decades Hungarians have played a most conspicuous role. A very broad public is aware of Leo Szilard and Edward Teller, who helped father the atom and hydrogen bombs; and of Albert Szent-György, the biologist. Any specialist will have heard also of Theodore von Kármán and John von Neumann, of George Pólya and Georg de Hevesy and Jenő Wigner, major figures in the history of modern mathematics, chemistry, and physics. The most surprising aspect of this galaxy of Hungarian "geniuses," [1] moreover, is that the larger number of them are Jews from Budapest, men who are related to one another by social milieu if not by blood, and who attended the same schools in their youth. And — to approach our subject — three of the more prominent, von Kármán, de Hevesy, and von Neumann, were sons of Jewish nobles.

If one moves into branches of the international intelligentsia of the past fifty years that border on science, one will again find large numbers of Hungarians. One may mention Karl Mannheim and Oszkár Jászi in sociology, Sándor Ferenczi and Franz Alexander in psychology, Georg

---

[1] According to some authorities, for example Eugene Wigner, Hungary has produced only one scientific genius, John von Neumann. In this study, however, as will appear below, the word "genius" is used in a slightly broader sense to describe a number of minds which have been both largely endowed with natural talent, and brilliantly creative. See on this problem Laura Fermi, *Illustrious Immigrants. The Intellectual Migration from Europe, 1930—1941* (Chicago: University of Chicago Press, 1968), pp. 4ff. and 53—54.

Lukács in Marxist philosophy, Karl Polányi in political economy, and his brother, Michael, who bridged with overriding brilliance both the natural and the social sciences. Once again, moreover, if one digs into the social background of such men, one is apt to find they were born into Jewish families of Budapest, and that they were related or grew up together; and once again one is apt to find here the offspring of Jewish nobles. Jászi's mother came from a Jewish noble family, for example; and Lukács' father was a Jewish noble.

This galaxy of brilliant scientific minds is one of the factors which has inspired this study of Hungary's Jewish nobles. The other appears when one turns to the study of Hungary herself between the wars. One learns that long before Admiral Horthy entered Budapest on a white horse in the autumn of 1919 as the symbol of conquering counter revolution, Baron Adolf Ullmann and other ennobled Jewish bankers had worked out in exile in Vienna the financial underpinnings of the restoration. [2] One learns also that when American and other Allied military representatives arrived in Budapest, the sons of Baron Weisz, Hungary's munitions king, greeted them, and along with Baron Groedel, another Jewish noble, instructed them about the iniquities Hungary had suffered at the hands of the Bolsheviks and Romanians. [3] Then as one gets into the details of the history of interwar Hungary, one finds looming behind the aristocrats who ruled the country an imposing cluster of capitalists. For example, one son-in-law of Fülöp Weisz, Hungary's leading interwar banker, was for a considerable time Foreign Minister, while the other was a leading member of Parliament. In two critical economic junctures, in 1920 and in 1931—1932, Baron Korányi, a major banker, was called in to be Minister of Finance. Admiral Horthy's bridge-partners, reputed members of his personal circle of advisors, were Leó Buday-Goldberger, the textile industrialist, and Ferenc Chorin, Hungary's leading coal magnate. It has been calculated that between the wars some ten families, closely bound by blood and marriage, controlled between them both of Hungary's leading banks, and thus in effect 50% of the national industrial establishment. [4] In 1944 the Germans allowed Baron Weisz's family free passage to Portugal in order to obtain a twenty-

---

[2] See Gusztáv Gratz, *A forradalmak kora* [The Age of Revolutions] (Budapest: Magyar Szemle Társaság, 1935), p. 194ff.

[3] See Harry H. Bandholz, *An Undiplomatic Diary* (New York: Columbia University Press, 1933), pp. 239, 262.

[4] See Iván T. Berend and György Ránki, *Magyarország gyáripara a második világháború előtt és a háború időszakában* [Hungary's Factory Industry in the Period Before the Second World War, and During the War] (Budapest: Akadémia, 1958), pp. 392—397.

five-year lease on their industrial holdings, so vital were these holdings to controlling Hungary. [5] Capitalists, in a word, played a very considerable role behind the aristocratic facade of interwar Hungary. Almost all these leading capitalists were Jewish, and a remarkable number of them were Jewish nobles.

This book is an historical and sociological study of Hungary's Jewish nobles, a group which has contributed substantially to the great efflorescence of Hungarian scientific geniuses of the past fifty years, and which for many years held overriding economic power within Hungary herself, and thus indirectly political power. There are some three hundred fifty families involved in the group. Their history spans the full breadth of the nineteenth century, and one or two of them played prominent parts in their homeland even after World War II and the catastrophe of German Fascism had wreaked havoc with the lives of most Central European Jews. Our objectives in this study are threefold. The first is simply to record the history of these people, telling where they came from, how they obtained their lofty positions in Hungarian society, and how they obtained their wealth. Our second purpose is to analyze why they became nobles. This is a question of considerable interest; for ennoblement in Hungary perhaps more than elsewhere in pre-1914 Europe implied political choice. It implied both a degree of social conservatism or "feudalization," [6] and a willingness to be considered Magyar as opposed to any other nationality.

Our third objective is more subtle. It is to explore whether the overall experience of the Jewish nobility can afford us some explanations of the galaxy of Hungarian geniuses to which the group contributed. This book is thus not only an essay in historical sociology, but also in cultural history. Naturally, since we will be working with a strictly limited sample, our conclusions will be designed not to close questions, but to stimulate further investigation. But we do hope to intimate in general terms that the economic and social phenomena of the nineteenth century in Hungary contributed more than is commonly suspected to the political and cultural phenomena of the twentieth.

---

[5] See Elek Karsai and Miklós Szinai, "A Weisz Manfréd vagyon német kézbe kerülésének története" [How the Manfréd Weisz Fortune Came into German Hands], Századok, Vol. XCV, no. 4—5 (1961), p. 686ff.

[6] For the literature on the "feudalization" problem in a German context, see the essays by Eckhart Kehr in Hans-Ulrich Wehler (ed.), Primat der Innenpolitik (Berlin: W. de Gruyter, 1968); and Hans Rosenberg, "Die Pseudodemokratisierung der Rittergutsbesitzerklasse am Ende des 19ten Jahrhunderts," in H-U. Wehler (ed.), Moderne Deutsche Zeitgeschichte (Cologne: Kiepenheuer u. Witsch, 1966), pp. 287—308.

* * *

To explain how one can identify Hungary's Jewish nobles is a major
task of this Prologue, and it is not difficult. The Hungarian National Archive
in Budapest contains the surviving records of all the ennoblement processes of Old Hungary, a rich store of biographical and economic information. [7] Moreover, outside the Archive a number of guides exist. Of these
the most important is a *Lexicon of Hungarian Jewry*, published by the Pest
Israelite Community in 1929, [8] which contains, apart from an impressive
number of biographical sketches, a list of 302 Jewish nobles. Another
major guide is a three-volume compilation of names and data relating to
the Jewish nobility which Béla Kempelen, the self-appointed genealogist
of the Hungarian noble class, published late in the 1930's. [9]

Nonetheless, there are two problems involved in identifying the Jewish
nobles which require mention. The first problem derives from the fact that
many of the families which acquired nobility converted out of Judaism. To
define the Jewish nobles, therefore, one must decide whether "Jewish"
denotes a religious or an ethnic quality. For purposes of this study it has
seemed sensible to prefer the ethnic definition. We will consider as Jewish
nobility, regardless of conversion, all those ennobled families which at
some time in the nineteenth century were still Jewish. It has seemed superfluous even to create an abstract standard such as Hitler formulated in the
Nürnberg Laws. Hitler, after all, composed his formula in the 1930's when
Jewish conversion and assimilation in Germany had been going on massively for a century. By then a succession of post-conversion generations

---

[7] The Archives contain three main sets of dossiers which relate to ennoblement.
First are the records of the Hungarian Minister-Attached-to-His-Majesty's-Person,
which were sent from Vienna to Budapest under the Treaty of St. Germain. These contain copies of the actual patents of nobility, documentation needed to obtain it, and materials relating to coats of arms. Unfortunately, much of this documentation was not kept,
and because of a peculiar filing system the dossiers are often impossible to locate. The
second set of dossiers, those of the Hungarian Minister of the Interior, are easier
to work with, and constitute the main archival source used in this study. The third set
of dossiers, those of the Hungarian Prime Minister, are often the most revealing. But
since the Prime Minister concerned himself only with the most important cases, his records
are strikingly incomplete.

[8] Péter Újváry. *A magyar zsidó lexikon* (Budapest: Pallas Nyomda, 1929). Cited
henceforth as *MZsL*.

[9] Béla Kempelen, *Magyarországi zsidó és zsidóeredetű családok* [Hungary's Jewish
and Jewish-Origin Families] (3 vols., Budapest: Viktoria Nyomda, 1937—1939). Cited
henceforth as Kempelen, *Zsidó családok*. Since my research has brought to light less than
30 Jewish nobles not published in *MZsL* or Kempelen, it has seemed superfluous to
burden this study with a list of them.

in once-Jewish families had thoroughly blurred the line between ethnic German and ethnic Jew. The present study is concerned above all with an earlier period, in a country where massive assimilation began only after 1867. Though a new generation of thoroughly assimilated Jews was coming to the fore in the final decades of the Monarchy, it seems highly improbable that anyone in Hungary who was adult enough to acquire nobility prior to 1918 could have been oblivious of Jewishness in his family within the past century.

Abstract definition of Jewishness seems superfluous in our study, also, because there was demonstrably a prevailing uncertainty in Hungary even in the 1920's and 1930's about whether a Jew could effectively cease to be Jewish. The Jewish *Lexicon* and Kempelen's work, for example, reflect efforts by wealthy and prominent originally-Jewish families to obtain the favor of omission from lists of Jews. [10] Kempelen even printed a number of apologies for implications he had published that one or another noble individual might have Jewish blood in his veins; and in one case he published a denial of rumors that a certain family was originally Jewish. [11] One can understand, given the political anti-Semitism of the interwar period, why it was important for the families in question to conceal their origins. But their efforts are *de facto* evidence that they were wholly aware of their Jewishness. Further, the Jewish *Lexicon* editors, reflecting the opinions of the 1920's, compiled their list of nobles according to the principle that anyone was Jewish who had once been Jewish. In the present study, which is historical as well as sociological, it seems only proper to follow the same conventions and, avoiding definitions, to list as Jewish all those families (but only those) which can be documented as such either in the Archive,

---

[10] For example, a family named Belatiny-Braun which made a fortune producing Hungarian champagne, is mentioned neither on the *MZsL* noble list, nor in Kempelen, *Zsidó családok*. Further, in another volume Kempelen does report on this family, claiming that its forebear changed his name from Brauner to Braun in the 1840's, and that the Brauner family originated in the Rhineland in the 1500's. Kempelen writes that "the family has documents proving it was Catholic at least from the 16th century in its possession." See *Nemesi polgárcsaládok* [Noble Bourgeois Families] (Budapest: nd.), pp. 40—41. In the *MZsL*, p. 391, however, buried in an article on "Industry," it is remarked that the Braun Champagne Firm was Jewish. Further, Gyula Mérei, *Magyar iparfejlődés 1790—1848* [Hungarian Industrial Development 1790—1848] (Budapest: Közoktatásügyi kiadó, 1951), pp. 291—292, reports what the Archives tell of the origins of a distiller family named Braun from Belatinc which came to Pest in the 1830's, and was Jewish. The story there is quite different from Kempelen's.

[11] In Volume II, p. 94, Kempelen volunteered that the prominent Independence Party Deputy, Géza Polonyi was "to his knowledge" not Jewish, although there were "rumors" o the contrary.

or in the *Lexicon*, or in some contemporary Jewish source such as the periodical *Az Egyenlőség* [Equality]. It is worth noting that our list of Jewish nobles is probably incomplete. [12]

The other major problem in identifying the Jewish nobility derives from the term *noble*, for as is well known there was a glittering variety of noble ranks and titles in Austria-Hungary. [13] The simplest solution to this problem has been to eliminate from consideration all Austrian ranks and knightly orders; to minimize the historically important distinction between untitled nobles and titled peers (magnates or aristocrats); and to concentrate on those families who became either Hungarian nobles or Hungarian peers through registration in the *Golden Book* of the Hungarian Crown. [14] This

---

[12] The famous *Semigothäisches genealogisches Taschenbuch...des gesamten Adels Jehudäischen Ursprungs* (Weimar: Kyffhaüser Verlag, 1912—1913) refers to a number of "Hungarian Jewish nobles" whom I have been unable to document; as does the Nazi, Klaus Schickert, *Die Judenfrage in Ungarn. Jüdische Assimilation und antisemitische Bewegung im 19. und 20. Jahrhundert* (Essen: Essener Verlag, 1937), pp. 95—96. Some of these nobles are demonstrably not Jewish, but since most stem from before 1850, it is difficult to be sure. Several Hungarian historians, most particularly the late Zoltán Horváth, have identified prominent late-nineteenth-century personalities as Jewish nobles whom I have been unable to document. It must be mentioned that in at least one case (Lajos György Losteiner-Arányi) *MZsL* has erroneously labelled a German as a Jew. See Pál Gulyás, *Magyar irók élete és munkái, új sorozat* [The Lives and Works of Hungarian Writers. New Series] (Budapest: József Kertész, 1939—1944), Vol. I, p. 799.

[13] The Austrian system of nobility differed from the Hungarian in that there were below the titled aristocrats two ranks instead of just one. The lowest, the *Edlerstand*, involved the right to place a "von" in front of one's name. The second, the *Ritterstand*, was more elegant though technically not very different. Further, in Austria the title "Baron" *(Freiherr)* was considered rather less aristocratic than it was in Hungary. For these distinctions see Nikolaus von Preradovich, *Die Führungsschichten in Österreich und Preussen, 1804—1918*, (Wiesbaden: Franz Steiner Verlag, 1955); and Berthold Waldstein-Wartenberg, "Österreichisches Adelsrecht, 1804—1918," in *Mitteilungen des österreichisches Staatsarchivs*, Vol. 17—18 (1964—1965), pp. 109—146. A convenient record of Austrian ennoblements is K. F. Frank zu Döfering, *Alt-Österreichisches Adels-Lexikon*, I Band, 1823—1918 (Vienna: Selbstverlag d. Verfassers, 1928).

[14] A useful handbook to the whole question of nobility in Hungary is Béla Kempelen, *A nemesség. Útmutató az összes nemességi ügyekben* [The Nobility. A Guide to All Matters Relating to the Nobility] (Budapest: Gyula Benkő, 1907). Apart from the original register in the Archive building, there are three aids to use of the Golden Book of the Dualistic Era. The first is incomplete: Béla Kempelen, *Magyar nemesi almanach* [Hungarian Noble Almanac] (Budapest: 1910). The second, and by far the most useful is József Gerő, *A királyi könyvek* [The King's Books] (Budapest: Belügyminisztérium, 1941). This is a prime source for genealogical data. The third aid is useful mainly for using the Archive, and for checking family relationships: József Gerő, *A magyar királyi belügyminiszter által igazolt nemesek, 1867—1937* [Nobles Confirmed by the Hungarian Minister of the Interior] (Budapest: Kovács és Szegedi, 1938).

means elimination of a number of Hungarian Jewish families who acquired noble rank through Austrian knighthood; but it also means elimination of all but two questions in the definition of a Hungarian Jewish noble. The first remaining question relates to the fact that after a Parliamentary reform in 1885 in Hungary, the King gave a number of Jewish persons either personal or hereditary membership in the House of Lords [15]. Since this membership brought glory and privilege in many respects exceeding ordinary peerage, it has seemed advisable to include such appointees. The second question emerges because parallel to personal nobility in Hungary, as in Austria, there was a table of court councilor ranks which were nonhereditary, but which at the higher levels brought status far exceeding ordinary nobility. On the whole it has seemed advisable to eliminate these categories from the Jewish noble group. Tradition has it, however, that in the final years of the Monarchy the King used the highest of these ranks, Privy Councilor, to reward prominent Jews without making them Counts. [16] Since the recipients were few, yet exceedingly illustrative of trends in ennoblement, it has seemed useful to honor this tradition, and to include them in our sample.

In such fashion it is possible to establish that the Hungarian Jewish nobility, created between 1800 and 1918, involved some thousands of male ndividuals in 346 different families. [17] Of these, 338 families acquired the

---

[15] There are numerous parliamentary records. I have used in particular: János Szerencs (ed.), *Főrendiház évkönyve, 1900* [House of Lords Yearbook] (Budapest: Pesti Könyvnyomda, 1900); Dr. Sándor Halász (ed.), *Országgyülési almanach 1886* [Parliamentary Almanac] (Budapest: Atheneum, 1886); Albert Sturm (ed.), *Országgyülési almanach* [Parliamentary Almanac] (Budapest: Pesti Lloyd Társaság, 1897, 1905, and 1910); and László Lengyel and Gyula Vidor (eds.), *Magyar országgyülési almanach* [Hungarian Parliamentary Almanac] (Budapest: Globus, 1932). There are incomplete lists of Jewish Upper House members in *MZsL*, p. 911, and in Schickert, *Judenfrage in Ungarn*, pp. 101, 103.

[16] These appointments, which were very numerous, are entered in the original Register of the Golden Book in the Archive. Privy Councilors were actually higher than counts, and together with the King's Ministers, the hereditary princes, and the highest-ranking state officials were addressed "excellencia." The counts, most generals, bearers of certain decorations, state officials of secondary importance, and some barons were addressed "méltóságos" (literally, "highness"). Most barons and officers were addressed "nagyságos" (literally, "worthiness"). The list of privy councilors used in this study is derived from the individual biographies in *MZsL*, and in *Országgyülési almanach*.

[17] There are two technical problems involved in counting nobles and noble families. The first emerges because married women sometimes boasted nobility after it was acquired by their parents, even though their husbands did not acquire it. This raises the question of whether one should consider the ladies' families "noble." In the present study such

rank *magyar nemes* [Magyar noble]: twenty-eight entered the peerage with baronial rank; seventeen acquired hereditary or personal membership in the Upper House of the Parliament; and ten became Privy Councilors. Of the Upper House members, only two neither acquired hereditary rank nor entered the nobility in some other fashion; [18] of the Privy Councilors, four acquired no other rank. [19] A chronological graph (Table 8 in Chapter V below) shows that only eight of these new nobles were created prior to the Austro-Hungarian constitutional compromises of the 1860's, and that 220, more than half of them, were created after 1900.

* * *

We must insert a word regarding the Hungarian scientific geniuses, a group about which the reader will hear a great deal in this study, but whose definition presents obvious difficulties. Sometimes people use the expression "scientific genius" in a broad sense to denote all conspicuous intellectuals. One student of the subject, for example, has collected the names of almost 100 conspicuous Hungarian academic intellectuals simply among the immigrants to the United States in the 1930's. [20] Here, however, we will use the expression "genius" in a more narrow sense to denote only extraordinarily gifted minds. This narrow definition may at first strike the reader as an attempt at evasion. This study places considerable weight on statistics regarding the Jewish nobles, yet there are only six or seven scientist offspring of Jewish nobles [21] in our collection — hardly enough to

cases are not considered "noble." On the other hand, when a male descendent or brother of some individual acquired nobility, that individual is considered a member of a noble family. The second technical problem emerges when several members of one family acquired nobility at different times. In the present study such cases are counted as different families only in the rare event that they acquired new and different *predicata* [surnames], instead of extending the original patent of nobility to cover new persons.

[18] The Upper House members with no other title were Ferenc Chorin, Ferenc Heltai and Zsigmond Singer. Leó Lánczy, who was in the Upper House, did not acquire nobility, but became a Privy Councilor. It is frequently reported that Chorin was about to be made a Baron when the Monarchy collapsed in 1918.

[19] The Privy Councilors with no other title were Károly Csemegi, János Teleszky, Vilmos Vázsonyi, and Béla Földes.

[20] See Fermi, *Illustrious Immigrants*, pp. 11ff. and 111. Other efforts at collecting names are Emil Lengyel, *Americans from Hungary* (Philadelphia: Lippincott, 1948); Sándor Incze (ed.), *Magyar Album* (Elmhurst, Ill.: American Studies Foundation, 1956), esp. p. 34ff.; and Tibor Szy (ed.), *Hungarians in America* (New York: Hungarian University Association, 1963).

[21] They are von Kármán, von Neumann, de Hevesy, Lukács, Maria Telkes, Frederick de Hoffmann and peripherally Oszkár Jászi.

establish a strong statistical connection between the two groups. Let us
remind the reader, therefore, of our purpose. Reference to the geniuses
is not intended to show that a numerical preponderance of Hungary's
brilliant intellectuals have come from our group of Jewish nobles, but to
suggest generally that the dynamic factors which produced the ennoblement of wealthy Jews in Hungary led also to the emergence of some outstanding scientists onto the international stage. In this context numbers
make little difference. It is significant only that though the Jewish noble
scientists are few, four of them — von Kármán, von Neumann, de Hevesy,
and Lukács — are among the eight or ten Hungarian scientists whose
names are world famous, and rank, indeed, among the outstanding minds
of our time.

Pertinent in this connection are two other problems. First, it is not
our purpose to suggest that all Hungarian scientists, much less all Hungarian
geniuses, are Jews. They are not. George de Békésy, to name but one scientist,
was not a Jew, but the son of a Christian Magyar new noble. Neither Béla
Bártók nor Zoltán Kodály, Hungary's musical geniuses, were Jews, nor
were many of Hungary's greatest modern writers. Suffice it to say that
Jews have been sufficiently important among Hungary's twentieth-century
geniuses to make it worth while to study the geniuses through a Jewish
sample. Nor, secondly, is it the purpose of this study to draw invidious
comparisons between the Hungarian geniuses and those of other nations,
or even to define numerically a sample of Hungarian geniuses. We wish
simply to premise that a layman looking back on the international intelligentsia of the twentieth century will usually recognize alongside Russians, Germans, Americans, Englishmen, Frenchmen, Italians, Austrians,
Swedes, Romanians, and Poles a respectable number of Hungarians.
And he will usually perceive that among the really outstanding members
of that international intelligentsia are the sons of some Hungarian
Jewish nobles.

*　*　*

The following study is based on cards bearing coded data accumulated
from many sources. The collection contains cards on approximately 1,500
identifiably Jewish families, mostly business people, and complements
rather than replaces the Jewish *Lexicon*, which concentrates on cultural
figures. For all the ennobled families, and for numerous non-noble families
which comprise this study's countersamples (about 800 families in all),
the cards summarize the information available in many published reference

works. They summarize in addition two large collections of cards compiled by Károly Vörös, of the Budapest Historical Museum, and also data
from his unpublished study of Budapest's virilists, or highest tax-payers
for the years 1873 and 1888. The cards draw further on a considerable
sampling of Archive material. To attempt footnoting all this data would
drown whatever useful digested material this study may contain. The footnotes will, therefore, in general not rehearse this material, which is described
in a bibliographical appendix.

CHAPTER II

THE BROAD ISSUES *

The Jewish Nobles — Important?

Let us introduce this study of Hungary's Jewish nobles by establishing with the aid of a statistical table (Table 1) their importance as a group. The table records the residential distribution of the Jewish nobles as between town and country, and their occupational distribution as between commerce and other professions. The lesson of the table is unambiguous.

TABLE 1
DISTRIBUTION CHART **

	1824—1859	1860—1899	1900—1918	1824—1918
Budapest	4	64	134	202
Commerce	4	47	103	154
Provinces	—	48	63	111
Commerce	—	32	48	80
Residence Abroad	4	5	12	21
Commerce	4	5	7	16
Military	--	1	11	12
Total nobles	8	118	220	346
Total commerce	8	84	158	250

** Data here relates to residence at the moment of ennoblement.

Of the whole sample of 346 Jewish noble families, 202 resided in Budapest at the time of ennoblement. Of these, 154 were directly associated with the world of finance, commerce, and industry. Further, of the 111 families who resided outside of Budapest in the Hungarian provinces at

---

* Parts of the material in this chapter have appeared in different form in articles published in the *East European Quarterly*, March, 1971, and the *Journal of Modern History*, March, 1972.

the time of ennoblement, 80 were professionally involved in the business world. Naturally one can find exceptions to the urban commercial character of the group. In 1893, 46 persons from the Jewish nobility figured among Hungary's 1,000 largest landholders, and three were then among the top 100 landholders. [1] Probably even in the later period most of these new nobles owned at least a country house. [2] But in the whole group only 29 families seem to have been entirely dependent on their estates for their living at the time of ennoblement, [3] and it may be added that prior to 1918 the tendency of family movement before and after ennoblement was almost exclusively towards Budapest and commerce, rather than towards rural residence and landed leisure. [4] In sum, the Hungarian Jewish nobles were, at least at the moment of their ennoblement, a middle-class urban group.

A second table tells us more of the economic import of Hungary's Jewish nobles, some of whom, as we know already, were immensely wealthy between the wars. This table deals with the directors of the leading Hungarian banks in 1881, [5] 1896, [6] and 1913, [7] with the leaders of the Budapest

---

[1] See the list in István Lörintey, *Magyarország nagybirtokosai* [Hungary's Great Landholders] (Szatmár: Szabadsajtó, 1893).

[2] One may detect landholding through comparison of the Jewish nobility list with the national landholding registers, save that smaller villas are not listed there. These registers are Gyula Rubinek (ed.), *A magyar korona országainak gazdacímtára* [Estate Directory of the Lands of the Hungarian Crown] (1st edit.; Budapest: Pesti Könyvnyomda, 1897; 2nd edit.; 1911).

[3] By "entirely dependent on their estates" it is meant first that the family demonstrably had estates; and second that the family name does not figure in the *Magyar Compass* business index for the years 1873, 1888, 1896, or 1913. A considerable number of Jewish noble families who listed themselves in one document or another as "landowner," turned out to have derived their fortunes from banking, local industry, etc., and even to be resident in Budapest. It is somewhat surprising that estates can be documented for only about half the Jewish noble group. This finding seems to contradict the trend among Hungarian Jews early in this century to increase their landholdings, for which see the anti-Semitic Géza Petrassevich, *Zsidó földbirtokosok és bérlők Magyarországon* [Jewish Landowners and Landrenters in Hungary] (Budapest: Stephaneum, 1904). Perhaps this countering of the trend towards land accumulation may be attributed to a political factor. The new nobles, as will be shown in later chapters, were predominantly from the governing Liberal Party. The new Jewish landowners may have preferred an opposition Independence Party affiliation, which excluded them from Governmental favors, i.e., ennoblement.

[4] See Table 7B in Chapter III below.

[5] The source is *Magyar Compass, 1881*. There are executives from the Austro-Hungarian Bank (henceforth OMB); from the *Pesti Magyar Kereskedelmi Bank* (Commercial Bank, henceforth PMKB); from the *Jelzálog-Hitel Bank* (Mortgage Bank, henceforth JB); from the *Leszámítoló Bank* (Discount Bank, henceforth LB); and from the *Hitel-Bank* (Credit Bank, henceforth HB). A complete roster of Budapest's most important

Stock Exchange [8] and the Budapest Trade and Industry Association in 1896; [9] and with the leaders of the Hungarian Industrialists' Association in 1905 [10] and 1917, [11] a total of 504 different positions (Table 2). The table categorizes the members of these leading organs of the Hungarian economy under five headings: representatives of foreign financial organizations; aristocrats and Magyar nobles; non-Jewish businessmen resident in Hungary; Jews; and Jewish nobles. Since strictly speaking it is not legitimate to consider these bankers, traders, and industrialists as just one group, the table shows no totals. By way of summarization, however, we may note that Jewish nobles constituted precisely half of the 148 Jewish families involved in these elite groups and only 24.1% of the total number of families; but that they represented 30.6% of the total number of persons involved, and held 36.5% of the total number of places — a concentration larger by far than that of any other category. Their prominence can seem all the greater when one recalls that the aristocrats in the table were as often as not *Paradegoyim* (persons brought in to make Jewish firms seem Christian), whereas the Jews were all economically important. The lesson of this table is that Jewish nobles were not only members of Hungary's urban middle class, but that long before the interwar period their numbers contained the capitalist elite of that class.

---

bankers would cover some banks not mentioned here. Testing has shown, however, that systematic inclusion of all the executives of those banks in this and the following samples would result in undesirably larger numbers without significantly different findings.

[6] The source is *Magyar Compass, 1896.* Included are executives from OMB, from PMKB, from, JB, from LB, and from the then newly founded *Hazai Bank* (Fatherland Bank, henceforth Hazai).

[7] The source is Leonhardt's *Compass, 1912.* Included are executives from OMB, from PMKB, from JB, from LB, from HB, from Hazai, and from the then newly established *Magyar Bank.*

[8] The source is Ágoston Félegyházy, *A Budapest tőzsde története* [The History of the Budapest Stock Exchange] (2 vols.; Budapest; Tőzsde Nyomda, 1896), Vol. II, pp. 238—239.

[9] The source is Jakab Pólya, *A Pesti Polgári Kereskedelmi Társulat és a Budapest Nagykereskedők és Nagyiparosok Társulata története* [The History of the Pest Citizens' Trade Association and the Budapest Large Traders' and Large Industrialists' Association] (Budapest: Franklin, 1896), pp. 522—525.

[10] Source is *A Magyar Gyáriparosok Országos Szövetsége választmányának második évi jelentése* [The Report of the Hungarian Factory Owners' National Association's Second Annual Meeting] (Budapest: Athenaeum, 1905). The GYOSZ was actually founded in 1903.

[11] The same for 1917.

TABLE 2
HUNGARY'S ECONOMIC ELITE
1880—1918

	Foreign	Aristo-gentry	Other non-Jewish	Total Jewish	(Jewish noble then)	(Jewish noble absol.)	Total places	Total persons	Total families
5 Banks '81									
places	12	11	21	20	2	10	64		
persons	11	11	20	19	2	9		61	
families	11	11	20	18	2	8			60
5 Banks '96									
places	10	24	23	38	17	27	95		
persons	10	22	22	36	15	25		90	
families	10	21	21	32	12	22			84
Stock Exch. '96									
persons	—	—	6	33	15	23	39	39	
families	—	—	6	32	15	23			38
Tr. Ind. Ass. '96									
persons	—	—	5	44	14	29	49	49	
families	—	—	5	36	11	22			41
GYOSZ 1905									
persons	1	3	12	28	18	20	44	44	
families	1	3	12	25	15	17			41
7 Banks '13									
places	19	31	23	79	51	—	152		
persons	19	30	21	73	46	—		143	
families	19	28	19	63	36	—			129
GYOSZ 1917									
persons	1	6	10	43	24	—	61	61	
families	1	6	10	36	20	—			57

A third table emphasizes even more strongly the presence of Hungary's capitalist elite in the Jewish nobility before 1918. This table analyzes the real-estate and stock holdings of the noble and non-noble Jews in Table 2 from the point of view of quantity (Table 3). The table identifies six categories of real-estate holdings according to whether or not the available Budapest virilist, or highest land-taxpayer, lists show the individuals involved

TABLE 3
WEALTH ANALYSIS: REAL ESTATE

I. Non-Noble Jews from Table 2 (77 persons)

	pre 1900 entry	post-1900	total
virilist	24	20	44
(large vir.)	(16)	(10)	(26)
estate owner	7	5	12
(large est.)	(5)	(—)	(5)
neither	12	15	27

II. Ennobled Jews from Table 2 (110 persons)

	pre-1900 entry	post-1900	total
virilist	55	38	93
(large vir.)	(39)	(30)	(69)
estate owner	35	21	56
(large est.)	(22)	(11)	(33)
neither	4	4	8

as paying a small or large tax; [12] and according to whether or not the available agricultural estate directories show them as owning medium (over 500 *holds* — one *hold* equals 1.42 acres) or large (over 2,000 *holds*) estates. [13] It must be emphasized that neither of these measures is perfect. The virilist lists, for example, were not compiled exclusively according to tax assessment; [14] and the incomplete data in the estate directories has

[12] By small tax it is meant that the individual, his father, or his son, figures on the virilist lists for 1888, 1904, or 1907—1917 in some capacity. By large tax it is meant that the individual, his father, or his son, paid over 900 Kr. in 1888, or figured among the top 200 taxpayers on one of the later lists. The inclusion of paternal and filial property seems appropriate because such a long period of time is involved, and because so often individual businessmen had the enjoyment of paternal or filial property through the family firm.

[13] Based on Lörintey's list for 1893 and the two Rubinek indices cited in footnote 1 above. Once again paternal and filial property is involved

[14] The virilists, to be precise, were the 1200 highest tax payers from whose number, according to a Law of 1872, one half of the 400-member Budapest Municipal Board was elected. The virilist lists were drawn up directly from the tax-lists, but are not an exact index of wealth for two reasons. First, the taxes fell most heavily on owners of houses within the city limits. Persons whose wealth lay primarily in stored goods and paper, or who owned factories outside the city, might thus easily not appear high on the tax-lists, even though they were among the richest men in the city. Second, after 1902 a law obliged all the virilists to stand in the municipal elections, but gave highest tax-payers the option of avoiding this obligation by abandoning their virilism. For details see Károly Vörös, "Budapest legnagyobb adófizetői" [Budapest's Highest Tax Payers], *Tanulmányok Budapest multjából*, Vol. XVII, pp. 145—196; and Vol. XX, pp. 249—308.

made it impossible to be absolutely sure about which individuals owned estates. Nonetheless, the table leads to the conclusion that the members of the Jewish noble families were far more wealthy than the members of the non-noble Jewish families. Of the 110 Jewish noble family members in Table 2, 84.5% were Budapest virilists, and 63% were high-ranking virilists. The corresponding figures among the 77 non-noble Jews who held property according to Table 2, are 59% and 35%. Furthermore, 56% of the ennobled Jews in Table 2 held rural real-estate holdings, and 33% held large estates. The corresponding figures among the non-nobles are 24% and 10%. We may add that in point of stock-holdings, Table 2 has already revealed the concentration of wealth among the ennobled Jews.

Some figures regarding the role of the Jews in modern Hungary can confirm in another fashion the importance of the Jewish nobles long before 1918. Jews were very far from being the only ethnic element in nineteenth-century urban Hungary. Indeed in 1800 they constituted hardly 1.5% of the nearly nine million inhabitants of Greater Hungary, and were then a negligible factor in her towns. [15] Even in 1910 they made up only 5% of the 18,264,533 people in the country, and only 23.2% of the population of Budapest. Apart from the Jews there were important Magyar, German, Serb, Slovak, and Greek elements in Hungary's urban stratum. Jews were, however, extraordinarily important in the leading economic and professional classes of Hungary's urban non-laboring society, or bourgeoisie, in the modern era. In Budapest by 1910, for example, Jews constituted 52.6% of all persons engaged in industry, 64.5% of all persons engaged in trade and finance, 58.8% of all medical personnel, and 61.5% of all persons practicing law. These statistics indicate fairly clearly that, though there were other ethnic groups in Hungary's urban society, the Jews were the most significant ethnic element in that stratum of Hungarian society by 1910, and insofar as the Jewish nobles were the elite of the Jewish community, they were Hungary's capitalist elite.

A little economic history can add a final touch to our initial view of the Jewish nobility. Early in the nineteenth century Hungary was a very "backward" land in comparison to the West, inhibited against change by the neo-serfdom of her peasants and the legal privileges of her nobility, cushioned against ideas of change by imperial Austria. At the turn of our

---

[15] The major source for statistics about Jews in Hungary is still Alajos Kovács, *A zsidóság térfoglalása Magyarországon* [The Take-over by the Jews in Hungary] (Budapest: Ernő Kellner, 1922). The most useful account of Hungary's population is József Kovacsics, *Magyarország történeti demográfiája* [Hungary's Historical Demography] (Budapest: Közgazdasági és Jógi Könyvkiadó, 1963).

own century Hungary was still economically "undeveloped" by West European standards. By then, however, Hungary was changing. The tentacles of modern capitalism had spread into many of her remotest corners, and Budapest, one of the most grandiose of Europe's bourgeois cities, with almost a million inhabitants, had sprung up at her heart. In the 1880's and 1890's Budapest was, next to Minneapolis, the second largest flour-milling center in the world. [16] Between 1867 and 1914 Budapest was the fastest growing city of Europe, and rose from 17th to 8th place among Europe's largest cities. [17] Just after the turn of the century Budapest's financial resources became sufficient to make her the only banking center of all Eastern Europe (excluding Austria and Prussia, but including Russia and Turkey) to limit and press back foreign "imperialist capital." [18] The bankers and industrialists of our tables were responsible for these feats of modernization and of economic independence. These Jewish nobles were the vanguard of Hungary's capitalist class in Hungary's age of modernization.

Businessman Ennoblement — An Anomaly?

Let us now review various historical factors in order to bring into focus the first special point which we must establish in this study: that the ennoblement of Hungary's capitalist elite was anomalous.

Reasons why ennoblement could have been attractive to these capitalists are deceptively simple to locate. One derives from the fact that Hungary was in several respects as "backward" politically in the nineteenth

---

[16] For details see Vilmos Sándor, "A Budapest nagymalomipar kialakulása, 1839—1880" [The Formation of Budapest's Milling Industry], *Tanulmányok Budapest multjából*, Vol. XIII (1959), p. 388; and his *Nagyipari fejlődés Magyarországon, 1867—1900* [The Development of Large Industry in Hungary] (Budapest: Szikra, 1954), p. 64ff. Hungarian authorities habitually compare Budapest to Chicago. Arthur J. May corrects this error in *The Habsburg Monarchy* (Cambridge: Harvard University Press, 1951), p. 246

[17] See Gusztáv Thirring (ed.), *Budapest félszázados fejlődése, 1873—1923* [A Half Century of Budapest's Growth], *Budapest Statisztikai közleményei*, 53 (Budapest: Statisztikai Hivatel, 1925), pp. 20—21.

[18] For details see Ferenc Eckhardt, *A Magyar közgazdaság száz éve* [One Hundred Years of the Hungarian Economy] (Budapest: Posner Grafikai Műintézet, 1941), p. 163ff.; and Iván Berend and György Ránki, *Magyarország gyáripara az imperializmus első világháború előtti időszakában* [Hungary's Manufacturing Industry in the Period Preceding the First Imperialist World War] (Budapest: Szikra, 1955), p. 130ff. Helpful also is Gusztáv Gratz, *A dualizmus kora* [The Age of Dualism] (2 vols.; Budapest: Magyar Szemle Társaság, 1934), Chs. 14 and 32.

century as she was in terms of economics. [19] Prior to the revolutionary events of 1848, Hungary was ruled by a Habsburg monarch through an antique estates "constitution." The powers of the King with regard to most of the citizenry were technically autocratic. But not only did he in practice dwell as often as not in Vienna, ruling through a lieutenant in Hungary and a minimal bureaucratic apparatus. Also, inside the Kingdom his control was limited by the role of the constitutional "nation," the "single and undivided" nobility. [20] It enjoyed manifold legal immunities, possessed almost absolute power over the enserfed peasantry, and its country assemblies were in entire control of all local administration. Under these circumstances, clearly, capitalists had a great deal to gain through ennoblement. As nobles they could approach the King. As nobles they could share in the nobility's privileges. They could even do better business, if as nobles they were immune from the tolls and taxes that prior to 1848 vastly inhibited Old Hungary's trade.

In 1848, of course, the legal privileges of the nobility were abolished, and the Diet devised a new liberal constitution which limited the power of the King, and gave most citizens civil rights. This constitution, in modified form, was finally accepted by the crown in 1867. In 1867 a new law gave even the Jews absolute civil rights. From then until the end of the Monarchy in 1918, therefore, the capitalists of Hungary had far less cause on paper to seek ennoblement than before. In practice, however, the old conditions lived on to a notable extent. Typically, the King saw no obstacle in 1849 to lifting the constitution of his Kingdom; and though in the 1860's circumstance forced him to relent, few people in Hungary doubted at the start of our century that, if he wanted to, he could defy the laws again.

---

[19] The classic work on the political history of Hungary is still Bálint Hóman and Gyula Szekfű, *Magyar történet* [Hungarian History] (8 vols.; Budapest: Egyetemi Nyomda, n.d.). See also the famous essay by Gyula Szekfű, *Három nemzedék* [Three Generations] (3rd Edit.; Budapest: Egyetemi Nyomda, 1934); and the recent Erik Molnár *et al.* (eds.), *Magyarország története* [History of Hungary] (2 vols.; Budapest: Gondolat, 1964). Standard surveys of the post-1867 period are the works by G. Gratz cited in the preceding footnote and Sándor Pethő, *Világostól Trianonig* [From Világos to Trianon] (Budapest: Enciklopédia, 1934). A comprehensive English-language account of Hungarian history since the eighteenth century is in C. A. Macartney, *The Habsburg Empire* (London: Weidenfeld and Nicolson, 1969).

[20] Apart from the general works just cited see the sociological analysis of the nobility in Ernő Lakatos, *A Magyar politikai vezetőréteg, 1848—1918* [Hungary's Political Leading Stratum] (Budapest: Élet, 1942); and the English language account of the background by C. A. Macartney in A. Goodwin, *The European Nobility in the Eighteenth Century* (London: Adam and Charles Black, 1953).

Until the end of his reign in 1916, Franz Joseph was a great deal more than a figurehead monarch in Hungary. Further, though the nobility as a whole never regained its legal privileges after the dramatic sacrifices of March and April, 1848, it retained enormous prestige. This nobility had fought for "world freedom" against "tyranny" in 1848; and though it lost that battle, it acquired in the process so firm a hold on the banners of political liberalism in Hungary, and particularly in the dominant Magyar community, that even under the ostensibly Liberal and tolerant laws of the *Ausgleich* (Austro-Hungarian Compromise) of 1867, the nobility wielded enormous social and political weight. Under these circumstances it is hardly surprising that urban capitalists who were busy making fortunes in Budapest continued to seek nobility.

Apart from this matter of social and political advantage which a bourgeois could derive from ennoblement in *Ausgleich* Hungary, there was a matter of attitudes. Today we tend to think of ennoblement as "snobbishness" — something ridiculous and without value. At the time, however, popular attitudes may have been rather different. The story of an iron merchant from Pozsony (Bratislava) named Weisz, who sought nobility in the 1880's suggests this. [21] Weisz originally petitioned the King (as was customary when one wanted nobility) to reconfirm a patent of nobility awarded in the seventeenth century to an alleged ancestor named Wajss. This attempt

---

[21] See for the following *Országos Levéltár* [National Archives] (henceforth cited as OL), K-148, B-Min. Eln. 1881, I-B 1928. In general terms the ennoblement process in Hungary began when a citizen drew up a petition in which a "lowliest of serfs" (leg-alázatosabb jobbágy) described his "merits and benevolences" to an All-Highest Majesty—the Habsburg Kaiser-King. Prior to 1848 the citizen forwarded his petition together with suitable documentation of his Hungarian citizenship, wealth, career, and charities, through the *Főispán* (Lord Lieutenant) of his county of residence to the King's Lieuten. ant in Hungary *(locumtenentiale,* or *Nádor).* The latter dignitary would make suitable investigations, and then forward the letter, if he favored it, to Vienna. There the Hungarian Chancellery would draw up a patent of nobility, which the King at his grace could sign. Each rank of the nobility and aristocracy had a fixed price, which one had to pay to the Crown. Payments were also due to an Office of Heraldry in Vienna, which drew up the new noble's coat of arms. After 1867 the ennoblement procedure altered somewhat. The *Főispán* now forwarded the petition to the Hungarian Minister of the Interior at Budapest. Both the *Főispán* and the Minister would, moreover, make investigations which were often quite thorough, and would add covering letters confirming the aforesaid merits and benevolences. The dossier would then go to the Hungarian Prime Minister, who after consultation with the Cabinet would forward it to the Minister-Attached-to-His-Majesty's-Person in Vienna. The latter would draw up the patent of nobility for the King to sign. For further details, see my paper, "Ennoblement in Dualistic Hungary," *East European Quarterly,* Vol. V, no. 1 (March, 1971), pp. 13—26, from which a part of the following discussion is excerpted.

failed, because the genealogical evidence Weisz submitted was slim. (He claimed the documents had been destroyed "in the Reformation disturbances.") But in the attempt Weisz had become acquainted with his county's *Főispán* (Lord Lieutenant — a Royal appointee who was head of each county's administration). Consequently, with the *Főispán*'s hearty recommendation of his "moral," "charitable," and "political" virtues enclosed, he now requested in lieu of a confirmation of the alleged old patent of nobility, a brand new patent. Once again he failed. The Ministers in Budapest, who after 1867 had to approve all cases of ennoblement, did not find in the amended petition sufficient documentation of Weisz' "merits." Thereupon, Weisz petitioned a third time, producing the required documentation and also an even longer letter from the *Főispán* about his "political" virtues; and now he succeeded.

The outrageous versatility with which this aggressive burgher attacked the Hungarian Royal bureaucracy leads one to wonder whether his understanding of society was the same as our own. This burgher behaved as if the bureaucracy was not a convenience to the citizen of a rational mobile society, but a fixed mechanism in a hierarchial world. To oil this mechanism was not for him, apparently, as it would be for us, a disagreeable obligation. This humble burgher of Hungary, apparently, saw the oiling of the bureaucracy as a virtue — as something that could be done, and which could enable him to approach the All-Highest Monarch, who was otherwise so inaccessible. In his petition, typically, this burgher failed entirely to request nobility for utilitarian purposes — for example as a means of social advancement for his children. He stressed that nobility was a rank which would befit his property — strictly medieval imagery. One may suspect that in using this imagery he reflected not only protocol, but also old-fashioned attitudes which were very widespread in Old Hungary's new capitalist classes.

A third factor which no doubt attracted the new classes of modern urban Hungary to ennoblement was the relative tolerance of the Magyar nobles. [22] These nobles were by no means open-minded. They were in no small degree anti-Semitic, and, as will appear later, they were reactionary on the whole in terms of social policy, and they were chauvinist Magyar nationalists. But they were also beleaguered. Old Hungary was a polyethnic land in which the Magyar nobles were only a fraction of the Magyar population, and in which the Magyars as a nation were only 46.7% of the

----

[22] On noble attitudes, see in particular Zoltán Lippay, *A magyar birtokos középosztály* [The Hungarian Landed Middle Class] (Budapest: Franklin, 1919), esp. p. 30ff.; and Győző Concha, "A gentry," [The Gentry], *Budapesti Szemle*, Vols. 400—401 (1910), pp. 1—34, 173—199.

total population as late as 1880, and 54.5% in 1910. Under these conditions, surrounded by a "sea" of Slavs and Vlachs, the Magyar governments were acutely conscious of the need to seek ethnic allies, and even the ordinary Magyar noble could see that his class might have trouble staying in command without some sort of help. The Jews in particular could give such help, because they often confessed themselves as only a religious group, not a nationality, and were willing to speak Magyar. [23] It is not surprising, therefore, that the nobility provided even Jewish new nobles (not to speak of recruits from other nationalities) with a modicum of satisfaction.

There were two major noble clubs of which we have a record, the aristocratic *Nemzeti* [*National*] *Casino*, and the gentry's *Országos* [*Country*] *Kaszinó*, both in Budapest. By 1913 the more aristocratic *Nemzeti* had admitted members of four families from the 23 in the first-generation (1860—1876) Jewish nobility; and six families from the 95 in the second-generation (1878—1900) Jewish nobility. [24] Meanwhile the gentry's *Országos* had admitted members of five families from the first generation, of nine families from the second generation, and of eight families from the third generation (post-1900) of the Jewish nobility. [25] This was not a record of overwhelming acceptance. Moreover, it is worth noting that in almost every case religious conversion preceded Casino membership, [26] and that even Casino membership did not entail complete social acceptance. [27]

[23] See István Bibó, "A zsidókérdés Magyarországon" [The Jewish Question in Hungary], in *Harmadik Út* [Third Road] (London: Magyar Könyves Céh, 1960), p. 317ff.

[24] *A Nemzeti Casino évkönyve*, 1913 [The Nemzeti Casino Yearbook] (Budapest: 1914). The families were Wodianer, Szitányi-Ullmann, Moskovicz, and Harkányi; Máday, Kilényi-Klein, Déchy, Korányi, *csatári* Grosz, and Königswarter.

[25] See *Az Országos Kaszinó évkönyve, 1913* [The Országos Casino Yearbook] (Budapest: 1914). The families were Harkányi, Lévai, Szitányi-Ullmann, Wodianer, and Zombory-Stein; Belatiny-Braun, Bíró-Brüll, Dóczy, Liebner, Máday, *megyeri* Krausz, *ráthonyi* Reusz, Wagner, and Pfeiffer, Fialka, Földvári-Basch, Lánczy, Létay-Landau, *szászi* Schwartz, Teleszky, Végh, and Walder. It may be noted that the Falk family, which did not acquire nobility, made this Casino.

[26] It may be noted also that the late Zoltán Horváth in his *Magyar századforduló* [Hungarian Turn-of-the-Century] (Budapest: Gondolat, 1961), p. 588, claims that the *Országos Kaszinó* never accepted even converted Jews as members. This statement is, as the above data indicates, and as Horváth has informed me in conversation, quite incorrect.

[27] I am indebted to Zoltán Horváth for this point; but the survival of prejudice is clear from such literary sources as Lajos Hatvany, *Urak és emberek* [Lords and People] (2 vols.; Budapest: Szépirodalmi Könyvkiadó, 1963), and Anna (Moskovicz) Lesznai, *Kezdetben volt a kert* [In the Beginning Was the Garden] (2 vols.; Budapest: Szépirodalmi Könyvkiadó, 1966).

Nonetheless, as Central European anti-Semites would discover to their distress after the first World War, the Magyar nobility accepted the Jewish community massively in terms of intermarriage. [28] The wife of one Prime Minister, Baron Géza Fejérváry, emerged from the Jewish nobility, [29] and the daughter of another, László Lukács, married into it. [30] Such inter-marriages, together with the fact that the Casino doors did on occasion open to persons of Jewish origin, could make what we, today, call vain snobbery seem serious business for the new classes of the last century.

There were, thus, in Hungary prior to 1918 many obvious inducements for middle-class ennoblement. But let us not lose perspective on reality! Even in the nineteenth century, and even inside Hungary one could detect loud criticism and mockery of the whole cult of the nobility. In 1884, to cite but one example, a Budapest newspaper, the *Pesti Napló* [Pest Daily], charged that the new nobles were stock exchange knights and gin nobles (börzelovagok és pálinkanemesek). The Jewish *Egyenlőség*, thereupon, polem-icized back that the old nobles of earlier centuries were pimp knights, stable nobles, and bandit counts (kerítőlovagok, istallónemesek, és zsivány grófok) — hardly a sign of reverence for the institution of nobility. [31] Under these circumstances we must wonder whether it is explicable that, as our statistics suggest, approximately half of the top Jewish capitalist elite ennobled. Was that not an anomaly?

To this we must add, moreover, that according to the classical liberal image of a "bourgeois" — the image which was current in Hungary as everywhere else in Europe in the nineteenth century — bourgeois ennoble-ment was incongruous. Figaro, for example, mocked the nobility and tricked the nobility, but did not join it. And even in Marx's post-liberal model, the "bourgeois" was supposed to be a creature of independent vigor, who sweeps away, even more than Figaro did, the ridiculous rem-nants of the old feudal system, grabs everything for himself, and establishes his own standards of behavior. We may recognize, of course, that from time immemorial in European history some capitalists had assimilated into the traditional nobilities by buying land and titles. From Balzac's novels

---

[28] See, for example, the remarks in Stefan Barta, *Die Judenfrage in Ungarn* (Buda-pest: Stadium, 193?), pp. 68—69.

[29] She was a member of the Biedermann family of originally-Hungarian Viennese bankers.

[30] Lukács' daughter married into the baronized sugar industrialist Hatvany-Deutsch family.

[31] See the *Egyenlőség*, 7 Sept., 1884, p. 7. Comp. the mocking sketches in Zoltán Ambrus, *Berzsenyi Báró és családja* [Baron Berzsenyi and His Family] (Budapest: Révai, 1906).

we learn that in the dynamic nineteenth century, even in Western Europe, the assimilation of capitalists into the nobility went on; and we know that from Molière's day at the latest these people were objects of public ridicule because of their assumed noble airs. Nonetheless, in the Western world in the nineteenth century the new capitalists seem on the whole to have preferred to remain middle class than to become new nobles. Even in imperial Germany and tsarist Russia, where middle-class ennoblement was officially encouraged, there does not seem to have been so massive an ennoblement of the century's new economic elite as our statistics show there was in Hungary. [32]

* * *

One may well inquire at this point whether the ennobled Jews in our sample were really so representative of all of Budapest's and Hungary's bourgeoisie as our earlier statistics have suggested above. Is it not possible, for example, that the Jewish nobles were old burghers, or a bourgeois aristocracy, having little or nothing to do with the new capitalism which in the late nineteenth century made bourgeois Budapest great? The question must be adjusted to the fact that these nobles were Jewish, and were emancipated only in 1867. But is it not possible that the Jewish nobles were Jewish "aristocrats" — old and distinguished people within Hungary's Jewish communities? In such a case it would be neither anomalous nor particularly significant that they came to side politically with the Magyar nobility.

Perhaps the simplest way to approach this question is to record that in terms of blood there were only a very few old Jewish aristocratic families in our group. The Lackó clan, for example, boasted descent from the famous fifteenth-century Prague talmudist, Akibá há-Kóhen, and had been in Hungary since immediately after its liberation from the Turks. [33] The Wertheimers [34] and Flesches were of ancient German-Jewish lineage. The Chorins, politically perhaps the most important family in our sample, boasted a rabbinical lineage extending well back into the eighteenth century. But

---

[32] For the Prussian case, see Lamar Cecil, "The Creation of Nobles in Prussia, 1871—1918," *American Historical Review*, Vol. LXXV, no. 3 (Feb., 1970), pp. 757—795. On the Russian case, see William L. Blackwell, *The Beginnings of Russian Industrialization* (Princeton: Princeton University Press, 1968), pp. 192 — 193, which cites N. P. Chulkov, "Moskovskoe Kupechestvo XVIII i XIX vv." [The Moscow Merchants of the 18th and 19th Centuries], *Russkii Arkhiv*, Vol. III (1907), no. 12, pp. 489 — 502.

[33] See the obituary of Antal Lackó in the *Egyenlőség*, 19 Aug., 1892.

[34] The well-known Budapest historian, Ede Wertheimer, who acquired Magyar nobility in 1899, was related to the famous German Wertheim and Wertheimstein banking clan.

these were exceptions. Far more typical of the Jewish nobility were the Brülls, grain merchants who made a pretence of descending from the famous imperial banker Samuel Oppenheimer, but actually descended from three penniless brothers who came from Galicia to Pozsony in about 1800, and had themselves adopted by the last of the original Brülls. [35] The Buday-Goldbergers, the textile kings, the proudest by far of the Jewish nobles of interwar Hungary, could trace themselves only to a poor goldsmith who immigrated, probably from Padua, before 1750. [36] The vastly important Hatvany-Deutsch [37] sugar-baron tribe, which left a print on Hungary's history even after 1944, had no record of their ancestry before 1810. Their pride in their blood depended on intermarriages, for example, with the Lackós; and their intimacy with aristocratic Hungary derived from family alliances. [38]

In the 1920's and 1930's when an extensive documentation was still available, historians could document an eighteenth-century Hungarian background for only 27 of the 346 noble families; and research could date most of the families less than 75 years back. [39] It would thus be quite

[35] See Sigmund Mayer, *Die Wiener Jüden* (Wien-Berlin: K. Löwit Verlag, 1917), p. 145ff.; and the exaggerated claims of Samu Bettelheim in *Mult és Jövő* [Past and Future], June. 1932, pp. 191—192.

[36] See László Kállai, *A 150-éves Goldberger Gyar* [The 150 Year Old Goldberger Factory] (Budapest: Székely. 1935), p. 13ff. .

[37] To understand the form of this name one must know that in Hungary nobility was not denoted by the addition of a particle before one's name (as in French with "de," and in German with "von"), but by adding a "y" to the end of it if, as is so common in Magyar, one's name ended in "i." If, on the other hand, one had a foreign name such as Deutsch, which did not end in "i," or if one wanted greater prestige, one could obtain (through additional petitioning and payment to the King) a *predicatum* (surname) derived most frequently either from an estate, or one's place of birth. Thus "*hatvani* Deutsch" originally indicated that the Deutsch family possessed an estate at the town of Hatvan. When, moreover, in the later nineteenth century many non-Magyars were systematically Magyarizing, it became popular among new nobles to take their *predicatum* (after suitable replacement of the "i" with "y") as their family name, although very often for an interim period they would hyphenate the new name to the old. The Hatvany-Deutsches hyphenated their name in 1897, and though they finally dropped the "Deutsch" after 1911, it seems convenient in this study to use the hyphenated form.

[38] Information from Bertalan Hatvany.

[39] This judgment is based on *MZsL* and on Kempelen's various works. Obviously, this "evidence" is not particularly strong. In the 1920's and 1930's prominent Central European families had good reasons to conceal anything Jewish in their pasts; and as mentioned earlier, there are internal signs in both the above sources that some well-known families induced the researchers to "forget" about them. My investigation suggests, however, that this sort of concealment was common mainly in families of humble origin. Those families who had Jewish "aristocratic" lineage seem, even after a conversion, to have boasted the fact.

false to argue that the Jewish nobles were aristocratic in terms of Hungarian Jewish society; or that its members acquired Magyar nobility late in the nineteenth century only because prior to the Jewish emancipation of 1867, as second-class citizens, they were ineligible for it.

Other indices of the newness of the Jewish nobility are easy to find. For example, only eight Jewish noble names figure among those of the 27 Jewish traders who helped set up the first large trader association in Pest in 1846. [40] By implication the other new noble families had not then become important. Comparably, only 86 individuals from noble families figure among the 325 identifiably Jewish persons who were among the 1,200 largest taxpayers in Budapest in 1888. [41] Yet in a subsequent list of only 707 top taxpayers from years 1904—1917 there were 116 Jews from ennobled families. [42] In this light it seems significant that 220 out of 346 new Jewish nobles acquired their rank after 1900, in the last two decades of the Monarchy's existence, when Hungary's industrial transformation finally became massive. [43] Evidently, they were the products of that transformation: and this means that their ennoblement was anomalous.

Another wealth-analysis table can reinforce this argument about the newness of the Jewish nobility. Table 4 shows that although the ennobled Jews were among those in our capitalist elite who gained their wealth early, they were not just an old class or even an elder generation of rich men. This table records the reappearance of names from the earlier, pre-1900 groups in Table 2 in the later, post-1900 groups. Patently, if the new nobles were an older generation element, their names would appear in great numbers in the earlier groups; and though they might reappear in great numbers in the later groups, they would *not* appear for the first time in the later groups. As it happens, the rate of reappearance is consid-

---

[40] For identifications, see the contribution by Antal Deutsch in Vidor Szirmai (ed.), *A magyar zsidóság almanachja. Védőirat* [The Almanach of Hungarian Jewry. A Defense] (Budapest: A Magyar Zsidóság Almanachja Szerkesztőségének kiadása, 1920), p. 144ff. In these calculations the expression "Jewish noble family" is used in a broad sense to include brothers, fathers, grandfathers, and in rare cases uncles of the gentlemen who eventually acquired nobility.

[41] The list of taxpayers is in Máté, *Magyar Almanach*. I am indebted to K. Vörös for use of his card collection, based on this list. Identification of Jews was mainly on the basis of Pest Israelite Community Suffrage lists (for which, see the bibliographical appendix below).

[42] This list was compiled by K. Vörös from the top 200 names on the virilist list of 1903, and 1907—1917. Identification of Jews was mainly on the basis of a Pest Israelite Community suffrage list of 1913, for discussion of which see the bibliographical appendix.

[43] See Table 1 for the pattern of ennoblement.

TABLE 4
WEALTH ANALYSIS: TIME OF ACQUISITION

I. Non-Noble Jews from Table 2

	pre-1900 entry	post-1900	total
no. of places	46	54	100
concent. (a)	—	1	1
repeats (b)	8	14	22
no. of persons	38	39	77

II. Ennobled Jews from Table 2

	pre-1900 entry	post-1900	total
no. of places	89	95	184
concent. (a)	3	5	8
repeats (b)	22	44	66
no. of persons	64	46	110

a. Concentration results when an individual holds more than one place in one of the bank-director samples — i.e., when he was in one year a director of more than one bank.

b. Repeats result when an individual appears in more than one sample — i.e., when he was a bank director in two different years; or when he was a bank director and a leader of GYOSZ.

derably higher among the new nobles than among the non-nobles. But this only implies that the nobles managed to retain their wealth after the turn of the century. Nobles and non-nobles divide about equally as between pre- and post-1900 new names. And it may be added that numerically, there were more nobles among the post-1900 (i.e., younger) generation. Unmistakably the Hungarian Jewish nobles were not just an older generation of their country's capitalist stratum. They represented a tendency towards ennoblement among Hungary's capitalists which was strong and continuous until 1918. And this finding makes it seem all the more puzzling that in Hungary there was so much bourgeois ennoblement.

* * *

One question remains in this discussion of whether or not the ennoblement of Hungary's capitalists was anomalous. There is considerable evidence that after they acquired nobility our Jewish businessmen and their families behaved in a fashion wholly reminiscent of the old nobles. The author Anna Lesznai, for example, has depicted her father, who was a Jewish noble, as a spendthrift, quixotic, conceited landlord, addicted to horseracing and mistresses, typically "gentry" (to use a Magyar expression which we will discuss in a later chapter); and her portrait is probably apt with regard to many of the Jewish nobility. [44] This sort of evidence suggests that through ennoblement our businessmen cast aside any connections they may have had with the rest of the Budapest bourgeoisie — that they became renegades wholly unrepresentative of their class. From this it might follow once again that the ennoblement of these particular capitalists was only to be expected — and that it tells us nothing of the inclinations of Hungary's capitalist bourgeoisie as a whole.

Even prior to 1914, moreover, a part of the Jewish nobility in Budapest was unmistakably becoming economically and socially a "bank aristocracy," clearly differentiated from Hungary's broader commercial world. [45] As early as 1900, for example, the Hatvany-Deutsch family (which already, with its in-laws the Schossbergers, controlled a quarter of Hungary's lucrative sugar production) nearly established a family cartel controlling the country's five largest banks. During the First World War Manfréd Weisz's family, which had built up a huge munitions complex on the Csepel Island in the Danube just south of Budapest, did establish a dominant hold on the second largest bank. As noted earlier, between the wars two groups comprising some ten, mostly Jewish noble families, controlled enormous industrial holdings. In view of these elaborate concentrations of wealth and power, which were paralleled by intermarriage and cliquish social behavior, one can hardly deny the emergence of a sharp stratification within Hungary's capitalist society. One need not be a Marxist to admit that such a "bank aristocracy," because of its great wealth, might behave politically in no way differently from the traditional aristocracy, and very differently from the rest of the capitalist bourgeoisie.

In evaluating this "bank aristocracy," however, one must bear in mind two factors. The first is its recent origin. Between the wars beyond question Hungary was dominated by a mere handful of banker and industrialist families. Between the wars it was possible for Hungary's Foreign Minister to be the leading Jewish banker's son-in-law, and for Jewish industrialists to be the reputed *éminences grises* of Admiral Horthy's regime. Between the wars nearly all the leading Jewish banker-aristocrats cut themselves off through religious conversion from the middle strata of the society from which they had emerged. Before the war, however, the banker aris-

---

[44] See the character named István Berkovics in Anna Lesznai, *Kezdetben volt a kert.*
[45] On the "bank aristocracy" see Péter Hanák's important "Skizzen über die ungarische Gesellschaft am Anfang des 20. Jahrhunderts," *Acta Historica*, Vol. X, p. 11ff.

tocracy in Hungary was only just forming. At the turn-of-the-century the Hatvany-Deutsch family's concentration of wealth was unique. The Manfréd Weisz family, the keystone of the interwar "bank aristocracy", was then only just becoming important, and was considered very *nouveau riche*. A major symbol of the detachment of the new "banker aristocrats" from the rest of the middle class was their foundation of a new social club as late as 1907. [46] And in the pre-war era the leading members of the "banker-aristocrat" families were nearly all still members of the Pest Israelite Community's leadership, indicating their continued homogeneity with the bulk of the Jewish middle class.

Beyond this, one must recognize that even between the wars, despite the ever clearer economic differentiation of the upper crust from the Jewish middle classes in Pest, the differentiation in social attitudes remained remarkably narrow. To see the evidence let us study the leadership of the major Hungarian economic institutions between the wars (Table 5). These reveal

TABLE 5

HUNGARY'S ECONOMIC ELITE

1920 — 1944

	Foreign	Aristo.	Other non-Jewish	Total Jewish	Jewish Noble	Jewish Other Dignit. (a)	Unknown Persons	Total Person
Stock Exch. 1921	0	1	4	36	7	6	0	41
7 Banks 1920	27	21	54	118	42	28	2	222
GYOSZ 1930	1	2	22	44	23	10	4	73
8 Banks 1935	9	19	68	98	26	30	7	201
Stock Exch. 1936	0	0	25	39	6	15	6	70
GYOSZ 1936	1	1	29	37	17	11	3	71
GYOSZ 1943	0	5	75	9	5	0	0	89

(a). The other dignitaries were holders of the ranks *Kincstári* (Treasury), *Kereskedelmi* (Commercial), and *Kormány* (Government) *Főtanácsos* (High Counselorship).

first a great turn-over even in the great capitalist circle. In the Budapest banks, for example, where in 1913 Jewish noble families had held 51 out of the 79 banking positions in Jewish hands, in 1935 they held only 26

---

[46] See Sándor Nádas, "A Lipótvárosi Kaszinó regénye" [The Story of the Lipótváros Kaszino], in the *Pesti Futár*, 1935, no. 7, pp. 11—16.

out of the 98 banking positions in Jewish hands. [47] In the Industrialists' Association, where Jewish noble families had held 20 out of 28 Jewish positions in 1905 (from a total of 44), they held only 17 out of 37 Jewish positions in 1936 (out of a total of 71). Only the very few wealthiest families retained their positions — and did so even after the Jewish laws of 1938—1940 had eliminated almost all other Jews from leading economic positions. The bulk of the Jewish nobility suffered catastrophe during the inflations and depression of the interwar period; and we may presume that for the urban middle classes as a whole, the same holds true. Nonetheless, despite this turn-over in the Jewish middle classes in Hungary between the wars, the leaders of the principal economic institutions were markedly consistent in point of social aspiration. The new people who rose to the top of the Pest business world in this period were just as avid for ranks and title as their predecessors had been. Among the leading Jewish bankers of 1935, 56 out of 98 were either nobles or holders of brand-new lofty ranks. In the Industrialists' Association in 1936, 28 of the 37 Jewish members were similarly distinguished. These were approximately the proportions which the Jewish nobles had attained in these groupings before the war. These data suggest that the Jewish banker aristocrats were far less differentiated in terms of social attitudes from the rest of the capitalist classes than they were in terms of absolute wealth. Old or new, high or simply rising, these middle classes "feudalized" by following the path of ennoblement.

The "feudalized" character of the Budapest bourgeoisie has been recognized, directly or indirectly, by major historians. Gyula Szekfű, for example, in one of the first major syntheses on modern Hungarian social history, propounded in 1920 that the "modernizer" urban stratum in Hungary's society somehow lacked moral integrity. [48] Szekfű described this failing *inter alia* in terms of an exaggeration, or "extremism" of the Magyar-speaking urban elements in over-supporting the "illusions" of the Magyar nobles, and he attributed it to a "foreignness" and particularly to a "Jewishness" of the stratum as a whole. There has been much disagreement with his explanations, but remarkably little with his description of the phenomenon. Oszkár Jászi, for example, writing a few years later from a political viewpoint diametrically opposite to Szekfű's, reached a remarkably parallel evaluation. He found that the middle classes not just in Budapest, but throughout the Monarchy had been "moral vassals" of

---

[47] These data are all derived from the appropriate yearbook of the *Magyar Compass*.
[48] See Gyula Szekfű, *Három nemzedék*, esp. p. 339ff.

the system. And he ascribed this quality specifically to their social climbing and enthusiasm for ennoblement. [49] Nor have the recent Marxist historians contradicted their predecessors on this point. One of them, Zoltán Horváth, has found that Hungarian capitalism as a whole was so far deficient in the pursuit of its "historic task", the establishment of "bourgeois democracy," that the proletariat had to teach it how. [50] This was a euphemism for saying that towards the end of the last century Hungary's "new class" gave its political allegiance not to the cause of "bourgeois democracy," but to the country's ruling noble caste. Anomalously it entered into "service" to the old regime. [51]

Ennoblement and Genius — Related Topics?

The author Anna Lesznai tells that when in about the year 1905 she first met the young philosopher, Georg Lukács, his ideas struck her, clear as a bolt of lightening, as extraordinarily modern and sensible. [52] Lukács himself has recalled that the poems of Endre Ady, the great turn-of-the-century Magyar poet, have always seemed to him miraculously and universally truthful. [53] In general when one studies Young Budapest — the new generation of intellectuals which was emerging after 1900 — one discovers a cosmopolitan modernity which contrasts sharply with the social behavior of the Budapest Jewish capitalists, parochial and old fashioned by most standards.

An awareness of this contrast can afford us major insight into the second special point we must make in this chapter: the significance of the fact that the Jewish nobility gave birth to a number of scientific geniuses.

---

[49] See Oszkar Jászi, *Dissolution of the Habsburg Monarchy* (paperback edit.; Chicago: University of Chicago Press, 1961), p. 153. For other interwar judgments of the Hungarian middle classes, see István Weizs, *A mai magyar társadalom* [Hungarian Society Today] (Budapest: Magyar Szemle Társaság, 1930), Chs. 5—7; and Lakatos, *A magyar politikai vezetőréteg*, p. 65ff.

[50] See Zoltán Horváth, *Magyar századforduló*, pp. 293—294. For a listing of other Marxist literature see the Erik Molnár (ed.), *Magyarország története*, Vol. II, pp. 607—610.

[51] Oszkar Jászi used the expression "service bourgeoisie" in an article published in the journal, *A Világ* [The World], on 6 July, 1911, and it reappears frequently in his later works. See the quotation in György Fukász, *A Magyarországi polgári radikalizmus története, 1900—1918* [The History of Bourgeois Radicalism in Hungary] (Budapest: Gondolat, 1960), p. 384; and Jászi's *Dissolution of the Habsburg Monarchy*, p. 153.

[52] See Lesznai, *Kezdetben volt a kert*, Vol. I, p. 683ff.

[53] See György Lukács, "Utam a magyar kulturához" [My Road to Magyar Culture] in *Kortárs*, Vol. XIII, no. 7 (July, 1965), p. 1018ff.

We may shortly discover that this was by no means Budapest's only clashing contrast, nor was the middle-class penchant for ennoblement the city's only anomaly. In effect, turn-of-the-century Budapest was a city of bizarre facades, where no one hesitated, for example, to change his name to suit his taste, where everyone concealed his past, and where no one went to the daily *corso* without dressing up. [54] And Budapest was a city of sharp social differences, where peasants and gypsies wandered palace-lined streets, and where everyone seemed to speak at least five tongues. There is evidence that the tensions of this theatrical social atmosphere translated themselves into Art. The great Parliament building, the most characteristic monument of bourgeois Budapest, is exciting not because it covers several acres with six stories of heavy mansarded Victorian masonry, but because perched incongruously on the bank of the Danube it is crowned with a forest of neo-Gothic pinacles and culminates in a distorted Renaissance dome resting on flying buttresses. The decoration is what counts! Similarly, what could be less probable but more stimulating than Ödön Lechner's *Art Nouveau* post-office, whose seven vertical stories are tiled from tip to toe with globular Japanese flowers in green, white, and gold; or than the creations of the painter Rippl-Rónai, who aped the style of Degas, Monet, Renoir, and Van Gogh, according to his mood? To come to our point, the atmosphere of anomalies in Budapest may have contributed to a cultural renaissance that took place in turn-of-the-century Budapest, of which our scientific geniuses were but a part. [55]

All at once Hungary and her capital gave birth to their own artistic "secession", and symbolism, their own psychology, their own female emancipation, as well as to their own mathematical revolution. They produced their own oriental scholarship, their own folk-art revival, and a thousand other "isms" of their own. Some of this cultural effervescence verged on irrationality. One is reminded, for example, of the painter Tivadar Csontváry, who painted Hebrew prophets among Sicilian cyprus against tropical sunsets in magnificently exciting colors. [56] In the Revolution of 1919, when asked in all seriousness by the commissars of education who were the world's greatest painters, Csontváry replied with his own name and "others to come." He died mad in that same year. But from the "demented" deca-

---

[54] For descriptions from different viewpoints, see Prince Louis Windischgrätz, *My Memoirs* (London: Allen and Unwin, 1921); and Manó Buchinger, *Küzdelem a szocializmusért* [Struggle for Socialism] (Budapest: Népszava, 1946), pp. 33ff. and 44.

[55] The most extensive study of the culture and politics of turn-of-the-century Budapest is Zoltán Horváth, *Magyar századforduló.*

[56] See Lajos Németh, *Csontváry* (Budapest: Corvina, 1964), p. 82.

dence of Budapest's cultural life before the war emerged also the greatest
Hungarian poet of the time. Endre Ady was as fair a specimen as one
could find in Europe of personal dissolution. He died in 1919 of syphilitic
complications. But he included in his poems a quantity of brilliantly rational social criticism, and he became the political hero of the war generation. Budapest's intellectuals would sit up all night before and during the
war reciting and listening to Ady's verse. Even in provincial towns there
was a cult of this brilliant poet. [57]

One may find suggestions that the Serious grew out of the Bizarre in
Budapest, even in politics. Old Hungary was in general a land of political
comic opera. A Count Andrássy could and would bound back and forth
from one party to another according to the dictates of his private aristocratic whims. Even the political "left" was fantastic in this land, accepting as its major leader during the first World War a Count Mihály Károlyi,
even though he was a magnate, a great land-owner, and a well-known rake
who had entered parliament in 1905 on the far "right" simply because he
was a magnate. It was not unusual to meet Károlyi, as Simon Krausz, a
new-noble banker once did, in a first-class carriage of the Orient Express
preaching land-reform; [58] or to find him mapping political strategy late at
night in a Munich night-club with a pretty girl at his side. [59] In 1913 he
was physically evicted from the Parliament as a noisy agitator. In 1918
when the Monarchy was collapsing, revolution was about to break, and
he was the leader of the radical opposition, Károlyi delayed appearing in
Budapest because he was hunting with other aristocratic politicians in
Transylvania. Yet Count Károlyi, perhaps precisely because he was so
strikingly anomalous a social figure, came more clearly than anyone else of
his class in Hungary to see what in Western Europe one might call "the
Truth." Count Károlyi was practically the only great landholder volun-
tarily to go out and distribute the land to the peasantry in Hungary where
even in the twentieth century almost feudal conditions survived in the
countryside. Károlyi was one of the few of any class in Hungary who both
spoke and acted at the end of the First World War for political democracy
and massive social reform in that land which was on the verge of a barricades revolution.

That Hungary's Jewish nobility gave birth to a number of distinguished
scientific geniuses is, under these circumstances, clearly not just a biolog-

---

[57] See the recent study by Erzsébet Vezér, *Ady Endre. Élete és pálya* [Endre Ady.
His Life and Career] (Budapest: Gondolat, 1969).

[58] See Krausz, *Életem* [My Life] (Budapest: Cserépfalvi, 1937), p. 292.

[59] See Ludwig Hatvany, *Das verwundete Land* (Leipzig, E. P. Tal, 1921), p. 293.

ical fact. It relates to why in Hungary there was a many-faceted cultural rennaissance after 1900, and also to the broad historical problem of how environment affects the development of new ideas. And these are main problems of this book. Earlier in this chapter we have underlined the importance of the Jewish capitalists' rise to wealth and power in Hungary, and the anomaly in their ennoblement. Henceforth, we must ask whether the ennoblement of those capitalists led to the emergence of Hungary's scientific geniuses.

PART II

DYNAMICS

CHAPTER III

MOBILIZATION

The Court Banker Ideal

The purpose of this and the following chapter is to explore the inspiration and social drive, first of the Jewish capitalists who ennobled in nineteenth-century Hungary, and later of the scientific geniuses who emerged from their midst. Let us begin with an account of two families whose shadow falls over the entire length of modern Hungary's economic history, the Rothschild and Sina families. Neither fits precisely into the Jewish nobility. The Rothschilds were most distinctly Jewish, but received their nobility in Austria, not in Hungary. The Sinas received nobility in Hungary, but were probably not Jewish. Nonetheless, one may intimate clearly from their histories a first major ideal which inspired the capitalists of Hungary all through the nineteenth century to ennoble. With this ideal in view we can proceed to the question of why men pursued it, and thence to the problem of what produced Hungary's geniuses.

As is known, the story of the Rothschilds began in the obscurity of the ghetto in Frankfurt am Main with the birth of Mayer Amschel Rothschild in 1744. [1] Despite the poverty of his family, and despite the restrictions on the lives and activities of Jews, harsher in Frankfurt than in many other towns of Germany, this forebear of nineteenth-century Europe's greatest banking clan obtained a respectable education. Then in the 1760's he became a dealer in old coins and established a small counter where traders at Frankfurt's great international fairs might change their money. As a numismatist he entered the association with Prince William of Hesse-Hanau (later Landgrave of Hesse-Cassel) which led to his eventual triumph.

---

[1] A useful account of the Rothschild family history is still Egon Count Corti, *Der Aufstieg des Hauses Rothschild* and *Das Haus Rothschild in der Zeit seiner Blüte* (2 vols.; Leipzig: Insel Verlag, 1926—1927). Further bibliography on the family, and on all the Viennese Jewish families mentioned below, may be found in Hanns Jäger-Sunstenau, *Die geadelten Judenfamilien im vormärzlichen Wien* (Vienna dissertation, 1950).

Prince William became one of the wealthiest rulers in Europe because he possessed in addition to a fat inheritance a businessman's acumen. Rothschild in the 1780's and 1790's became first his numismatist, then his money-changer, then his general factor, and finally when Napoleon in 1806 drove him into exile, the guardian of Prince William's wealth. With this vast fortune to deploy, Rothschild, who by now had five sons, developed an international organization which enabled him to make the best of the smuggling, broking, and supplying opportunities of the Napoleonic wars. By 1811 the family was embarked on gigantic international financial operations such as supplying gold to the British pay-masters in Spain. In 1812 when Mayer Rothschild died, he had a son in London, a son in Paris, a son in Spain, and a successor in Frankfurt, who together possessed the best economic intelligence system in Europe and constituted a major international financial power. Six years later, at the Congress of Aix in 1818, the Rothschild offspring usurped a French state loan from the established international bankers of London, Paris, and Amsterdam, and thus converted their real power into recognized power.

The far-flung Rothschilds are relevant in this chapter on the inspiration of the Hungarian Jewish nobility because of their peculiar social behavior. In technique and in the scale of their operations they represented all that was new and dynamic in one of the greatest ages of West European financial capitalism. They never abandoned, however, the traditional role of court banker which the father of their line assumed to Prince William of Hesse. Even in middle-class England and bourgeois France they aspired to become barons. At Frankfurt and in Central Europe, the center of their operations, they were content with outward humility to be not the "fifth power of Europe," but "Metternich's bankers." In reality independent, they ostentatiously stood behind the throne just as had Samuel Oppenheimer, Samson Wertheimer, and the other great "exceptional" Jewish imperial factors of the past. [2] By the nineteenth century, of course, the court Jews of Central Europe no longer required "exceptional" privileges in the same sense as in the past. Napoleon had breached the ghetto walls all through Western Germany, and enlightened despots had done so to some degree even in the East. [3] In Austria, however, many Jewish disa-

---

[2] On the court Jews, see Selma Stern, *The Court Jew* (Philadelphia: Jewish Publication Society of America, 1950); Howard Sachar, *The Course of Modern Jewish History* (New York: World, 1958), p. 40ff.; and Werner Sombart, *The Jews and Modern Capitalism* (reprint; New York: Collier, 1962), p. 73ff.

[3] See the account in S. M. Dubnow, *Die neueste Geschichte des jüdischen Volkes* (3 vols.; Berlin: Jüdischer Verlag, 1920), Vol. I, pp. 10—31.

bilities remained; and besides, Joseph II and his successors had found a new degree of "exceptionality" with which to attract wealthy Jews to the throne. In Vienna in the 1780's the Habsburgs had started giving patents of nobility even to nonconvert Jews; [4] and by 1815 the cluster of ennobled court factors represented by the Arnsteins, the Eskeleses, the Hönigs, the Wertheimsteins, and the Pereiras was one of the most famous features of that city which was reputed for the aristocratic pretensions of its Christian middle classes. [5] The Rothschilds in 1816 accepted such a patent of nobility from Kaiser Franz, signalizing their willingness to work within the "system." Moreover, Salamon Rothschild, who in 1819 established a branch of the family firm at Vienna, was not above accepting most of the legal disabilities which the old regime there imposed upon his race. In 1822, he was grateful to become the first non-convert Jew to become an Austrian baron, though it was only twenty years later that he received the landowing privilege usually concomitant on such a rank. [6] So doing he established definitively the admirability of the new, ennobled court bankers in the eyes of many less powerful Jewish financiers of Central Europe.

The Sina family came from Moschopolis in Greek Macedonia. Legend has it that they were of Sephardic, or Spanish Jewish origin, [7] but converted to Greek Orthodoxy. In actuality they were Armenians. Regardless, they embarked upon the trail of wealth in a way which historically in Danubia is identified as "Greek." In 1718 under the treaty of Passarowitz between the Emperor and the Turks, Ottoman and Austrian subjects gained the right to trade in each other's countries. Austria's subjects, as it turned out, proved quite unable to cope either with Ottoman backwardness or even with the competition of the Turkish subjects, mainly Greeks, who were used to Ottoman corruption. The main result of the Treaty, therefore, was that Greeks such as the Sinas established virtually without opposition a profitable commerce in handwares, tobacco, and cotton from the Balkans

---

[4] See the data in Jäger-Sunstenau, *Die geadelten Judenfamilien*, pp. 38—39.

[5] A recent account of the life of these ennobled Jews is Hilde Spiel, *Fanny von Arnstein* (Frankfurt a/M: S. Fischer Verlag, 1962). On the pretensions of the Vienna bourgeoisie, see the study by Ilse Barea, *Vienna* (New York: Knopf, 1967), pp. 84ff.

[6] The Rothschilds received the right to purchase noble land in Austria and Bohemia only in 1843; and they had to wage a lengthy and costly struggle even to obtain the right to own real estate in Vienna. See Corti, *Aufstieg*, p. 296ff; *Blütezeit*, p. 247ff.

[7] The legend was sufficiently strong to merit the Sina family a listing in the *Semigothäisches genealogisches Taschenbuch* of 1912. Although objections were made, the name was listed in the *Semigotha* of 1914 as non-Jewish with a question mark — one of six such question marks in a list of 300 apologies.

to Central Europe and managed even to gain a stranglehold on freshly liberated Hungary's local trade. [8] The very word for "trader" in that country became for a time "Görög" or "Greek." [9]

When Simon Georg Sina, [10] who was born in 1753, came of age the Ottoman State was entering its era of disintegration and the Empress Maria Theresa was cracking down on these foreign traders in Hungary. Sina's career is a record of what happened to the Greeks after they were deprived of their hold on the local trade (which incidentally fell almost entirely into the hands of Jews). Simon Georg Sina stayed in the Balkan commerce, but did so by joining the Greek community in Vienna itself, and opening a cotton-goods counter there, building on the opportunities opened for Greek traders by the Russo-Turkish treaty at Küçük Kaynarca in 1774, which let Christians in the Ottoman dominions sail under a Russian flag. By the time the vengeful Turks had let Albanian robbers sack Moschopolis in the 1780's, Sina was sufficiently rich to be invulnerable to this disaster, which ruined many of his compatriots. He had expanded beyond foreign trade into banking; and in the ensuing period of revolution and war he acquired not only a vast fortune but a private bank network of his own in the Balkans, which, although not the equal of the Rothschilds' system in Western Europe, was of very considerable importance for the European South East. So powerful did he become, that in the Napoleonic wars he could take major credit for keeping Austria's Balkan trade going despite the political disturbances. He is important to our topic, because he like the Rothschilds elected to fit in with Vienna's new court banker tradition. In 1818 he acquired nobility in Austria, and his son, George Simon Sina, obtained baronage in Hungary in 1832.

The Rothschilds and George Simon Sina were highly conspicuous economic figures of Austria and Hungary during the forty years after 1820. The Rothschilds were western oriented (and of course richer by far).

---

[8] On the Greeks in Hungary see Ferenc Eckhardt, "Kereskedelmunk közvetitői a 18-ik században" [Our Commercial Middlemen in the 18th Century] in the *Századok*, 1918, p. 359ff.; and also the recent discussions by T. Stojanović, "The Conquering Balkan Merchant" in *Journal of Economic History*, 1960, p. 237ff.; Anton Spiesz, "Die orthodoxe Handelsleute aus dem Balkan in der Slowakei," in *Balkan Studies*, V (1968), p. 381ff.; and Mihály Pásztor, *A százötvenéves Lipótváros* [The Hundred-Fifty Year Old Lipótváros] (Budapest: Statisztikai Hivatel, 1940), pp. 59—68.

[9] See László Kállai, *A 150-éves Goldberger Gyár*, p. 14ff.

[10] See Const. von Wurzbach, *Biographisches Lexikon des Kaiserthums Österreich*, Vol. XXXIV (1872), pp. 351—358; David Landes, *Bankers and Pashas* (New York: Harpers, 1969), pp. 11, 23ff, and 43; and Georg Franz, *Liberalismus* (Munich: Callwey, 1955), pp. 64—65.

The Sinas were considerably more involved in Hungary and the East. But in Vienna they fought on a par, first within the framework of the great Austrian National Bank, founded in 1817, then in the 1830's over who should build in Austria some of the first railroads on the Continent, and over who should open the Danube to shipping. Later, in the 1840's they fought over who should help Count Széchenyi finance the chain bridge over the Danube between Pest and Buda. Meanwhile, both families set about dynasty building. The barons Rothschild married not only other barons Rothschild, but also British and German ennobled Jews. The Baronesses Sina married Prince Mavrocordato and Prince Ypsilanti, a Duc de Castries, and a Count von Wimpfen. With all their economic power and prestige, in a word, both families reinforced the court banker tradition of Vienna's past — a tradition whose outward sign was now ennoblement.

In order to obtain as clear as possible a view of what the court banker tradition meant for nineteenth-century Hungary, it is convenient at this point to recount briefly the histories of three Jewish families which made fortunes in three main branches of Hungary's early capitalist economy. The first are the Wodianers, who came to Bács county in Southern Hungary from Bohemia in the middle of the eighteenth century, attracted evidently by the Balkan trade from which the Greeks were being evicted. [11] By 1796 the Wodianers had established a firm in Szeged on the Tisza, and they made fortunes first by trading in cotton, grain, and tobacco during the Napoleonic boom, and then by manipulating their capital to the disadvantage of the Hungarian nobility in the ensuing years of depression. [12] Sámuel Wodianer, the founder of the family's *kapriorai*, or older branch, [13] established a trading house in Pest in 1828. In 1841 this constituted the nucleus of the *Pesti Magyar Kereskedelmi Bank*, Hungary's first publicly

---

[11] The Wodianers were a complex clan. The elder, *kapriorai*, branch comprised Sámuel Wodianer, his sons Mór and Albert, and his grandson, Albert. As is described in the text, they grew by mid-century to be one of the great powers in Viennese banking. The younger, *maglódi*, branch, headed by Sámuel's nephew, Béla Wodianer, stayed in Pest. This branch was far less important, and got its nobility because of its prominent cousins. See OL. K-128, B-Min Eln. 1867, I B 2595.

[12] A major account of Hungary's commercial economy in this period is Mérei, *Magyar iparfejlődés*. Useful also are Béla G. Iványi, "From Feudalism to Capitalism: The Economic Background to Széchenyi's Reform in Hungary" in *Journal of Central European Affairs*, Vol. XX, no. 3 (Oct., 1960), pp. 270—288, which updates an earlier archival study by the author published in Hungarian; and Molnár *et al.* (eds.), *Magyarország története*, Vol. I, Part IV. Ch. 3, which reflects recent views.

[13] On Sámuel Wodianer and his sons, see Mérei, *Magyar iparfejlődés*, pp. 36, 38 and 170—171; Lederer, *Az ipari kapitalizmus kezdetei*, esp. pp. 73—75 and H. Jäger-Sunstenau, *Die geadelten Judenfamilien*, pp. 186—187.

owned bank. But it was in Vienna that Sámuel Wodiander found the most favorable opportunities for business. By 1829 he had established a wool-classification house there, and had formed close relations with Metternich's bankers, especially with the Rothschilds. Eventually he became a principal exporter of Balkan cotton and Hungarian wool to the mills of England. The natural movement of the international trade sector of Hungary's economy bore this businessman to Vienna, and there he quickly fell in with the traditions of the town. In 1844, having converted, he acquired Hungarian nobility. In 1863 he became a baron in Austria, and later on his sons, who possessed gigantic Hungarian estates, became barons in Hungary too.

The Biedermann family made its fortunes in another sector. [14] Hersch Freistädtler, the founder of this clan, was an engraver who came from Germany to the ghetto at Pozsony [Bratislava, Pressburg] in the mid-eighteenth century. Pozsony played, as it happens, a peculiar role in both Jewish and economic history in Hungary. In the first place, being directly on the frontier of Moravia and Austria, it formed a convenient settling place for Jews who were expelled from Vienna and the Austrian dominions in the seventeenth and eighteenth centuries. Consequently, although after the battle of Mohács (1526) the Hungarians had expelled all Jews from the town, by the early eighteenth century it had the largest Jewish community in Hungary and the country's most significant ghetto. [15] In the second place, while the Turks dominated Hungary and long afterwards, until 1848, Pozsony was the country's political capital, the seat of the Diet. And in the eighteenth century the Jewish ghetto, swollen with immigrants from all over Europe, came to dominate the capital's thriving market. Hersch Freistädtler's family leaped to affluence because of this market.

Freistädtler's son, Michel Lazar, although initially an engraver like his father, dealt in jewels and clocks also, and mediated loans to the aristocratic Magyars who attended the Diet. Yet the longer he did this, and the richer he grew, the more it became apparent that the logical place for him to operate was not provincial Pozsony, but Vienna, where his clients

---

[14] On the Biedermanns, see apart from Jäger-Sunstenau, *op. cit.*, pp. 111—112; Sigmund Mayer, *Die Wiener Juden, 1700—1900*, pp. 139ff., and 282ff.; *Encyclopedia Judaica*, Vol. IV, pp. 778—779; and Hans Tietze, *Die Juden Wiens* (Leipzig, Vienna: E. P. Tal, 1933), p. 152ff; and Wurzbach, *Biog. Lexikon*, Vol. I, p. 386ff.

[15] There were also ghettos in a number of other west Hungarian towns, but these were relatively small; and elsewhere in the country the Jews either had no right to dwell in towns at all, or else they arrived in number only in the nineteenth century. On the history of the Jews in Hungary and on their situation prior to 1848 see Venetianer, *A magyar zsidóság története*; [History of Hungarian Jewry] (Budapest: Fővárosi Ny., 1922); and Zsigmond Groszmann, in *Magyar Zsidó Szemle*, Vol. 53 (1936), p. 231ff.

actually lived. Consequently, he took advantage of the legislation of Joseph II to change his name to Biedermann, [16] and obtain a dispensation to live in Vienna. There he established his own banking house, and the first Viennese wool-sorting firm. Michel Lazar Biedermann was, until his death in 1843, a pious Jew, and a leader of a Jewish community, so he remained aloof from the more profane aspects of being a modern court banker. But both his sons, who were in mid-century very important bankers, converted. The elder, Simon, became an Austrian *Ritter* in 1860 and later a baron, while the younger, Gustav, won Hungarian nobility in 1867.

The Todesco family history can afford us insight to a major sector of Hungary's early nineteenth-century capitalist economy from which Jews were excluded: the guild-dominated industrial sector. Hermann Todesco was born in 1792 into a Jewish family from Breslau in Silesia which had settled, as had the Biedermann forebears, in Pozsony. [17] By his day a new factor had come to determine the economic life of that city, apart from the Diet-inspired market which launched the Biedermanns on their path to riches. Maria Theresa and her son Joseph II had both firmly encouraged their subjects to manufacture. In their western lands the result had been a decided boom, particularly in textiles, but in recently liberated Hungary the consequences were quite different. In lieu of pressing taxation upon the Hungarian nobility, Maria Theresa had early in her reign erected a customs frontier around her eastern kingdom; and the more she encouraged manufactures after this, the more her Hungarian subjects found the customs regime a fatal obstacle to competition with the more favored manufactures of Austria and Bohemia. [18] By the end of the century Hungary had fallen far behind the western Habsburg lands in manufactures, and indeed had become a fertile market for those other lands. Only Pozsony, strategically located on the frontier, had profited from the system. The inhabitants of its ghetto had come to monopolize the wholesaling of Austrian textiles in much of northern and western Hungary. The Todescos,

---

[16] Under one of Joseph II's reforms all the Jews in the Empire had to adopt surnames, preferably German. Unlike some of his other reforms, this was both effected and lasting. See S. M. Dubnow, *Die neueste Geschichte des jüdischen Volkes*, Vol. I, p. 234ff.

[17] On the Todesco family, see apart from Jäger-Sunstenau, *Die geadelten Judenfamilien*, pp. 174—175; Mayer, *Die Wiener Juden*, p. 141ff.; *Jewish Encyclopedia*, vol. XII, p. 172; and Wurzbach, *Biog. Lexikon*, Vol. XLV, pp. 224—227.

[18] The classic essays on the Austrian exploitation of Hungary are two volumes by Ferenc Eckhardt, *A bécsi udvar gazdaság-politikája Magyarországon*, Vol. I., *Mária Terézia korában*, and Vol. II. *1780—1815* [The Vienna Court's Economic Policies in Hungary in the Time of Maria Theresa, and 1780—1815] (Budapest: 1922 and 1958). For the following, see also Mayer, *op. cit.*, p. 261ff.

who were silk merchants, thrived thus off Central Europe's first great push towards industrialization, even though paradoxically, as Jews they were barred from most manufacturing activities within Hungary.

Hermann Todesco was the member of his family who most clearly reflected the dilemma of early nineteenth-century Hungary's manufacturers. His family as early as the 1780's had obtained a dispensation to live in Vienna, since their business required them to maintain close contacts with the manufacturers of silk in Habsburg Italy. Hermann Todesco, unable to manufacture inside Hungary, simply left that county altogether. In 1830 he established a cotton mill at Marienthal near the Austrian capital. His enterprise succeeded so well that in 1835 he was able to establish a textile mill on a former state domain near Padua. Eventually this became one of the largest in Europe. Meanwhile he gambled in stocks and when he died in 1844 he left his sons a very considerable fortune. The lesson of this family chronicle is that industrialists in early nineteenth-century Hungary, like the international traders, and the borderland merchants, gravitated sensibly towards the economic center of the Habsburg realm, Vienna. And the result was the same. Hermann Todesco became a banker. Although he remained a pious Jew, his sons shortly swam with the general trend. In 1861 they acquired knighthood in Austria, and in 1869, having converted, they became barons.

In evaluating the court banker tradition of Vienna one must bear in mind that the numbers of the court bankers were relatively few. Prior to 1848 there was in Vienna an unofficial, "illegal" Jewish population of many thousands, but the number of "tolerated" Jews, who possessed the legal right to live there, was less than two hundred, and by no means all of them were ennobled bankers. [19] Nonetheless, the gravity which drew capitalists in virtually every sector of Hungary's economy to Vienna worked effectively to make the weight of this tradition far greater than numbers can suggest. And the dominating international importance of the Roth-

---

[19] There is a great deal of imprecision among historians about the number of ennobled Jews in early nineteenth-century Vienna. It seems useful to make a sharp distinction between the convert Jews who were ennobled, and the non-converts. In the first category, according to Jäger-Sunstenau's list, there were 20 between 1746 and 1848, of which four each were created by Maria Theresa and Joseph II, one by Leopold II, nine by Franz, and two by Ferdinand. In the non-convert category there were ten: Hönig (1789), Popper (1790), Wertheimstein (1791), Eskeles (1797), Herz (1797), Lämel (1812), Rothschild (1816), Leidesdorfer (1817), Liebenberg (1817), and Hofmannsthal (1835). It seems fairly clear from these dates that ennoblement of non-converts took place primarily at times of considerable financial stress. All save the Rothschilds converted prior to 1848.

schilds and the Sinas, who had accepted the tradition early in the century, made it decidedly influential among the capitalists of nineteenth-century Hungary.

Mobilization of Peoples

The court banker tradition, then, was an ideal of sorts which inspired our nineteenth-century Hungarian Jewish capitalists when they ennobled. We shall see later that it was not the only such ideal. In this chapter we are concerned generally with the dynamics of the ennoblement trend, however, not just with its inspiration. Consequently it is pertinent at this point to inquire why this first ideal was powerful in its effects; and to this end it is convenient to recite the chronicle of the Ullmann family, one of the earliest in our sample to acquire nobility.

The Ullmanns are known first in mid-eighteenth century Bamberg, where a forefather was court factor who went bankrupt. [20] Their history is one of constant movement. From Bamberg they fled to Moravia. Thence they moved to Pozsony, where the first important Hungarian member of the family, Mór János Ullmann, was born about 1780. Mór János himself moved even further, first out onto the southern *Alföld* [Great Plain] as had the Wodianers, participating in the Balkan trade from which the Greeks had been evicted, then to Pécs, then to Pest. And to this pattern of geographical mobility Mór János Ullmann added an element of economically upward mobility. During the Napoleonic period the Imperial army was cut off frequently from traditional sources of supply in the West and outside Europe, yet was constantly at war, and was forced accordingly to fall back on Hungary for provisions. The period became accordingly one of boom in that land, and Mór János Ullman and other traders were able to accumulate small fortunes through speculation in grain, wool, leather, and other natural produce. Even after 1815 Mór János' wealth grew. By the 1830's, he owned the principal hotel in Pest and was a major processor of tobacco. In the 1840's he was involved in a financial battle with Baron Sina over the placement of the first Hungarian railroad.

---

[20] There were three branches of the Ullmann family. The oldest, *szitányi*, branch founded by Mór János (born Moizes) is discussed here. The cadet branches both derived from Károly Ullmann, a cousin a brother of Mór János who settled in Pécs and traded there until about 1840. His son Károly moved to Pest about then and received nobility with predicatum *erényi* in 1867. Another son, Mór György, moved to Pest later, and received nobility with the predicatum *baranyavári* in 1889. See the *Egyenlőség*, no. 16, 1887; 20 Jan., 1889; 26 June. 1891; and 14 Aug., 1896.

In 1841, together with his cousin Károly Ullmann, he was a leader in the founding of the *Pesti Magyar Kereskedelmi Bank*.

This pattern of mobilization suggests why in 1826 Mór János Ullmann converted and sought Hungarian nobility. In Hungary in that day Jews were subject to a great variety of legal restrictions. Almost all the country's inhabitants, moreover, were subject to taxes, and to tolls if they desired to move about. Only nobles were really free to travel, and nobles in addition were free of taxes. Through ennoblement thus Mór János released the chains which inhibited his movement both around the country and upwards towards greater wealth.

As it happens a simple desire for increased mobility was not the only reason why this first Ullmann stepped into the court banker tradition. [21] He acted also apparently because of a scandal which had broken out in connection with his activity as an elder of the Pest Israelite Community. Accused of malpractice by other elders with whom he had been feuding, he impulsively broke with his religion, and also with his wife, a mother of ten so pious and longsuffering that she insisted on remaining Jewish though it meant losing contact with all her offspring. One may guess that there were also economic reasons for Ullmann's ennoblement. Land was then still overwhelmingly the main form of property in agrarian Hungary. Jews could not own land. [22] With his patent of nobility Ullmann both could and did immediately acquire considerable estates (as did, we may insert, very many other early Jewish nobles in Hungary).

From outside evidence one may confirm, however, that the mobility achieved through ennoblement was a dominant motive in the behavior of Mór János Ullmann and probably most of the other cases of ennoblement among Jews in Hungary prior to 1848. For example, a professional table of the Jewish nobility (Table 9 in Chapter VI below) shows clearly that these Jewish capitalists were not following the age-old West European rule of escaping their middle-class origins, and sanctifying their wealth by acquiring nobility, investing in estates, and retiring from trade. Almost all the earlier ennobled Jews in Hungary remained until the end of their lives in business, and though some of their children did retreat into the countryside, eventually losing their money alongside the old nobility,

---

[21] For the following see the *Egyenlőség*, 9 Apr., 1921, p. 10.

[22] The first legislation enabling Jews to own real property in Hungary was issued in 1840; but it was not executed until 1860. Until then Jews could control land only through complex financial processes. See Mérei, *Mezőgazdaság és agrártársadalom Magyarországon, 1790—1848* [Agriculture and Agrarian Society in Hungary] (Budapest: Globus, 1948), p. 33ff.; and *MZsL*, "Birtokképesség."

the bulk of these children seem to have remained in business also. Characteristically, both Mór János Ullmann's grandson and one of his great-nephews were key figures in the Budapest banking world in the years before the First World War, three-quarters of a century after his ennoblement. [23] Evidently businessmen in nineteenth-century Hungary regarded patents of nobility as concommitants of business, not as an escape from it.

Since even the great Viennese court banker careers discussed earlier in this chapter reflected considerable geographical and social mobility, it seems logical at this point to suggest a conclusion. Perhaps behind the ennoblement trend we have been studying was that dynamic mobilization of men, called the "urban" or the "industrial" revolution, which has been changing the world from their time to our own.

* * *

It is important to mention here that in the eighteenth and early nineteenth centuries the Jews were a particularly uprooted, mobilized element in the population of Greater Hungary. There had been Jews in Pannonia even before the arrival of the Magyars way back in the ninth century. Some of modern Hungarian Jewry may have descended directly from these "pre-Magyar" Hungarians. By the end of the Turkish wars in 1715, however, their number was minuscule, [24] and an immigration, thereafter, of Jews into "liberated" Hungary was certainly one of the major population movements of modern European History. In the eighteenth century many of these immigrant Jews came to Hungary from Austria, Moravia, and Bohemia, fleeing persecution, driven away by the rigid official inhibitions against Jewish marriages, [25] or following the general migration of settlers into the "liberated" Hungarian territories. Later in the first half of the nineteenth century, after the toleration edicts of Joseph II, there was a massive Jewish

---

[23] Ödön Szitányi was President of the *Hazai Bank* and Adolf Ullmann was President of the *Hitelbank*.

[24] A recent study has tended to confirm older estimates that there were very few native Jews left in Hungary by 1700; that there were some 13,000 Jews in Hungary in the 1730's, and perhaps 20,000 by mid-century. See Fülöp Grünvald and Sándor Scheiber (eds.), *Magyar-Zsidó Oklevéltár*, Vol. VII (Budapest: Egyetemi Ny., 1963), esp. p. 45. Another study, however, has cast these figures in a new light by showing that the general population of Hungary early in the eighteenth century was not 2,500,000 as had previously been thought, but perhaps 4,000,000. See Kovacsics, *Magyarország történeti demográfiája*, [History of Hungary's Demography] (Budapest: Közgazdasági és Jógi Kiadó, 1963), pp. 148ff. One must recognize, of course, that the Jews were very far from the only people who immigrated in large numbers into Hungary in the eighteenth century.

[25] See Schickert, *Judenfrage*, p. 50.

influx from partitioned Poland. [26] Sometimes these immigrants came to
Hungary via Moravia. More usually they came over the Carpathians.
Always they were fleeing the appalling poverty of the ghetto in the once-
Polish eastern lands.

This mighty movement left the Jews of Hungary with far less of an
institutional inhibition against secularization than Jews in other East European lands. In the Polish-Lithuanian lands, for example, and to a lesser
extent in Bohemia and Germany, the Jews of the nineteenth century were
held back and inhibited from a free participation in Christian secular
society by the existence *inter alia* of entrenched Jewish Orthodoxy and
the physical ghetto. In those lands it was difficult for a Jew to escape his
"mediaeval state" without an exhausting break with everything Jewish.
In nineteenth-century Hungary, on the other hand, there was (outside
the Austrian frontier) virtually no ghetto; and even in the heavily
Orthodox Carpathian region, close to the Galician homeland, the congre-
gations were so new and few in number that it was not uncommon early
in the century for Jews even to be born without inscription in any
congregation's records. [27]

Patently a Mór János Ullmann who had wandered all his life, and
who thus faced no entrenched religious institution, was much more ready
for conversion and ennoblement than the inhabitant of a Polish ghetto.
In effect, historians have often generalized that this sort of movement in
the lives of Hungary's Jews was broadly responsible for "exaggeration"
in their social behavior there; [28] and considerable evidence does suggest
that this Jewish migration was important in the background of the ennoblement trend, particularly in the earlier part of the nineteenth century.
Significantly, the known immigrations of Hungarian Jewish nobles occurred
generally after 1770 but without exception prior to 1850. Thus precisely

---

[26] Any precise knowledge of the immigration from Galicia is inhibited by two factors.
First, prior to the 1850's estimates of the population of Hungary are based exclusively
on very faulty Royal conscription and tax lists, and on a famous one-man census by
Elek Fényes. Secondly, in order to escape the legal restrictions upon them, many Jews
lived "invisibly," in the sense that Government officials were persuaded to take no note
of them. A most famous case of this "invisibility" was in Vienna in the 1820's and 1830's,
when some 10,000 Jews were present, but under 200 were officially recognized. See Mayer,
Wiener Juden, Part II, Chs. 3 and 4.

[27] See, for example, Ármin Vámbéry, *Küzdelmeim* [My Struggles], (Budapest:
Franklin, 1905), p. 1.

[28] Even so fair an observer as Robert Kann has stressed the relevance of this problem.
See his "Hungarian Jewry during Austria-Hungary's Constitutional Period," *Jewish
Social Studies*, Vol. VII, no. 4 (October, 1945), pp. 380—386.

in the age of Mór János Ullmann the Jews of Hungary were most conscious of the perspectives opened by personal immigration, and least bound
by settled and established institutions. We can recall indeed that even
the Rothschilds and the court Jews of imperial Vienna were in a physical sense "immigrants" to Austria. When these Jews, thus uprooted,
became in addition rich, and consequently migrants between the two
wholly separate worlds of Jewish and Christian medieval society, they
could easily have found it attractive to seek compensation and security
in the court banker ideal.

* * *

While thus acknowledging the significant impact Jewish migration had
in the making of the Jewish nobility in Hungary, we must emphasize
that this sort of mobilization was neither the only form, nor the most
important form of mobilization which affected the Jewish nobles. The
migration of the Jews into Hungary was limited in time. Alajos Kovács,
an anti-Semitic statistician who published in 1920 a still unsurpassed statistical study of the Jews in Old Hungary, deduced that the famed immigration from Galicia took place mainly in the 1830's and 1840's, and became
inconsequential after the 1870's. [29] A table based on the first known location of all the Jewish noble families makes fairly clear, moreover, that
migration was not directly responsible for the trend to ennoblement in
Hungary in the later nineteenth century (Table 6). This table shows that
most of the Jewish nobility came from the earlier, western immigration.
Of the 126 nobles created prior to 1900, about 64 are known to have
come from Germany, the Austrian crown-lands, or from the Hungarian
counties adjacent to the crown-lands. [30] Only 26 came demonstrably from
the north-eastern counties of the Galician immigration, and from Transylvania. Of the 220 post-1900 creations, 91 came demonstrably from the
west or the western counties, while only 33 came from the northeast. Our
information about the family origins of the Jewish noble group is unfortunately incomplete. Moreover, the fact that in no case can Galician birth
be proved may attest less the truth than a considerable concealment of the
truth. The figures just mentioned do suggest, however, that whereas most
of the Jewish ennoblements took place after 1900, most of the immigra-

---

[29] Alajos Kovács, *A zsidóság térfoglalása Magyarországon*, p. 13ff.

[30] An exact figure is not available because of fluctuation within the Jewish noble
group. For example several families from Western Hungary emigrated to Vienna early
in the nineteenth century and then reimmigrated in order to buy estates in Hungary
late in the century.

TABLE 6
FAMILY ORIGIN

	1820—1899	1900—1918	1820—1918
Unknown	1	4	5
	(1)	(4)	(5)
Germany	—	7	7
Austria	8	5	13
Moravia-Bohemia	18	8	26
N.W.	7	17	24
W.	13	25	38
S.W.	15	19	34
Croatia	2	6	8
	(64)	(91)	(155)
S.E.	8	18	26
Budapest	21	51	72
E.C.	7	27	34
	(36)	(96)	(132)
N.E.	21	19	40
Transylvania	4	12	16
Galicia	1	2	3
	(26)	(33)	(59)
Totals	126	220	346

Code: N.W.: Western Slovakia
      W.: Dunántúl north of Balaton
     S.W.: Dunántúl south of Balaton

S.E.: Tiszántúl south from Szeged and Arad
E.C.: Pest, Nógrád, Heves, Jász, Bihar, and Hajdu counties
N.E.: Borsod, Szabolcs, Szatmár, Ung, Bereg, and East Slovak counties

tion was in the earlier period. To this one may add a quantity of evidence that it was simply not the immigrant Jews in Hungary, even in the later period, who entered the assimilation movement which led to ennoblement. In 1900, for example, when two parliamentary deputies, Ede Egan [31] and Miklós Bartha, [32] "discovered" and publicized information regarding the

---

[31] Egan was an agricultural expert of Scottish origin. As a member of the Hungarian Parliament in 1897, at the behest of the Minister of Agriculture, he made a tour of certain Ruthenian estates rented by the Hungarian treasury from the Count Schönborn family. In his report Egan attributed the poverty of the area to the primitive agriculture practices; to the total absence of state officials and of modern commercial institutions; and to the usurious behavior of the Jews. Egan started what turned into a crusade to transform the Slavic peasants into Magyars by sending in Magyar officials; by modernizing the local economy; and by reducing the power of the Jews. The affair became celebrated

usurious domination of immigrant Jews over Ruthenian peasants in the Carpathian region, they made it clear that these "Kazars" themselves did not assimilate. They found that only the "Kazar" children did so, who were born in Hungary and moved to Budapest.

The writer, Lajos Hatvany-Deutsch confirms this observation in an extensive and partially autobiographical account of a family named Bondy, which began its career early in the nineteenth century with penniless immigration to Hungary, and then through pure drive ended late in the century very wealthy.[33] Hatvany describes the vigor with which the Bondy's sought wealth. Each generation was meticulous and single-minded in its pursuit of money and power, in its worship of the family firm, and in its disregard for interfering human considerations. In this chronicle, however, the immigrant grandfather remained all his life at Miskolc, the point of his original settlement, wholly isolated from the great world, humbly absorbed in his business. It was the second generation of the family — the generation which saw the 1848 revolution — that first sent a member to Pest, and even he was German-speaking and rigidly middle-class in his outlook. Only in the third generation, educated in Pest at Magyar schools after the Jewish emancipation of 1867, and wholly oblivious of the grandfather's immigration, did assimilation and care for wordly fashions catch on. The hero of this generation acquired immense riches, a castle, and a countess for a wife.

The very evidence which demonstrates, thus, that the immigration perhaps did determine the early ennoblement wave among Jewish capitalists in Hungary, strongly suggests also that in the later years of the nineteenth century, immigration probably did not play a signal role in stimulating a Jewish craving for ennoblement.

The history of a latter-day Jewish noble emphasizes the sort of up-rooting, or mobilization, which lent real force to the ennoblement of Jews even in Mór János Ullmann's day early in the nineteenth century, but

---

when Egan was shot down on a subsequent visit to the area by unknown (but, by anti-Semites, easily guessable) snipers. I am indebted to Professor József Perényi, of the East European Chair at the Eötvös Lóránt University, for a typescript copy of Egan's original and never accurately published report in the National Archive (VKM. Eln. 1897, 3286). There is an account of the affair in Professor Perényi's Russian lanquage study of the Ruthenian question, *Studia Historica Academiae Scient. Hung.*, Vol. XVI, p. 136ff.

[32] Bartha was a well-known journalist who took up Egan's cause and injected a rather vicious anti-Semitism. He published an account of his own travels in Ruthenia under the title *A kazár földön* [In the Land of the Kazars] (Budapest: F. Buschmann, 1921, orig. published 1907).

[33] See Hatvany, *Urak és emberek.*

particularly after mid-century. Henrik Ohrenstein clearly sought nobility
in 1908 because out of crushing poverty he had suddenly risen to enormous wealth. [34] Ohrenstein was born, penniless, in 1857 by his own account
in a Banat Village, by popular tradition in Galicia. With a brother he
launched himself on the road to wealth by renting clay-pits from the
Serbian Monastery at Beocsin in Syrmia and establishing a cement plant
there. By gouging his workers and by minute accounting he managed to
buy the Beocsin pits and to rent others. Then he married the daughter of
a cement manufacturer of Újvidék (Novi Sad) and converted this family
link into control of his father-in-law's firm. By the mid-1890's, he was
one of the major cement producers of all southern Hungary, able to mount
a display at the great exhibition of 1896, and to acquire a contract for
enlarging the Margaret Bridge in Budapest. With this he began to expand
into other branches of the construction industry. By 1912 he controlled
three-quarters of Hungary's cement production. Meanwhile he had moved
to Budapest, had occupied a villa on the fashionable *Andrássy-út*, and had
become a director of the *Hitelbank* [Credit Bank] — the most important
bank in Hungary. In 1908 he acquired nobility and in 1910, now one of
the leaders of the Hungarian economy, he became a baron.

Ohrenstein, one may suppose, sought titles and other outward signs
of affluence because abhoring his past, yet not comprehending his present,
he suffered the loneliness of the modern city. Basing his values on material acquisition, deprived of any old community by his participation in
the industrial and urban revolutions of his day, cast into a social environment new and strange and gross which cared for him not a whit, he com-
pensated for his isolation by adhering to the baron-banker ideal.

A quantity of evidence suggests that Ohrenstein was far from the only
case in the Jewish nobility wherein ennoblement resulted from modern
urbanization. Table 7 shows that of the 126 Jewish nobles created prior
to 1900, only 16 were definitely born in Budapest and only 17 are first
heard of in Budapest. Yet 51 of the 93 born outside Budapest eventually
moved there. Of the 220 Jewish nobles created after the turn of the
century, 42 are known to have been born in Budapest and 43 are first
heard of there. Fifty-seven, however, are known to have moved there. In
the whole group of 346 new nobles, almost 33% are known to have moved
from the provinces or abroad to the booming Hungarian capital. Many
others, whose history is hidden, may also have done so. To their number

---

[34] See on Ohrenstein the *Egyenlőség*, 31 July, 1896, p. 5; and Jenő Varga, *A magyar
kartellek* [The Hungarian Cartels] (Budapest: Világosság Nyomda, 1912), p. 41.

TABLE 7
PERSONAL ORIGIN

	1820—1899	1900—1918	Total 1820—1918
7A			
Budapest born	16	42	58
Budapest first heard of	17	43	60
	(33)	(85)	(118)
Foreign first heard of:			
Croatia	1	6	7
Aust. Bohemia	10	11	21
Galicia	—	—	—
	(11)	(17)	(28)
Province born	50	59	109
Province first heard of	32	59	91
	(82)	(118)	(200)
Totals	126	220	346
7B—FAMILY MOVEMENT			
To BP pre-ennoblement	38	53	91
To BP post-ennoblement	13	4	17
	(51)	(57)	(108)
From BP pre-ennoblement	2	2	4
From BP post-ennoblement	24	2	26
	(26)	(4)	(30)
To Vienna—individual	4	—	4
To Vienna—family	11	3	14
	(15)	(3)	(18)

one must add all those new noble families, including the Ullmanns and the Vienna bankers of the early part of the century, who changed their whole style of life in the transition from poverty to urban and industrial riches. Such movement within the lives of the men who sought ennoblement must be regarded as a primary reason for their craving for ranks and titles.

Mobilization of Ideas

The history of the Telkes family suggests with remarkable clarity the degree to which the nineteenth-century social mobility we have been discussing contributed not only to capitalist imitation of the court banker ideal in Hungary, but also to the formation of Hungary's scientific geniuses.

The first of this clan we know of was Simon Rubin, who was born in 1845 at Szeged in the heart of the great Hungarian plain on the Tisza River. Schooled in mathematics as was both usual and necessary in the Jewish community in that day, because of its business orientation, young Rubin began his career in 1867, the year of the *Ausgleich*, after moving to Budapest by joining the staff of the new National Statistical Office. As an economist and writer he made a distinguished career. Eventually he rose to be a respected minor official in the Ministry of Trade. Meanwhile, however, he ardently embraced the cosmopolitan new life open to assimilationist Jews in Dualistic Hungary. He became a leading figure in the patriotic Name-Magyarizing Movement — whose significance we will see in the next chapter. And finally, after changing his own name to "Telkes" he acquired in 1907 Magyar nobility, thus dramatizing the degree to which he had escaped his humble Jewish past.

Of Telkes' eight children one son in particular carried on the father's record of social mobility. Béla Telkes, born Rubin, became towards the turn of the century a Unitarian minister, removing himself culturally from the whole of this family's past; and as if this did not satisfy him, he moved also to Nicaragua and became there a plantation director. Two more of Telkes' sons seem to have been less mobile. Although they converted, they both became bank-directors in Budapest where they were born. The fourth son, however, moved to the United States, and eventually became Hungarian consul in Cleveland.

Maria Telkes, the physical chemist, was born in Budapest in 1900, the daughter of one of Simon Telkes's banker sons, and though the start of her career reflected no more mobility than was present in her family environment, she later became as "uprooted" as her uncles. [35] Educated at a convent school she displayed even as a girl a marked interest in, and ability at, the natural sciences. She studied at the University of Budapest, and eventually in 1924 obtained her doctorate there. But then in 1925 she visited her uncle in Cleveland, and decided to leave her homeland for good. She worked first as a biophysicist at the Cleveland Clinic Foundation. A decade later she moved to the research department of the Westinghouse Electrical and Manufacturing Company at Pittsburgh, and in 1939 she moved to the Massachusetts Institute of Technology, where she remained. Meanwhile her talents developed apace. In the thirties she conducted experiments which resulted in the invention of a photoelectric mechanism capable of recording the emanations of energy sent out by the human

---

[35] See the biographical sketch in *Current Biography*, 1950, pp. 563—564.

brain. During the war she was concerned with applied uses of solar energy, developing first a system for converting sea water to drinking use by means of solar heat; and later constructing a solar heating system for residential buildings.

Naturally it would be gross exaggeration to attribute the success of Telkes' scientific investigations to the social mobility of her family. The evidence does lend, however, to a general supposition that a family atmosphere in which mobility and mobilization were taken for granted could be conducive to fruitful scientific experiment. Other forms of evidence exist, moreover, which are suggestive in this same direction. Let us recite, for example, the career of John von Neumann, a genius whose incredible memory allowed him to retain volumes of historical facts, and who could juggle huge numbers and resolve the most complex mathematical problems in his head. [36] Von Neumann was born in Budapest in 1903, the son of a banker who had evidently hardly been known prior to the middle nineties, when he began work at the *Jelzáloghitel Bank* [Mortgage Bank]. [37] The elder Neumann had prospered greatly, *inter alia* because Kálmán Széll, the chief of his bank and his personal protector, became in 1899 Prime Minister of Hungary. By 1913 when he acquired nobility, he was as redolent of new wealth as the new baron Henrik Ohrenstein or as József Lukács, the philosopher's father, his colleagues in the banking community. When at the end of the war John von Neumann was about to embark on his professional training, his family was in a position to move abroad — and did so temporarily during the Commune of 1919 and the anti-Semitic counterrevolution which followed. Consequently von Neumann studied chemistry at Berlin, and physics at Zurich; and though he did return to Hungary to take a degree in Mathematics at the University of Budapest in 1926, he found employment the following year as the youngest *Privatdozent* in the history of the University of Berlin. Then he moved to Hamburg. By 1930 he was sufficiently well known to be invited to Princeton; and by 1933 was sufficiently respected there to become the youngest member of the newly established Institute for Advanced Study.

---

[36] Useful characterizations of von Neumann are in *Current Biography*, 1955, pp. 625—627; *Bulletin of American Mathematical Society*, Vol. 64, no. 3, Pt. II (May, 1958); *International Encyclopedia of the Social Sciences*, Vol. XVI (1968), pp. 385—387; National Academy of Sciences, *Biographical Memoirs*, Vol. XXXII (1961), pp. 438—457; and *Life*, 25 Feb., 1957, pp. 89—104. Unfortunately von Neumann died when still young, and prepared no intellectual memoirs.

[37] On the elder von Neumann, see the *Pesti Tözsde*, 26 Aug., 1926, p. 9; and 6 June, 1929, p. 4.

In the twenties von Neumann developed the field of mathematics applied to social science which is known today as game theory. During the war he was at Los Alamos, associated with the development of the atomic bomb. After the war he became a founder of modern computer science. In the years prior to his death he was an advisor in several capacities to the United States armed forces and a member of the Atomic Energy Commission. And if we may judge from the record of Hungary's other scientists, von Neumann was not alone in benefitting from a wide-ranging educational experience. Very many of them seem to have traveled abroad for their higher education, particularly to Austria and Germany, but also to France and England. [38] One of them has even communicated that the key to his career as a computer specialist and sociologist is the fact that as a Jew he could not obtain the university training he wanted in Hungary after 1918, and consequently had to seek his training abroad, wandering from country to country all over Europe. [39] The changing scene, he claims, inspired the scientific imagination of his country's physicists, opened their eyes to new perspectives, and encouraged experimentation.

Lajos Hatvany was not a scientific genius; but his family is very important to our story of Hungary's Jewish nobility, and he himself looms large in the background of the tale of our scientists. We may conveniently recite his career at this point, as a further key to how the social mobilization of late nineteenth-century Budapest contributed to the formation of Hungary's great scientists.

Hatvany was born in 1880, the son of Sándor Hatvany-Deutsch, flour-miller and sugar baron. [40] Raised in the lap of *nouveau riche* luxury, Hatvany while still young flatly refused to follow in his father's business footsteps. He embarked instead upon a career of academics and became a philologist, completing a doctoral dissertation about the letters of Pliny. But then he grew bored and changed fields. He turned from academics to literature and composed a satire against philologists entitled *Die Wissenschaft des Nichtwissenswerten*. A fertile imagination and material independence now

[38] Mrs. Fermi claims on the basis of her list of some hundred prominent Hungarian emigre intellectuals that apart from the "most brilliant ones," most of them were educated largely at home. But "at home" means within the old frontiers of the Habsburg Monarchy — i.e., including Vienna. See *Illustrious Immigrants*, pp. 111—112.

[39] Letter from Alexander Szalai to WOMc Jr., 3 April, 1969.

[40] There are appreciations of Hatvany in all the recent publications and republications of his literary works. The most extensive published biography, however, seems to be in Benedek (ed.), *Magyar irodalmi lexikon*, Vol. I. The history of his family is discussed in detail in Chapter VI, below.

led him to diverse exploits, the most famous of which was his sponsorship and editorship of a journal of modern Magyar literature entitled *Nyugat* [West] to symbolize the cosmopolitan ideas he wished to stimulate. [41]

Nyugat, the very antithesis of the stuffy late-romanticism which still then passed for literature in Hungary, began publishing young writers such as Zsigmund Móricz, Mihály Babits, and Frigyes Karinthy in 1908. It became a principal vehicle of the Ady cult. Proudly and consciously it assumed the mission of "revolutionizing" Hungarian culture. All that was bright, young, and original in Hungarian literature crowded into its pages. But then in 1910 Hatvany came to feel that his journal was too precocious, too remote from society, too febrile. Cautiously he announced that, to encourage a spirit of independence in the literary revolt, he would withdraw his financial backing. [42] The response was a brawl. Several writers took umbrage at the implication that they were "ivory-tower intellectuals": they accused Hatvany, the millionaire, of trying to make profits out of culture and of harboring hypocritical values. Other factions, thereupon, published manifestos supporting Hatvany, and a minor war broke out over who would control *Nyugat*. In the end Hatvany fled to Berlin, where he helped found and for some time edited a journal which let him propagandize the new writers of the Budapest renaissance while remaining beyond the range of their barbs.

In later years Hatvany's career took a more serious path which vindicated his earlier dabbling. He turned now from culture to radical politics. In 1917 he purchased a daily newspaper, and as its editor played an important role in the preparations for the revolution of 1918. He was a member of Count Károlyi's National Council in the autumn of 1918, and did what he could to keep it on a sober course. When the Bolsheviks seized power, he went into exile, but he did not (as did so many others) change his principles. In the later twenties he was brave enough to come home, to force the Horthy Regime to put him, a baron, on trial, and to put its slander of the revolutions of 1918 and 1919 to scrutiny in a court of law. In general, however, Hatvany's record illustrates how the social mobilization of turn-of-the-century Budapest led to a characteristic versatility in intellectuals there.

Hatvany's social mobility was far from the only factor in producing his versatility. The city itself and the society which dwelt in it were, as we remarked in the preceding chapter, naturally stimulating to diverse

---

[41] For the *Nyugat* affair, see Horváth, *Magyar századforduló*, p. 425ff.
[42] For the following, see *ibid.*, p. 447ff.

and experimental activities. Simon Krausz, a banker recounts how he once financed a mad effort to introduce bull-fighting in Budapest as a tourist attraction; and how in the pre-war days even he lived gaily in a *Art Nouveau* villa, entertaining artists and musicians. [43] Further, as will appear in later chapters, a leading profession of many Budapest intellectuals, young and old, was journalism, which by its nature encourages versatility. Yet the main factor in Hatvany's versatility was obviously his wealth. His wandering from field to field was essentially dilettantism, a luxury made possible not just for him, but for the whole society he represented, by the sudden affluence which he and it enjoyed.

Let us consider in this light the career of Michael Polányi, perhaps the most representative of the scientists with whom modern Hungary has startled the world. Born in 1891 in Budapest, there can be little doubt that Polányi was stamped from his childhood by the mobilization of his time. His father, Michael Pollacsek, was a railroad planner and professional engineer who had been born in the Carpathian region. His mother, Cecile Wohl, was from Kovno in Lithuania, the daughter of an old rabbinical family there. [44] Both parents were highly educated. The father studied at the Zurich *Technische Hochschule*. The mother, a woman of extraordinary talents, emancipated herself as a girl by migrating with a school friend to Vienna and insisting on making her own living. The family experienced all the vicissitudes of modern business. The parents began in Vienna, moved to Budapest in the eighties, acquired a fortune building Hungarian local railways, and settled for a time on the *Andrássy-út*, and then in 1900 lost all. Michael Polányi and his two elder brothers were thus direct products of migrations across frontiers, into cities, upwardly towards wealth, and outwardly towards ideas.

Michael Polányi was also the product of a considerable international cross-fertilization of ideas, acquired in part through travel, of which the family did a lot, but also through peculiar educational experiences at home. The husband of his mother's school friend was a Russian emigré *narodovolets*—a populist revolutionary—named Samuel Klatschko. Though Klatschko lived in Vienna, the Pollacsek boys saw him during their annual summer vacations at Baden and learned from him of the exotic Russian

[43] See Simon Krausz, *Életem*, especially p. 138ff. Other pertinent recollections of the versatile intellectual life of turn-of-the-century Budapest are in the early chapters of Arthur Koestler, *Arrow in the Blue* (London: Hamish Hamilton, 1952); and in the portrait of Ferenc Molnár by S. Behrman in the *New Yorker*, 21 May to 8 June, 1956.

[44] See *The Logic of Personal Knowledge. Essays Presented to Michael Polányi on his Seventieth Birthday* (London: Routledge and Kegan Paul, 1961), p. 15ff.

intelligentsia of Bakunin, Chaikovsky, Nechaev, Plekhanov, and Axelrod, as well as of Dostoevsky and Tolstoi. The influence of Klatschko determined Michael Polányi's older brother, Karl, to become a founder and first president of the Galilei Circle, the center of intellectual and social revolt among Budapest's university students after 1908. Klatschko also strongly influenced the Polányis' first cousin, Ervin Szabó, to become a socialist and sociologist and Budapest's most original radical intellectual in the pre-war years.

And then at home in Budapest Michael Polányi experienced another sort of contact with cosmopolitan ideas. There his mother, both before and after the family fortunes decayed, presided over an intellectual salon to which the city's radical *literati*, old and young, flocked, and at which every new idea, every new trend from the West was assiduously cultivated. While Michael Polányi was attending the gymnasium in the pre-war years, therefore, he was in continuous contact with Lajos Hatvany, with Oszkár Jászi, with Georg Lukács, and with all the other bright young people of Young Budapest. With this background not only of family mobilization, but of *demi-monde* intellectual adventure, it does not seem surprising at all that Michael Polányi effectively developed his prodigious scientific talents.

Polányi's characteristic, however, has been not only the successful development of his talents, but the sheer diversity of his accomplishments. A testimonial volume prepared for his seventieth birthday in 1961 characteristically begins with an "index" of his contributions to science. They include the development of a theory of adsorbtion, and work on the plasticity and strength of materials, on X-ray analysis, and on reaction mechanism. They fall within the disciplines of physics, mathematics, and biochemistry. [45] In addition, he is celebrated as an authority on the social sciences, philosophy, morals, and even history. The reason for this diversity

---

[45] There are surprisingly few published biographical sketches of Michael Polányi, although his *curriculum vitae* is available in *Who's Who* and other gazetteers. There is helpful material on his brother, Karl Polányi. however, in portraits by Hans Zeisel in *International Encyclopedia of the Social Sciences*, Vol. XII (1968), pp. 172—174; and by Paul Bohannan in *American Anthropologist*, New Series, Vol. LXVII (1965), pp. 1508—1511 Further, there is a good deal of interesting material on the Polányi family background in Fermi, *Illustrious Immigrants*, pp. 113—114, which is based on material from members of the family; in Oszkár Jászi's memoir fragment in *Látóhatár*, Vol. VIII, no. 1—2 (April 1957), p. 62. and in the invaluable memoir by Ilona Duczinska and Zoltán Horváth, "Polányi Károly és a Galilei Kör," [Karl Polányi and the Galilei Circle] in the *Századok*, Vol. CV (1971), no. 1, pp. 89—104. I am indebted for further details to Mr. Samuel Goldberger, who encountered them in his research on Ervin Szabó.

is adequately clear. Polányi has never hesitated to cross the walls between disciplines. In fact, in 1947, after some years holding a chair at the University of Manchester in physics and chemistry, he deliberately changed to a chair in social studies.

Nor is such versatility Polányi's alone among the Hungarian scientific geniuses of this century. Leo Szilard, to name but one, had the most enormous scope, experimenting at times in mathematics, at times in physics, at times in politics, and even in the joys of literary composition. [46] Versatility, in fact, has in no small degree been the attribute of the Hungarian geniuses of our century, which has made them seem to be a cohesive group in the eyes of the world. And it seems no stretch of the imagination to attribute this extraordinary common quality to the mobilized, *nouveau riche* affluence of Lajos Hatvany's Budapest.

It is not in the competence of this book to compose laws of history, much less of cultural history whereby one phenomena leads "inevitably" to some other. From our investigation in this chapter, however, it does seem that the mobilization of peoples, which in the nineteenth century inclined Hungarian Jewish capitalists to imitate the court banker ideal, stimulated in the early twentieth century a readiness in Budapest intellectuals to explore new scientific realms; and specifically to slip easily from discipline to discipline in the realm of ideas, exaggerating with their versatility the glitter of their natural genius.

---

[46] See the portrait of Szilard by Wigner, in National Academy of Sciences, *Biographical Memoirs*, Vol. 40 (1969), p. 337.

CHAPTER IV

WESTERNIZATION

The Magyar Noble Ideal

The court bankers of early nineteenth-century Vienna were not the only ideal which inspired Hungary's Jewish capitalists to ennoble. The Magyar nobles also were an inspiration for these capitalists. Let us approach an explanation of why this was so through the career of Mór *Iudasi* Gans, the first Jewish intellectual to acquire nobility in nineteenth-century Hungary.[1]

Born at Komárom on the Danube between Pest and Pozsony in 1829, Gans followed a career determined by his experiences as a university student in Pest. There in 1848 he was smitten by the revolutionary fervor which was sweeping all Europe. As was natural for a revolutionary in that springtime of the nations, moreover, he took up a specifically national cause, the Magyar cause. [2] In the spring of 1849 he even became editor

---

[1] Five books are particularly helpful in reconstructing the careers of Gans and the other Hungarian Jewish intellectuals discussed below. These are János Kosa, *Pest és Buda elmagyarosodása 1848-ig* [The Magyarization of Pest and Buda Prior to 1848] (Budapest: Általános Ny., 1937); Zsigmond Groszmann, *A magyar zsidók V Ferdinánd alatt, 1835—1848* [The Hungarian Jews under Ferdinand V] (Budapest: Egyenlőség, 1916); the same author's *A magyar zsidók a XIX század középen* [The Hungarian Jews in Mid-19th century] (Budapest: Egyenlőség, 1917); Rózsa Osztern, *Zsidó újságírók és szépírók a magyarországi németnyelvű időszaki sajtóban... 1854-ig* [Jewish Journalists and Writers in the Hungarian Press of the German-Language Period... until 1854] (Budapest: Ferdinand Pfeiffer, 1930); and Nikolaus Laszlo, *Die geistige and soziale Entwicklung der Juden in Ungarn in der ersten Hälfte des 19. Jahrhunderts* (Berlin: Michel, 1934). See also Gyula Farkas, *A "Fiatal Magyarország" kora* [The "Young Hungary" Era] (Budapest: Magyar Szemle Társaság, 1932), esp. Part II. Both the latter named works are moderately anti-Semitic.

[2] For the background of the political relationship between Jews and Magyars in Hungary, see László Simon, *A zsidókérdés a Magyar reformkorban* [The Jewish Question in the Hungarian Reform Era] (Debrecen: Dr. Bertók Lajos Kiadása, 1936), p. 43ff. For the role of the Jews in the revolution of 1848—1849, see Béla Bernstein, *A negyvennyolcas magyar szabadságharc és a zsidók* [The Hungarian war of Independence of 1848 and the Jews] (2nd. edit.; Budapest: Hungária, 1939).

of a short-lived Magyar revolutionary journal; and in the end this rebellion against his King led, paradoxially, to his ennoblement.

In the quiet early decades of the century the Magyar national cause had been in many senses identical with that of the Hungarian nobility. [3] Nobles had been then virtually the only articulate social class in Magyar society. As privileged members of the old constitutional Hungarian *natio*, moreover, these nobles had had a sense of corporate identity and political mission which far excelled the leadership of many other East European linguistic nationalities at the time. In the great decades of reform from 1830 to 1847, nobles had led virtually every political trend in Magyar society. Széchenyi was an aristocrat, Deák was a noble, Kossuth was a noble. And in the revolutionary years, 1848 and 1849, once again the nobility was in the lead in Magyar Hungary, though students, such as Gans, and members of the non-noble social classes now began to play a role. The nobility, voting in the traditional Diet, devised and pushed through the modern, liberal constitution of March and April, 1848. The nobles in the Diet emancipated the Hungarian serfs. [4] The nobility were the most conspicuous social element which fought for Hungary in the revolutionary war.

In the 1860's therefore, when in many other countries of Europe noble leadership was losing its appeal, the ideal of a "noble nation" lived on among the Magyars and led nationalists such as Gans to join its ranks. [5] When at Világos in August, 1849, Russian armies accepted the surrender of the Magyars, and afforded Austria an opportunity to stifle the revolutionary nationalism of Pest, Gans despairingly moved away from Hungary to Vienna, where scribbling could afford him a living. There in 1860 and 1861, when Franz Joseph first abandoned the absolutism with which he ruled in the years after 1849, and restored

---

[3] Recent literature on the development of Magyar nationalism may be found through the essays in Andics (ed.), *A Magyar nacionalizmus kialakulása és fejlődése*, and through the contribution of George Barany in Peter Sugar and Ivo Lederer (eds.), *Nationalism in Eastern Europe* (Seattle: University of Washington Press, 1969), p. 259ff.

[4] Radical and Marxist Hungarian historiography has shown that the nobility emancipated the serfs to a considerable extent not because of liberal convictions, but out of naked self-interest. See Ervin Szabó, *Társadalmi és pártharcok a 48—49-es magyar forradalomban* [Social and Party Struggles in the 1848—1849 Hungarian Revolution] (Vienna: Bécsi Magyar Kiadó, 1921), Chs. 9, 10, 11; and Emil Niederhauser, *A jobbágyfelszabadítás Kelet-Európában* [The Emancipation of the Serfs in Eastern Europe] (Budapest: Akadémia, 1962), p. 139ff. In Magyar nationalist historiography, however, as in the eyes of contemporary observers such as Gans, the liberal convictions of the nobility seemed more important than self-interest in the emancipation.

[5] The aristocratic character of Magyar nationalism is emphasized by Peter Sugar in Sugar and Lederer, *Nationalism in Eastern Europe*, pp. 48—50.

certain constitutional forms in Hungary, Gans went to work publishing a pro-Magyar political journal. The leaders of the Vienna Magyar community as it happened, were aristocrats. Indeed, Gans undertook this patriotic enterprise specifically for Count Apponyi, a leading Hungarian magnate. Subsequently as a Magyar publicist Gans moved into ever more elevated social circles. It was thus that finally, in 1867, as press-secretary for Count Gyula Andrássy, one of the founders of Austro-Hungarian Dualism, Gans was rewarded for his Magyar nationalism with nobility.

Mór Gans was not a particularly important Magyar nationalist intellectual. Indeed, few of the Jewish intellectuals who were really important as Magyar nationalists in the nineteenth century ennobled. [6] At this point, accordingly, we had best touch on the history of one of these important nationalists, Miksa Falk, to test our finding that the ideals of Magyar nationalism favored ennoblement.

Born in Pest in 1828 of rich, convert-Jewish parents, Falk was thrown onto his own resources early in life by the bankruptcy of his father. [7] Like Mór Gans he turned his talents to journalism and became involved in the Magyar national cause. In 1848 he was studying philosophy in Vienna, and he participated in the revolution there, not in Pest. After the collapse of the revolutions, however, his superior writing talents won him a singular position in the Magyar national movement. He became the intimate of Széchenyi in the latter's last years. He became a firm friend of Deák and Eötvös and stood by their side in the critical years of negotiation with Franz Joseph in the middle sixties. On their recommendation he became the Magyar-language tutor of the Empress Elizabeth, and thereafter remained a personal friend of the royal couple. After 1867 he became editor of the *Pester Lloyd*, a famous German-language Budapest daily paper which served as unofficial organ, at first for the business circles of Budapest, and later for the Hungarian Government. Although on the side he acquired a fortune speculating on railroad construction and the stock market, he also joined the Hungarian Academy of Sciences and produced until his death in 1908 a steady stream of patriotic literary, economic, and political publications. In the 1890's he was a parliamentary deputy for several years, and throughout the Dualistic Era he was in on the political councils of the Governement in Budapest. Falk epitomized perhaps more than any other man the success of Jewish and Magyar cooperation in the Dualistic Era.

---

[6] See Table 9 in Chapter VI below for the record.

[7] For the following see Miksa Falk, *Kor és jellemrajzok* [Sketches of the Times and of Contemporariesl (Budapest: Révai, 1902).

Miksa Falk did not acquire nobility, although he was a Magyar nationalist. But because of his court connections and the decorations he received from Franz Joseph, Falk had personal rank far exceeding nobility. Further, his brother possessed nobility in Austria, his son became a member of the "gentry" *Országos Kaszinó* in Budapest, a club even more exclusive with respect to Jews than the magnates's casino. And, thirdly, Hungary was a land where intellectuals were greatly respected. That Falk failed to ennoble is not, therefore, a symptom that as a Magyar nationalist he despised nobility, but simply that like many other distinguished nationalist intellectuals of the Magyar nation he felt formal ennoblement superfluous.

There is abundant documentary evidence even from the very end of the nineteenth century, that the Magyar nationalist meaning of ennoblement in Hungary remained very much alive. Exemplary is a *feuilleton* published in the daily *Budapesti Hirlap* [*Budapest News*] in January, 1896.[8] It told of a Budapest Jew named Berger, whose father had acquired in the course of business a large estate, established a beet-sugar refinery thereon, and sent him out to manage it. Young Berger sought to become a citizen of standing in his new location. He introduced scientific agricultural methods, paid more taxes than most of the local gentry, and contributed palm trees and flowers from his greenhouse to the county balls. The local gentry, however, laughed at and despised him until, as a sign of Government favor, his father acquired Magyar nobility. At the following county assembly the gentry youths expressed accumulated indignation over the Bergers' supposed intrusion into their rural world. Fisticuffs ensued, and blood was shed on both sides. Thereupon, the gentry observed that young Berger's now-noble blood looked as "Magyar" as their own; indeed, that it mixed indistinguishably with their own. As a result the gentry accepted the Bergers as Magyars and invited them to join the local casino. In ennoblement, in sum, the Bergers sought nationality, and through ennoblement they acquired it.

One may laugh at this tale of nationalism in the ennoblement movement in Hungary, no doubt, but one should not ignore its seriousness. The author was Viktor Rákosi, and its original publisher was his brother Jenő Rákosi, the Social Darwinist.[9] These two were among the leading exponents of Magyar nationalism in the late nineteenth century. What is

---

[8] See the *Budapesti Hirlap*, 24 Jan., 1896.

[9] There is a lengthy chapter on the Rákosi circle in Jenő Pintér, *Magyar irodalomtörténet* [History of Hungarian Literature] (8 vols.; Budapest: Stephaneum, 1930—1941), Vol. VII. See also Gyula Farkas, *Az asszimiláció kora a magyar irodalomban* [The Assimilation Era in Hungarian Literature] (Budapest: Franklin, n. d.), p. 90ff.

more, there is strong evidence that the *feuilleton* expressed a broad range of assimilationist Magyar opinion. The Rákosi brothers were both ethnic Germans from Western Hungary who became Magyar chauvinists. Jenő Rákosi, indeed, acquired Hungarian nobility himself in his efforts to seem more Magyar. Further, the Pest Israelite Community, the largest and most important Jewish community in Hungary, republished the tale with enthusiastic endorsement in its semi-official journal, the *Egyenlőség*. [10] All this occurred at the start of Hungary's national Millennium, during which Jenő Rákosi established the national goal as a Magyar nation of 30 million souls to be achieved, in part, through Magyarization.

Further contemporary evidence of the legitimacy of considering ennoblement a matter of Magyar nationalism in Old Hungary is a clever argument which the assimilationist Jewish weekly newspaper, the *Egyenlőség*, published in 1905 (which, as will appear later in our study, was a year of mass-produced Jewish ennoblements). [11] According to this argument it did not matter that some Jews actually paid money for noble rank. In the first place, ennoblement was allegedly an external matter which had nothing to do with making people "better"; and in the second place, allegedly, even those people who purchased nobility were "apt to be someone anyway" (azok rendszerint úgy is valakik). It followed, according to the *Egyenlőség*, that purchased nobility did nothing to degrade the Nation's leading stratum, but actually contributed to its brilliance. The trick of the argument was, of course, its assumption that there was nothing un-Magyar about an ennobled Jew. Here, just as in Rákosi's fable, ennoblement was shown to entail Magyarization.

Nor was it only among Jewish and German assimilees and in the "yellow press" that ennoblement was considered a means of satisfying Magyar nationalism in Old Hungary. In the middle 1890's, Gyula Pick, a landowner from Fejér County whose wife was a member of the recently ennobled Hevesi-Bischitz family of Budapest, decided he wanted nobility.[12] He had converted. A cousin of the same name had acquired nobility in 1888; his wife was related to the baronized Schossberger family; and he based his petition to the Government on a contribution to "stopping the spread of socialism in the countryside." There seemed, therefore, no great

[10] The *Egyenlőség*, 31 Jan., 1896, pp. M. 1—2. It is interesting that the *Egyenlőség* resurrected the fable later on also, at a time when Jewish confidence in Magyar Hungary was severely shaken. See the issue of 22 Jan., 1921, pp. 16—17.

[11] For the following anecdote, see the *Egyenlőség*, 19 March, 1905, pp. 2—3. Compare the arguments in the same journal for 27 May, 1889, p. 8; 21 June, 1895, p. M-1—2.

[12] See OL K-26, Min. Eln. 1898, IX 729.

obstacle in his way. In the Prime Minister's office, nonetheless, his suit got held up. It turned out that the Government "now always recommended" that new nobles Magyarize their names. In 1898, therefore, Gyula Pick became Gyula Pajzs; whereupon the King rewarded his services with a grant of Magyar nobility. The Government, it may be noted, did not always succeed in persuading ennoblement candidates that they should Magyarize their names. [13] By 1918, however, in all 155 of the 346 Jewish noble families had radically Magyarized their names. [14] Clearly the Hungarian Government itself considered ennoblement as a "distinction, donated only to citizens of Hungary who had expressed their patriotism." [15]

Magyar Nationalism

Let us now look into the history of Mór Bloch-Ballagi, the very eminent uncle of an insignificant government official who acquired Hungarian nobility in 1918. Ballagi himself never became a noble, but his career points with surprising clarity to a major source of that nationalism which encouraged the Hungarian Jewish capitalists to pursue the Magyar noble ideal.

Ballagi was born in the northeastern county of Zemplén in 1815. [16] Though his parents were poor he managed to attend the yeshivas (Jewish schools) at Nagyvárad and Pápa and, discovering Christian Europe, began a lifetime participation in West European culture. He became one of the first Hungarian Jews to learn Greek and Latin, as well as several modern languages. Then he took up mathematics at the University of Pest. Unable to receive a fitting degree there because he was Jewish, he proceeded in 1839 to Paris to continue his search for knowledge. Later he studied philosophy and botany at German universities. In part because of his lready remarkable scholarly virtuosity he became, in 1840 at the age of 25, the first Jew to be elected to the newly founded Hungarian Academy of Sciences. The real reason for his election, however, was that even then he was laying particularist roots which contrasted with the breadth of his European scientific endeavor. He had become an exponent of the systematic and radical reform of Judaism through Magyarization. In 1840 he

---

[13] In 1900 the Government failed in an effort to impose the precedent of the Pick-Pajzs case on a family named Rosenfeld. See OL K-26, Min. Eln. 1900, IX 3014.

[14] This figure does not include minor Magyarizations such as from Schwab to Sváb.

[15] For this wording see the definition in OL K-26, Min. Eln., 1904, XI 4422.

[16] Ballagi is discussed in all the works in footnotes 1 and 2 above.

was the major Jewish propagandist of a Magyar Liberal project of that year for total assimilation of the Jews. And after the grateful Magyars enshrined him in their Academy he placed his talents even more fulsomely at their disposal. First, he translated the Pentateuch into Magyar for Baron Eötvös. Then in 1843 he left Judaism entirely, and after an experiment with Lutheranism, became a minister of Calvinism, the "pure Magyar" faith. He participated in the Magyar struggle of 1848 for a time as secretary to Arthur Görgey, Kossuth's great rival for leadership of the revolution. He devoted the last 36 years of his life to the defense of Magyar Calvinism and to the study of Magyar literature.

Ballagi's Magyar nationalism is interesting to us because it bore such an obvious relation to his participation in the secularized, rationalistic culture of modern Western Europe. The eighteenth-century Enlightenment struck down the medieval religious and social barriers which could have kept Ballagi from exploring on the frontiers of modern knowledge, emancipating his intellect. And his Magyar nationalism in a sense served the function of imposing new limits upon his intellectual wanderings. It would be venturesome to define too narrowly how in particular nationalism served this function. We might speculate that he felt the intellectual horizons of the West were too broad, and from some sort of loneliness in the great world of Europe sought to find a new "home" in a Magyar national community. We might speculate equally that after his experience with Western knowledge he felt so alienated from the cultural environment into which he had been born, that he craved a reinforced particular identity. Or we might speculate that he felt simply the existence of undesirable cultural contrasts between his homeland and Europe, and that he became nationalistic in a deliberate effort to raise up his own people. [17] Regardless of which of these or other sorts of narrow explanations apply, it seems clear that nationalism emerged in Ballagi to a significant extent not just as a combination of such tribal loyalty and religious particularism as had contributed to pre-Enlightenment patriotism, but also as an accompaniment to his contact with the modern, specifically secular and analytical culture of the West.

---

[17] For sample discussions of the origins of modern nationalism in Eastern Europe see the recent essay by Peter Sugar in Sugar and Lederer, *Nationalism in Eastern Europe*, Ch. 1; Hans Kohn, *The Idea of Nationalism* (paperback edit.; New York: Macmillan, 1961), Ch. 8, which adopts a traditional cultural approach; and Karl W. Deutsch, *Nationalism and Social Communication* (paperback edit.; Cambridge: MIT Press, 1966), esp. Chs. 4—6, which adopts a strictly sociological approach.

By way of confirmation of this connection one may conveniently recall the peculiar cultural "backwardness" of Hungary at the beginning of the nineteenth century, and then point out that Ballagi was not alone. [18] Eastern Europe in general had suffered cultural disasters in the post-Renaissance period because of wars and social troubles, on the one hand, and the drastic character of its Counter-Reformation on the other. Poland, however, and Bohemia and Austria had at least remained within Europe, whereas the Turks had ripped Hungary out. Into Hungary's Western border, and into the Transylvanian hills the Turks had seldom penetrated, but for two centuries they had reduced the bulk of the country to a waste; and since the Habsburgs "liberated" Hungary in a spirit more of the Counter-Reformation than of the Enlightenment, this land remained, until the French Revolution, a cultural as well as an economic "fallow field" (to use Count István Széchenyi's expression). In Ballagi's day, moreover, despite the existence of a university at Pest, and of enlightened salons at Pozsony, Metternich's "Reaction" was doing what it could to stifle any spirit of inquiry. And under these condition even the great Széchenyi, who, we may point out, was relatively uninhibited by the "Reaction" because of his wealth and magnate status, felt shaken when he perceived the contrast between the Western Cosmos and Hungary, and opened his heart to his benighted Magyars with a nationalist passion recalling that of the truly lonely Russian intellectuals.

The record of the "little man" nationalists in Ballagi's and Széchenyi's Hungary confirms that modern (i.e. secular) nationalism emerged in that country in close relation to the advent of Westernization. [19] Ballagi and Széchenyi were moderates in their nationalism, for example, alongside István Horváth, a Magyar cleric who after discovering Europe came home and scientifically "proved" the greatness of his unlettered countrymen by dubbing them "relatives" of the Jews and of many other Asiatics. Ballagi was certainly no extremist either next to Jan Kollár, the Slovak priest, who, after studying in Germany and after witnessing the romantic bonfires on the Wartburg, wrote about an essential "interchange-

---

[18] For the background of the following, the best accounts are still Szekfű's volumes in Hóman and Szekfű, *Magyar történet* and his early chapters in *Három nemzedék*. But see also early chapters of the detailed Marxist account, Endre Arató, *A nemzetiségi kérdés története Magyarországon, 1790—1848* [The History of the Nationality Question in Hungary] (2 vols.; Budapest: Akadémia, 1960).

[19] For the following, see apart from the work by Arató just cited, Fran Zwitter, *Les Problèmes Nationaux dans la Monarchie des Habsburgs* (Belgrade: Akademia, 1960), which refers to the vast literature on the subject.

ability" of all the Slavs, and went on to "prove" the greatness of Pan-
Slavic culture by "demonstrating" the Slavic origin of the place-names not
just of Elbian Germany, but of all Southern Italy and Sicily. And one
may mention in this connection even Ljud'ovit Gaj, the cosmopolitan
journalist and savant of Zagreb, who, while seeking so elementary a platform for modern education as a standard language for all his beloved
Croats, expounded their cultural "unity" with a great, albeit mythical,
Illyria. Such utterly consistent resort to messianic nationalist explanations in these Westernized men seems to confirm our point. Westernization transformed traditional patriotism into secular and analytical forms
of nationalism in Hungary.

* * *

One must ask at this point whether the loneliness of a culturally "backward" land explains adequately why a pioneer of Westernization in Hungary such as Ballagi should have become a modern nationalist. France
and Germany, by way of contrast, were "backward" by modern standards
in the seventeenth and eighteenth centuries, yet the lonely pioneers of the
French Enlightenment remained prior to 1789 universal and European in
their outlook rather than national; and in enlightened eighteenth century
Weimar *bloss deutsch* could be considered *nicht deutsch*. Why was is not
so also in "backward" Hungary? To fortify our argument against such
attack let us turn now to the career of Karl Beck, a cousin of three most
eminent banker-nobles of turn-of-the-century Budapest. Beck's career recalls
some of the particular ways in which modern nationalism emerged from
Westernization in Hungary.

Born at Baja on the Danube in 1817, Beck attended a gymnasium at
Pest and then began to study medicine, the only discipline in which Hungary
then granted Jews a university degree. [20] Emancipated by his education
from Jewish Orthodoxy, he turned to expresssing his soul on paper, became
a poet, and wandered abroad. He made known the beauties of his native

---

[20] Beck was only one of several Jewish intellectuals in this early German-language
"Great-Hungarian" strain of nationalism. One may refer also to the poet and dramatist
Karl Hugó (Bernstein), who in the 1840's thought of himself (and was thought of) as the
"Hungarian Shakespeare," though he had to be translated for Magyar audiences. He car-
ried the banner of Hungary to the banks of the Seine in 1848 and eventually went mad.
For bibliography on these people, see footnotes 1 and 2 above. For other references to
the "Great Hungarian" strain of nationalism see the works of Béla Pukánsky, "Wand-
lungen und Abwandlungen des deutschungarischen Bewusstseins," *Ungarische Jahrbücher*,
Vol. XIV (1934), pp. 144—164; and *Német polgárság magyar földön* [German Citizenry
on Magyar Territory] (Budapest, 1940).

land the length and breadth of Germany. He wrote the poem to whose words Strausz later composed the Blue Danube Waltz. Yet then in 1848 Beck like Gans, Falk, and Ballagi, joined the Revolution. Though a poet, he carried the political banner of Hungary to barricades on the Elbe and the Rhine. Even far from home, he expounded with exuberance his passion for a political cause.

Beck was certainly not a very important poet, and because he wrote in German Magyars do not always consider him "Hungarian." But his case recalls that in each and every one of the different linguistic "reawakenings" of Hungary, poets played a great role, and *nota bene* left their imprint upon the jargon of their people's political nationalism. The reason for this was first of all, of course, that in the peculiarly "backward" society of Hungary, where the great bulk of the population was comprised of ignorant serfs, where there was hardly any urban middle class, and where even the nobility hovered on the edge of illiteracy, writers in general found themselves not only the first social element to be affected by Westernization, but also in many cases the only social element in their nationality group to be affected. Among the Slovaks and the South Slavs in particular, but to some extent even among the Magyars, it fell to poets actually to mold the paths of modernization which their nations would tread.

In addition, both the form and the circumstances under which Westernization came to Hungary encouraged the development of a specifically poetic jargon of modern political ideology there. Karl Beck and other apostles of Western culture in Hungary were products not directly of the French Age of Reason, but of the Romantic Era which followed it; and they received their ideas not from France directly, but from Germany through the agency of the German romantic poets and the German exponents of idealistic philosophy. Not Voltaire and Condorcet, but Schiller, Schelling, and Hegel were the forebears of the nationalistic intellectuals of the thirties and forties of nineteenth-century Hungary; and their ideas derived not from Locke and Montesquieu, but from Herder and Fichte. [21] These were ideas which stressed organic unities and beautiful romantic feelings rather than the cool reasoning of the liberal European West. Moreover, because Western culture came to Eastern Europe and to Hungary, not just as an intellectual phenomenon, but as a movement associated with revolutionary political aims, the Karl Becks were often beleaguered

---

[21] For an excellent detailed discussion of the education of an East European intellectual of Beck's era see Martin Malia, *Alexander Herzen and the Birth of Russian-Socialism* (paperback edit.; New York: Universal Library, 1965), esp. Chs. 5, 6, and 10.

men. East of the Rhine, and most particularly East of the Leitha, the
tasks of Revolution were considerably more difficult and dangerous than
in the West, and as noted above, its social bases were weaker than in the
West. What is more, the enemies of Enlightenment and of Revolution
were incomparably stronger in these feudal Eastern lands than in the West,
if only because the despotic rulers of the area could subsume the tools
of Reason to Reaction. Such factors made the cause of Revolution East
of the Rhine in the nineteenth century a matter of loneliness and isolation,
stimulating outpourings hot and emotional, rather than rational, of poetic
faith in one or another nation.

To this one may add the complicating factor that Western culture
came to Hungary from outside in the nineteenth century. Even at Weimar
after 1792 *Kultur* had become compulsively German once men perceived
that Reason might be French. In Hungary, correspondingly, in the degree
that Reason turned out to be "foreign," its advocates like Karl Beck
compulsively reinforced their particularism with often irrational emphasis
on their love for their nebulously conceived homes.

To sum up, the doctrines of modern political ideology in Hungary,
were molded importantly by writers and poets, who in the great age of
European romantic idealism were appalled by the dangers of the political
missions which circumstance had forced upon them, and who were reacting
irrationally against the foreignness of the European world. The jargon
of modern ideology in Hungary became, therefore, characteristically imprecise, reflecting fear as much as reason. Given this heritage of imprecision,
perhaps it is not so surprising that the Magyar nationalism of Budapest
Jewish capitalists late in the nineteenth century still focused foggily on a
syllogistic identification of the term "Magyar" with "noble" which was
typical of the patriotism of the past.

*   *   *

The career of József Rosenfeld-Rózsay clarifies a factor which alongside the fears of the poets lent a specifically irrational character to the
modern nationalist doctrines of all Greater Hungary's peoples, though
particularly to those of the Magyars.

Born in 1815 in German-speaking western Hungary, Rózsay was the
son of a personal physician of the princely Festetich family. [22] Following
his father's career, he studied medicine at the best German universities.

---

[22] There is some material on Rózsay in the *Egyenlőség*, 24 May, 1885, p. 7; and
OL K-126, B-Min Eln. 1882, I B 463.

In about 1840 just as a political alliance between Jewish reformers and Magyar liberals was coming about, Dr. Rosenfeld settled in Pest. There in 1843, unlike Karl Beck but like Mór Ballagi, he rejected German Great-Hungarianism. He helped found a "Magyarization Society" among the Jewish medical students, one of the major organizations of the 1848 student revolution in Pest. Hereafter, Rosenfeld was regularly and ever more enthusiastically Magyar. In 1848—1849 he was Chief Physician in a Magyar military hospital. After the revolution he buried himself in his greatest work, the introduction of modern hospitalization in Pest; but in the 1860's when political conditions permitted, he reorganized the Jewish "Magyarization Society" and took an active part in the Jewish reform movement. In 1864, as titular Chief Doctor of the City and County of Pest, Rosenfeld Magyarized his name and was elected to the Hungarian Academy of Sciences; and in 1884 in somewhat round-about fashion he acquired nobility. [23]

Rózsay's career recalls that there was no easy "natural" way for the men of Reason and Revolution to describe their nationality in early nineteenth-century Hungary. In England and France there had existed from times long past a linguistic culture coterminous with the state; and searchers for a modern secular national identity could use the old states without excess of contradiction. Immediately East of the Rhine, however, the Germans who sought a national identity faced very considerable difficulty; for though there was a myth of a single German state, there were in practice several; and what was worse, Austria and Prussia, the strongest of those states, were in no way exclusively German in population, nor were they politically Liberal. Modernizers could not easily tell, thus, which Germany should be their home or how any of the Germanies could be made free. The ideologists of modern Germany responded to these knotty problems evasively, by resorting to passionate nationalism and to an organic Reason which beclouded the issues. And in Hungary the dilemmas facing modernizers were even worse.

Despite the thousand-year-old dominance of Magyars in the thousand-year-old Hungarian state, modernizer Hungarians faced dilemmas because the language of that state was Latin, and because Magyars ruled it not as Magyars, but as members of a medieval constitutional noble nation. Indeed, though Magyar was the vulgar language of much of the ruling class, the King and his aristocracy spoke German, and in the polyglot provinces even nobles might grow up speaking Slavic or German instead

---

[23] Rózsay received Austrian nobility with a Hungarian predicatum. His family eventually obtained nobility in Hungary.

of Magyar. [24] Consequently, any effort to develop a modern identity in Hungary implied recognizing the country's polyglot character, and questioning the rights of the ruling class. Difficulties notwithstanding, decisions were made. Hungary's constitutional "nation," the nobility "one and undivided," began to call itself Magyar, building on the coincidence of "Hungarian" and "Magyar" in the Magyar tongue. Some of the non-noble elements of society, for example Rózsay and other Jewish Magyar nationalists, followed the noble example. But this involved willful acceptance of the nobles' nationalist doctrines; and other non-noble elements began to seek non-Magyar linguistic identities. For all alike there was an element of identity conversion; and for all alike, we may recognize accordingly, Westernization generated in Hungary as in Germany a need for willful beclouding of the inequities of identity choice.

As time passed, this need to sacrifice rationality for the sake of modern identity became for the noble "nation" of Greater Hungary more and more urgent. The old "Hungarian nation," like the Ottoman ruling caste in Turkey, held power in its vast land exclusively because of a tissue of feudal charters and medieval institutions. [25] Even the process of building a modern linguistic nation was, therefore, for this "nation" just as for the Ottoman caste, highly corrosive to every aspect of its power base. Moreover, since by the 1840's the feudal privileges which gave that "nation" its identity were a burden around Magyar Hungary's neck, it had to endure a new crisis. In 1848 Kossuth, Deák and Széchenyi persuaded the Hungarian nobles to demolish the constitutional rights by which they possessed the whole of Saint Stephen's land (i.e., Greater Hungary). Thereafter the old "nation" ruled in Greater Hungary not by right, but on the premises, less than acceptable in terms of modern Liberalism, that it possessed power, and that it was somehow superior to the other nationalities. Claiming to be Hungarian and Liberal, the noble "nation" now excluded as non-Magyar half of the Hungarian population from actual enjoyment of citizenship, using para-legal methods. Claiming to be Magyar, this "nation" excluded also most of the Magyars. With good reason under

---

[24] That the Magyar nationality was a "convert" nationality was a favorite argument of the *Egyenlőség* late in the nineteenth century. See, for example, its issues of 31 Dec., 1882, pp. 4—5; 7 Sept., 1884, p. 6; and 27 May, 1889, p. 8. Some confirmation of this view, drawn from contemporary memoirs, are in Schickert, *Judenfrage*, pp. 18—19.

[25] For the dilemma which modern nationalism posed the Ottoman caste, see Bernard Lewis, *The Emergence of Modern Turkey* (London: Oxford University Press, 1961), esp. Ch. 10; and Sugar's comments in Sugar and Lederer, *Nationalism in Eastern Europe*, pp. 49—52.

these circumstances even convert Magyars such as Rózsay became nationalistic without much regard to non-organic Reason. In the light of cool
western Reason the myths and legends on which their adoptive nation's
power rested would have withered away.

In significant part modern Magyar nationalism strikes us today as foggy
and syllogistic because its makers were members of an older nation who in
modernizing had to reject their identity and to demolish at infinite risk
their older basis of power. Their seeming fogginess derived also, of course,
from the archaism of the legal formulae which in the past had placed their
nation among the most clearly defined in Europe. It is no slur on their
intelligence that they failed to "see through" those formulae, which though
archaic were in their day still strong. One must admit, however, that they
did not want to "see through." The fears of this nation, like those of the
poets, put a pathological stamp on the jargon of modern Magyar nationalism which can account for a prevailing confusion in Budapest late in
the nineteenth century of the words "Magyar" and "noble."

Neolog Jewish Nationalism

The Jewish nobility contained not only intellectuals, but Jewish religious figures. In 1863 the very first Hungarian Jew since the Middle Ages
who, as a Jew, acquired Hungarian nobility was Simon Vilmos Schossberger, the Chairman of the ardently *Neolog* [Assimilationist] Pest Israelite
Community. In 1885 Schossberger's successor in that semi-religious office,
Dr. Ignác Hirschler, became the first Jew who, as a Jew, entered the Hungarian House of Lords. In 1868, 10 of the 37 men who organized the Jewish
Congress, which determined the whole subsequent history of Hungary's
Judaism, were members of families who had already joined, or would
join the Magyar nobility. [26] This directly religious leadership of ennoblement among the Jews was a limited phenomenon. There were no descendants of great reformer rabbis such as Lipót Lőw of Szeged and Lőw
Schwab of Budapest in the nobility, for example. Further, few chairmen
of the Pest Neolog Community acquired nobility, despite the business and
political careers which often made them especially eligible for ennoblement.
These men, the most important of the Neolog Jewish religious leaders,
contributed less to the new nobility than to a burgher spirit, which perhaps

---

[26] See the list in *MZsL*, p. 998.

even in the final years of Dualism was strong in the poorer business world of Pest.

Nonetheless, of the entire group of 346 Jewish noble families, only two were Orthodox in point of religion at the time of ennoblement. [27] Furthermore, particularly in the provinces, one discovers time and again that the new nobles were leading figures in the local or regional Neolog Jewish Community. The Gutmans of Nagykanizsa were a case in point. [28] So were the *jánosi* Engels and Schapringers of Pécs, Izsó Rósa of Szeged, the *végvári* Neumann family of Arad, the Kohn-Kunffys of Kaposvár, the Kánitzes of Eger, and the *peskodari* Engels of Nyitra. The Dereras of Temesvár headed the Sephardic Jewish reform in that city. The Freudigers of Óbuda, one of the two Orthodox noble families, were likewise the head of a reform movement. Beyond this, the Pest Community, unmistakably the most important Neolog community in Hungary, was a central rallying point of the ennoblement movement. From the early 1880's on, there were regularly several new nobles among the senior councilors of this community. Its organ, the *Egyenlőség*, regularly defended the practice of ennoblement. Twenty-three out of 29 Jewish nobles created between 1887 and 1896 were members of this community. [29] Throughout the period of Dualism many, even of the provincial Jewish nobility, affiliated themselves to this community. To this degree it seems demonstrable that to fathom the reasons why nationalism inclined the bourgeois elite of turn-of-the-century Budapest to ennoblement, we must turn our attention to the Westernization of the Jews in Hungary.

Let us approach this complex and difficult subject through an account of the career of Aaron Chorin, the grandfather of a distinguished lawyer and politician, Ferenc Chorin, who became a Hungarian peer in 1903, and the great-grandfather of one of the key industrialists of Admiral Horthy's interwar Hungary. This elder Chorin was born in 1766 in Moravia, and attended the Yeshiva at Mattersdorf near Sopron in Hungary. [30] He then moved to Prague to study in the circle of the famous teacher Ezekiel Landau; and there he learned literary German and discovered the European Enlightenment. At the age of 17 he married, and became for a

---

[27] Freudiger, 1909; and Schönberger-Sebestyén, 1912.

[28] This and the following data are extracted from the articles in *MZsL* on the towns mentioned.

[29] This may be deduced through comparison of the list of ennobled Jews in the *Egyenlőség*, 24 April, 1887, pp. 5—6 with the information in the *Egyenlőség*, 31 Jan., 1896, p. 3.

[30] There is an extensive biography of Aaron Chorin in the *Jewish Encyclopedia*, Vol. IV. See also the *Egyenlőség*, 31 May, 1896, pp. M. 4—5.

while a trader. This did not suit him, however, and after 1789 he accepted an invitation to be rabbi at Arad in eastern Hungary, got involved in a bitter dispute with Orthodox rabbis about whether sturgeon must be considered ritually impure, and embarked on a campaign for the drastic "rationalization" of all areas of Jewish ritual and way of life. In particular he advocated until his death in 1844 Jewish acceptance of the German language in place of Yiddish and Hebrew in all but the most sacred prayers. Chorin carried out, in a word, in the Habsburgs' eastern lands the mission of Moses Mendelssohn and other great German Jewish reformers, and this turned out to be a Germanizing mission.

Chorin's career recalls that the national cultural awakening among the Jews late in the eighteenth century, and their revolt against medieval religious and political authority, was different from those among the other linguistic nationalities of Europe. [31] The difference stemmed largely from the emphasis the nineteenth century placed on land. Most of the European peoples possessed in one fashion or another historic lands, and consequently focused their revolt on secularization and nationalization of their territorial medieval authority. The Jews could not do this. In terms of language, religion, custom, and even of "medieval state" the Jews were prior to 1789 probably the most self-conscious and distinct nation of Europe: but they lacked land. Consequently, enlightened Jews of Aaron Chorin's generation in Central and Eastern Europe chose to rationalize their Jewish nation's life by assimilating into the cultural and territorial German nation in which they lived. They tended to assert that Jewry was not a nation, and that a Jew differed from his fellow citizens only in religion. Theirs, in a word, was a strain of nationalism which, like the Hungarian noble and Ottoman variants, was inverse. With convert zeal Chorin and his fellow reformers attacked the Jewish distinctness of the past at the very moment when other national reformers were insisting on ever-heightened distinctness.

Historians may at first consider Chorin's act of national identity-rejection strange, for customarily they view nationalism as a matter of positive identity-assertion. Even Karl Deutsch's illuminating sociological treatment of modern nationalism deals largely with the rise of positive nation-syn-

---

[31] On the Jewish reform in general see, apart from Dubnow, *Neueste Geschichte des jüdischen Volkes;* Howard Sachar, *The Course of Modern Jewish History* (New York: World Publishing Co., 1958), Ch. VII; and the very stimulating address by Gershom Scholem to the World Jewish Congress in Brussels in 1966, variously reprinted, but published in English under the title "Jews and Germans," in *Commentary*, Vol. XLII, No. 5 (November, 1966), p. 31ff.

dromes as a result of the mobilization of people out of their traditional "homes." Deutsch reduces nationalism to a matter of communications. He premises that a "nation" may take many forms, recognizing the existance of old (or "historic") nation-syndromes as well as new ones. He allows for successful adaptation of old syndromes to new conditions, and also for their failure. But in no detail does he discuss under the heading of nationalism the emotion-laden strivings of mobilized individuals from such an old nation to locate a path of adaptation. His nationalists are all builders, followers, or converts: they are not adjustors and diluters, although Aaron Chorin was, and so were many others, not just among Europe's Jews, but in other nations also.

The career of Dr. Ignác Hirschler illustrates one fateful way in which such inverse nationalism among Neolog Jews in nineteenth-century Hungary led to Magyar peerage. Hirschler was born in the Pozsony ghetto in 1823 and trained in Vienna and Paris in ophthalmology. [32] He returned to Pest in the 1850's as Hungary's only major eye specialist, and presumably because he had lived in emancipated France, he plunged promptly into the struggle for Jewish emancipation at home. He found enlightened Jewry there embattled. On the one hand, the German-speaking world had proved untrustworthy. German burghers had led pogroms in Pozsony and Pest in 1848, [33] and Austrian Absolutism had drastically taxed the Jews after its victory in 1849. On the other hand, the reformer Jews were faced with Orthodoxy. As recently as 1843 Orthodox Jews in Pozsony had petitioned the King against emancipation on the grounds that the Jews were not citizens of Hungary, but of Palestine. [34] In general, Orthodoxy preferred continued political oppression to a sacrifice of religious purity. [35] Orthodoxy was, moreover, not only entrenched in such old West Hungarian ghetto towns as Pozsony, but among the newly-immigrant rural Jewish population of the North and East; and it could rely on the traditionalist Jewish authority across the mountains in Poland. Against both the Germans and Orthodoxy the logical ally for the Neolog Jews was the Magyar nobility. [36] This

---

[32] See the biography in the *Egyenlőség*, 17 July, 1896, p. 8.

[33] On the development of anti-Semitism in Hungary, see Venetianer, *A magyar zsidóság története*, p. 140ff. and Part III; and Schickert, *Judenfrage*, p. 117ff.

[34] See Groszmann, *A magyar zsidók V Ferdinánd alatt*, p. 24.

[35] A reasonable explanation of the Orthodox position is in Sándor Büchler, *A zsidók története Budapesten* [History of the Jews in Budapest] (Budapest: Franklin, 1901), pp. 439—440.

[36] On the Magyarizer reform in Hungary, see Venetianer, *A magyar zsidóság története*, p. 123ff.; Groszmann, *A magyar zsidók V Ferdinánd alatt;* and Kosa, *Pest és Buda elmagyarosodása*, Ch. 6.

nobility had a reasonable record in the past for helping Jews. [37] It had
recently committed itself to ideological Liberalism. Its only price for help
was complete Jewish assimilation. The reformer Jews of Pest had already
in 1848 told the Magyars that in order to obtain emancipation they would
cast their still new Germanism aside and Magyarize to the extent of cele-
brating the Sabbath on Sunday. [38] Hirschler in the 1850's had no hesita-
tion casting his lot in the same direction. In 1860 he was elected Chairman
of the Neolog Pest Israelite Community as the ally of noble Magyar Liberalism, and though in 1861 the Austrian authorities removed him from that
post, he resumed it in 1867 at the time of the *Ausgleich*. [39]

In the aftermath Hirschler's advocacy of Jewish Magyarization led
him to fateful acts. In December, 1867, the Hungarian Parliament abolished
all laws which denied the country's Jewish inhabitants civic and political
rights equal to those of the Christians. [40] Some weeks later the Hungarian
Government organized a conference designed to prepare the institutional
framework for relations between the State and the "Jewish Religion," and
late in 1868 it convoked a Jewish Congress to ratify the conference's work.
These developments placed Hirschler and his fellow Magyarizers in a delicate position. On the one hand, the State was insisting that the emancipation law recognized only one "Jewish Religion." On the other hand, the
Orthodox Jewish leaders in the country were prepared to resist the establishment of any central Jewish authority which might subordinate them
to Neolog reformers. In this situation Hirschler and his fellow reformers
accepted a Governmental suggestion that they deal with the State exclusively in a "secular" capacity, leaving "religious" matters for later determination by appropriate "religious" authorities. In the peculiar context of
Judaism this classic Liberal distinction between "secular" and "religious"
affairs was not very meaningful. On the strength of it, however, Hirschler
and his friends excluded the rabbinate, the pillar of Orthodoxy's strength,
both from the preparatory conference, and from the Jewish Congress,

---

[37] This means simply that particularly in the eighteenth century, when the Jews
were excluded from Hungary's towns, they frequently found haven on the estates of the
aristocracy.

[38] See Venetianer, *A magyar zsidóság története*, p. 154ff.

[39] See Büchler, *A zsidók története*, p. 489ff.

[40] On the following see the recent essay by Nathaniel Katzburg, "The Jewish Congress
of Hungary, 1868 — 1869," in Randolph L. Braham (ed.), *Hungarian Jewish Studies*,
Vol. II (1969), pp. 1—34. There are extensive reports on the Jewish Congress in the works
of Venetianer and Büchler just cited; in the *MZsL* article on "Zsidó Kongresszus" and
in the *Egyenlőség*, 10 Jan., 1929, p. 11.

which as a result fell under Neolog influence. [41] Hirschler himself became president of the Congress. The Orthodox decided to act on their own. In the end the State was obliged to accord formal recognition to both trends among the Jews; and Hungarian Jewry went into the late nineteenth century split into three [42] hardly communicating factions.

In retrospect it is easy to condemn Hirschler's management of the Jewish Congress; at the time, of course, it was far less so. Today it appears elementary that any people who shared so many cultural and historic bonds as the Jews did in mid-nineteenth century Europe should stick together rather than expose themselves to the mercies of the other nationalities of the region, which were all rigorously intensifying their unity. Today it may seem unreasonable that a Jewish national leader such as Hirschler could advocate a cultural and legal regime which was alien to the majority of his people. [43] In 1868, however, modern anti-Semitism, whose record determines our modern attitudes towards Jewish affairs, was only just beginning to loom on the horizon. The great battle of that time was still the struggle of Enlightenment, whether Jewish, British, German, or Magyar, against medieval barbarism, whether it assumed the form of Christian anti-Semitism, or Jewish religious Orthodoxy. In the not yet democratic world of 1868, moreover, it could seem largely irrelevant to Jewish leadership considerations that the majority of Hungarian Jews still

---

[41] Technically, the delegates to the preparatory conference were appointed by Baron Eötvös, the Minister of Cults and Education. But according to Venetianer, *A magyar zsidóság története*, p. 287, Hirschler actually compiled the list of delegates, and though Katzburg, who has recently reexamined the sources, finds no clear proof of this allegation, he admits its probability; and these delegates laid down the principles on which the rabbis were made ineligible for election to the Congress.

[42] After the Jewish Congress Hungarian Judaism split into "Congressional" (Neolog), Orthodox, and "Status Quo" communities. The latter were explicitly unable and unwilling to make a choice between Reform and Orthodoxy, and consequently pretended the Congress had simply not taken place. It was quaintly characteristic of the Dualistic Era that the State, though desirous of achieving a united Jewish Representation, ended up according formal recognition to both Neolog and Orthodox organizations, but not to the "Status Quo," which alone of the three groups stood for the informal but practical unity of all Jews of the pre-*Ausgleich* centuries. See *MZsL*, p. 804.

[43] The Magyar governments continued after the factionalization of the Jews in 1868 to contend that in the eyes of the Law there was only one Jewish religion. Accordingly, the census figures never made a distinction between the various factions, and there is no way of telling precisely how the Jewish population split. It was seldom denied, however, that on a countrywide basis the Orthodox until the inter-war period had a majority. See the remarks by Alajos Kovács, the statistician, in the *Egyenlőség*, 24 Jan., 1931, p. 3, which question a claim that the Orthodox were 37.4 per cent of Hungarian Jewry.

were Orthodox, and German or Yiddish speaking. What were leaders for, it was then habitually asked, if not to guide their benighted and ignorant peoples to the light of Reason? And for Hirschler it was particularly natural to try and guide Hungarian Jewry into Magyarization and into denial of Germanism and Yiddish Orthodoxy, because the Magyars had granted emancipation exclusively on the premise that Jews were a religious group and not a nationality. To have acknowledged Jewishness as a nationality in Hungary in 1868 would have been in Hirschler's eyes to reject the emancipation and to return to the fearful past.

Hirschler in effect failed to achieve the concordat which he hoped for at the Jewish Congress. He remained until 1883 at the head of the Pest Neolog Community. But perhaps in part because he failed, and certainly in part because the law itself forced his people to choose between unreformed orthodox religiosity and over-reformed Neolog secularism, he became more ardently Magyarized than ever. Unable to go back, he went forward. In return in 1885 the Government had him appointed to the House of Peers. After his death the Government gave his son formal nobility. [44] His case illustrates how easy it was for Hungarian reformer Jews to solve their embattled political situation "inversely" through denial of Jewish nationality, through Magyarization, and if necessary through ennoblement.

Official Nationalism

Our objective in these pages has been to suggest how in Hungary Westernization contributed to the syllogistic, seemingly irrational confusion in turn-of-the-century Magyar nationalist doctrine of the terms "Magyar" and "noble." We have observed several factors which could have contributed to this confusion, particularly the fear which Hungarian circumstance instilled in the romantic poets, and the willful passion of the identity conversion which the Enlightenment imposed on all Hungarians, though particularly on the country's noble "nation" and on the reformer Jews. For another, and in some ways decisive, factor let us look now at the career of Aaron Chorin's grandson, Ferenc Chorin, who was one of the most prominent and wealthy men in Hungary during the Dualistic and interwar periods. [45]

---

[44] Dr. Ágoston Hirschler obtained nobility in 1909.

[45] There seems to be no adequate biography of the elder Ferenc Chorin, despite his major importance in late nineteenth- and early twentieth-century Hungarian history

This elder Ferenc Chorin was born in Arad in 1842, two years before Aaron Chorin's death, the son of a doctor. Following the teachings of his grandfather, Ferenc was exposed in his youth to the secular world. He studied abroad and in Budapest to be a lawyer. As a result, of course, he became like Hirschler not a Germanizer, but a Magyarizer Jew. Even grandfather Chorin in his old age saw that the Magyar nationalist movement in Hungary might require Reform Jewry to make a second shift of culture and language; and for the younger Chorin, who grew up in the shadow of 1849, and who witnessed at Pest the thrilling Magyar reawakening of the 1860's, Germanism was repulsive. Ferenc Chorin began his public career accordingly as founder-editor of a Magyar-language, Kossuthist, ardently anti-Austrian political journal in Arad. In 1869 as a parliamentary deputy, he tended even to question the Magyars' need for the *Ausgleich*, which Count Andrássy and Ferenc Deák had made with their Habsburg King; and in general, the religious zeal of his grandfather flamed in him in the secular form of Magyar nationalism.

Chorin in his early years as a deputy was guided in his enthusiasm for the Magyars as was Hirschler by the fact that in 1867 just after the *Ausgleich* the Magyar Parliament emancipated the Jews. For example, he never felt able to join the most extreme independence-minded, anti-Austrian Magyar politicians, whose call for upsetting the *Ausgleich* altogether might lead to questioning the emancipation. After 1868 Chorin did side with Kálmán Tisza in moderate opposition to the new constitutional system. After 1875, when as we will see in a later chapter Tisza made his own compromise with Austria and became Hungary's Prime Minister, and when in renegotiating the customs *Ausgleich* in 1876—1877 Tisza failed to insist on the establishment of an independent Hungarian national bank, Chorin, outraged by these "betrayals," split with the Government Party, and helped organize a parliamentary opposition. But in 1884, at the climax of an anti-Semitic outburst in the Independence camp of Magyar politics, Chorin decided to reenter Tisza's pro-*Ausgleich* Government Party. In this Ferenc Chorin acknowledged that he was still like his grandfather a Jew, and that his Magyar nationalism was still an assimilationist strain of Jewish nationalism.

Even in the 1880's, however, Chorin was following his Magyar nationalism into a more and more secular crusade. As a parliamentary deputy in the 1870's he had seen it in the country's interest to lobby for her struggling industries. He had become involved accordingly in the Salgó-

tarján Hard Coal Company, one of Hungary's larger mining concerns. [46]
By 1890 his economic Liberalism had borne him so far into coal affairs,
that he became president of the Salgótarján Company. By 1901 he was
not only Hungary's leading coal magnate and very wealthy, but also he
was posing as Hungary's industrial "grand old man" and was about to
organize a Hungarian National Association of Manufacturers (the GYOSz).
At this point he was forced by an incompatibility law to leave the parliamentary chamber of deputies. In order to retain his influence on the formulation of legislation, therefore, he accepted a life-peerage; and in the course
of this high act of Magyar patriotism this grandson of Rabbi Aaron Chorin
became a Catholic.

One should not regard Chorin with complete lack of sympathy. Magyar
nationalism had in general become formalistic by his day due to a peculiarity
of those secularizer times in Europe. All through the early and middle
years of the century a growing state of hostilities with Vienna had impas-
sioned Magyars and Jews alike and made political nationalism a matter of
immediacy to them all. The peace after 1867 relaxed the tension. In the
new circumstances individuals had other problems to resolve apart from
saving the nation. There was at least an opportunity for Magyar society
to come to grips with concrete problems, leaving the mouthing of nationalist
slogans to someone else. Unfortunately, a "someone else" was available . . .
the Press . . . who would not let the slogans die.

Even before the *Ausgleich*, publicism had played a disproportionate role
in the fate of the Magyars. [47] Kossuth, for example, made his name as a
journalist who published the debates of the Hungarian Diet. Budapest in
1848 was almost as well equipped with popular patriotic and revolutionary
journals as was Vienna, although its intelligentsia was far smaller. In the
era of the *Ausgleich* one could find attached to many of the leading Magyar
politicians a publicist, [48] and as early as 1878 a publisher named Légrády
founded Budapest's first daily mass-readership newspaper, the *Pesti Hirlap*.

---

[46] On the Hungarian coal industry, see Eckhart, *A magyar közgazdaság*, Part III;
Sándor, *Nagyipari fejlődés*, pp. 118—138 and 403—418; Berend and Ránki, *Magyarország
gyáripara 1900—1914*, p. 174ff; and Jenő Varga, *A magyar kartellek*, p. 17ff.

[47] Pintér, *Magyar irodalomtörténet*, Vol. VII, contains a lengthy chapter on the Budapest press. See also for discussions of the press, Horvath, *Magyar századforduló*, p. 152ff.;
and Gyula Farkas, *Az asszimiláció kora a magyar irodalomban* [The Assimilation Era in
Hungarian Literature] (Budapest: Franklin, nd.), p. 90ff.

[48] One may note the following relationships: Széchenyi and Miksa Falk; Kossuth
and Ignác Helfy; Görgey and Mór Ballagi; the elder Andrássy and Mór Gans and Lajos
Dóczy; Deák and Manó Kónyi; Kálmán Tisza, István Tisza and Ödön Gajáry; and perhaps also Albert Apponyi and Henrik Béla.

He started with a daily edition of 8000 copies, and by 1890 was publishing 30,000 copies daily. [49] How extraordinary the role of the press thereupon became is suggested by an estimate of 1884, that Hungary's intelligentsia — i.e., those who had more than an elementary education — amounted to only 128,000 persons, or approximately 0.9 per cent of the total population; that only a quarter of these actually read seriously; and that 10% of these serious readers were themselves writers. [50] A modern press "hit" the Magyar world thus before a reading public had been formed there; and since the press brought about the emergence of a literate public, rather than as in Western Europe responding to it, a vicious circle emerged. The press lords, to support themselves, had to rely for financial support on the nationalist political parties and had to appeal on a low intellectual level to the public. The result was pompous nationalistic jingoism which disastrously encouraged imitation both by the public and by the politicians.

With time, no doubt, the sophistication of the Magyar public grew, and politicians such as Chorin perhaps should have found the means for escaping the tyranny of the press. But with time, as it happened in Budapest, the press also grew. By 1896 there were 22 daily newspapers in the city. [51] And meanwhile the press acquired a moral dictator: that same Jenő Rákosi, whom we have mentioned early in this chapter as the propagandist of new nobility. [52] Rákosi combined a rigid, uncritical devotion to Social Darwinism with considerable literary talents. He lent the Press, whether Government or oppositional, a tone of seemingly intellectual and highly moral nationalism which was very difficult for contemporaries to see through, much less defy. One may estimate that as a result of Rákosi's moral imprecations, Magyar nationalism acquired a strong injection of what today we call "bourgeois morality," and became an official, ritualistic nationalism. Perhaps in that secular era, when old religions were losing ground anyway, the emergence of such a ritual could lead men to think nationalism was a worthy new Faith.

Such contributory explanations of Ferenc Chorin's conversion aside, however, the lesson of his career is that successive identity rejections wasted the faith of Westernizer Jews in Hungary. The transitions first to Germanism and then to Magyar nationalism were initially sources of great

---

[49] See Pintér, *Magyar irodalomtörténet*, Vol. VII, p. 43—44, comp. pp. 60, 73.
[50] See Szekfű, *Három nemzedék*, p. 254, note, quoting from Gusztáv Beksics, who would certainly not have minimized the facts.
[51] See Horváth, *Magyar századforduló*, p. 163
[52] See above, footnote 9; and Horváth, *Magyar századforduló*, p. 593.

passion for reformer Jews. But in the end they more than once led to a patriotic Magyar ennoblement which excluded Judaism altogether, and which, to hammer our point home, reduced religion and nationalism alike to materialistic formalism wherein it was admiralbe if "Magyar" was confused with "noble."

"Gentry" Nationalism

We may approach a final factor which made ennoblement in nine-teenth-century Hungary a matter of Magyar nationalism through an account of her father by the author Anna Lesznai.[53] Gejza Moskowitz was the son of Dr. Mór Moskovitz, a physician who became the personal attendant of Count Gyula Andrássy, and who acquired nobility in 1867 when Andrássy became Prime Minister of Hungary. Gejza's career began early in the 1870's when Count Andrássy, now Imperial Chancellor, asked Dr. Moskovitz what his son would do for a living. Receiving no clear answer, Andrássy suggested the youth come to Vienna as his personal secretary. Young Mos-kovitz had been raised to hobnob with the best families of Hungary, and was wildly excited with this opportunity to penetrate the core of aristocratic Europe. He soon found, however, that Viennese politics were unheroic, and consequently when Count Andrássy commanded him one day to "get a cab," he perceived an offense to his honor. Thereupon he rushed home to Budapest, married the rich daughter of József Hatvany-Deutsch, retired to an estate, and largely to spite Andrássy joined the political opposition. By modern standards, his behavior was wholly foolish; and it may seem idiotic when one learns that Gejza Moskovitz had not the slightest interest or ability in estate management and spent the rest of his life in boredom. Yet Gejza Moskovitz does not figure as a fool in the Moskovitz family chronicle. As a member of the nationalistic anti-Government opposition he paraded around deploring Kálmán Tisza's "fell sacrifice" of Hungary's independence to Austria. Dogmatically and irrationally he lauded the virtues of the "1,000-year old Hungarian State" and of its "Holy" Constitution. And in general, he appeared to his contemporaries and children as a heroic, albeit sometimes quixotic patriot.

Lesznai most perfectly intimates the quality of Magyar nationalism in the late nineteenth century when she has a scion of an old Magyar family

---

[53] The following is based on Lesznai, *Kezdetben volt a kert*, Vol. I. Although this extensive novel is not a *roman à clef*, one of the two fictional families whose history it chronicles approximates, according to sources close to the author, her own.

(now in serious financial straits) visit her father, a new-noble Jew, to obtain the latter's backing for a Government-sponsored railroad which will connect their county at last with the outside world. She has Moskovitz reject the scheme on principle, because it is Government-sponsored: and then she has him cry out in lieu of explanation: "With your pure Magyar heart, Peter, clink glasses to the old world!... A toast to the opposition of honorable men against the rogues! Even you should be able to drink that!" Peter replies with politeness, but recalls how the greatness of the modern English State emerged, not from noble slogans, but from a "mercantile spirit" — and the building of railroads. Moskovitz replies: "England?... A Jew country! Everyone's a filthy miser[Grajzler]there, even the lords!But here, through the Grace of God, the likes of us and even Jews are gentlemen [úriember]. We are on Hungary's soil." To this Peter replies: "you of the opposition are the country's Bayards, celà va sans dire. But people misunderstand your slogans! You are stirring up the Budapest rabble and the greenhorns at the university; and what is infinitely worse, you are driving even the socialists at our necks! Can you deny it?" Whereupon Moskovitz effectively closes the exchange by crying: "Our folk will never become socialist! Ours is an honest, good folk!" [54]

Lesznai's account brings to mind a major divergence between the course of Magyar ideology in the late nineteenth century and that of ideological strains elsewhere in Europe. In Hungary, as in most of Central Europe in the 1870's, 1880's, and 1890's a new generation of ideologists came of age. [55] It developed in the shadow of Bismarck's anti-Liberal, conservative, and nationalist *Reich* and differed from its Western equivalent by rejecting Liberalism in favor less of social radicalism, than of national radicalism. But in most of Central Europe the general trend in this radical generation was towards further articulation of programs and ideas. In Austria and Bohemia both, for example, there was a major split in the 1880's between "old" liberal nationalists and "young" radical nationalists. In both these lands,

---

[54] *Ibid.*, Vol. I, pp. 350—351.

[55] For the background of the following insofar as it regards Germany, see Koppel S. Pinson. *Modern Germany* (2nd edit.; New York: Macmillan, 1966), Chs. 9 and 10; and George L. Mosse, *The Crisis of German Ideology* (paperback edit.; New York: Universal Library, 1964), Part I. For Austrian developments see Karl Eder, *Der Liberalismus in Altösterreich* (Vienna: Herold, 1955), Chs. 3 and 4; the later chapters in Georg Franz, *Liberalismus* (Munich: Callwey, 1955); and Peter Pulzer, *The Rise of Political Anti-Semitism in Germany and Austria* (New York: John Wiley, 1964). For the Bohemian pattern, see the essay by Joseph Zacek in Sugar and Lederer, *Nationalism in Eastern Europe*, p. 166ff.

moreover, analytic socialism sprang up from a seed within the national-liberal movements in the generation of the 1880's. And while towards the end of the century in Austria there was a strain of specifically demagogic nationalism, even Karl Lueger had something of a social platform; and Georg von Schönerer, who depended entirely on myth-spewing, emotional, anti-Semitic Germanism, seldom spoke for more than a fraction of the population. Not so in Hungary.

In Magyar Hungary there was no split in the 1880's between "old" and "young." [56] The "young" Magyars of the 1880's simply took over without question the old "constitutional" Deákist and Kossuthist causes of their fathers and grandfathers. The issue of "independence" simply drowned all the social issues which other European nationalists took into account. The reasons for this stand-still character of Magyar ideology are not fully clear. Some authorities have attributed it to the peculiarities of Kálmán Tisza's political system, which we will discuss in a subsequent chapter. Others have explained the lag as a fatal consequence of the Austrian repression of the Magyars after 1849; as a reflection of the strength of the Hungarian noble nation's "old ideology;" and as a function of the emergence of a convert-Magyar press. It seems useful to recall also the Magyar political class nurtured its political ideas in the 1870's and 1880's still far less in the modern city of Budapest, than in the un-intellectual environment of feudal estate, military barrack, and county casino. Regardless of the explanation, Gejza Moskovitz, with his foggy dogmatism, was characteristic of the entire Magyar political opposition and much of official Magyar nationalism in his day. In his myth-bound syndrome of nationalism it was not even ironic if a decadent feudal noble had to defend modernization against a decadent Jew; and it was undeniable that something God-given and special about the Hungarian people and State deprived the peasant question, the nationalities question, and the socialist question of existence.

The dogmatic character of Magyar nationalism alone makes it simple to understand why even early in the twentieth century Magyar nationalists could accept a syllogistic identification of "Magyar" with "noble." However, another circumstance contributed even more heavily to the same result. This also emerges from Anna Lesznai's account of her father. She refers to him and his sometimes hysterical social behavior as typically "gentry." Thus she recalls the single sociological development of late nineteenth-

---

[56] For the following see in particular the chapter by Szekfű in *Három nemzedék*, p. 265ff; and the essays noted in footnote 3 above.

century Hungary which Magyar national ideologists did attempt to rationalize. [57]

Under the pre-1848 constitution of Hungary the nobility, landed and "undivided," had possessed the right to serve in the county administrative system which substituted for a "State" and ran the country; but the nobles had been under no obligation to serve in those days. After the constitutional revisions which culminated in 1867, the nobility possessed no special legal right to participate in the national administrative system, but came under a very great pressure to do so. [58] Unable even to keep their land in the changing economic world of the late nineteenth century, large numbers of nobles needed administrative offices simply to eat. And, long before the twentieth century began, the Magyar nobility lost its old identity as a class dependent on land and became, in one degree or another, dependent on bureaucratic income, which in the long run came from the State.

Magyar nationalist ideologists responded to this sociological development by gradually, in the latter decades of the century, producing a new definition of the national leadership which took into account the nobility's new bureaucratic condition. They observed that in enlightened, liberal, and successful England a "gentry" led the nation, which was as in Hungary partly landed, but partly employed in public administration. Blandly ignoring, therefore, the blatant difference between the public spirit of the English gentry-bureaucrats and the involuntary service of the ruined Hungarian nobility, they imported the expression "gentry" to Hungary, and inferred that neither all the Magyars nor all the Great-Hungarians, but the "gentry"-staffed State constituted the identity of the Nation. To emphasize this they even founded a "gentry" casino in Budapest which provided the new, state-employed national leadership a "home" distinct from the *Nemzeti Casino* of the aristocrats.

One must exert caution in generalizing about the "gentry" doctrine in late nineteenth-century Magyar nationalism, for its ambiguities were very great. The most detailed efforts at defining the meaning of "gentry" in Hungary focus vaguely on people who had lost their land, but who indulged in a careless, land-holders' way of life; who considered "trade" and Jews

---

[57] On the development of the "gentry" ideal in Hungary, see Győző Concha, "A gentry"; and also Zoltán Lippay, *A magyar közbirtokos középosztály és a közélet.*

[58] A most useful essay in the relations between nobility and bureaucracy is Andrew János, "The Decline of Oligarchy: Bureaucratic and Mass Politics in the Age of Dualism" jn A. János and W. B. Slottmann (eds.), *Revolution in Perspective*, (Berkeley: University of California Press, 1972); and Dezső Buday, "Magyarország honoratior osztályai" [Hungary's Professional Classes], in the *Budapesti Szemle*, Vol. CLXV (1916), no. 470, pp. 238—249.

below them; but who served in the state bureaucracy. The most famous single definition proclaims that: "He who has land is a noble, whereas he who is landless is "gentry." [59] And it is usually agreed that the antithesis of the word "gentry" in Hungary was the word "Jew." [60] In practice, however, inconsistencies with these rules were innumerable. A most glaring example is Anna Lesznai's regular reference to her father as "gentry," although he was both landed and Jewish. In the family chronicle from which we have been quoting she does this through the mouth of the sociologist, Oszkár Jászi, whose habitual precision of language she knew well, because she married him. And repeatedly one intimates from Hungarian memoirs and Hungarian histories that the only constant in the "gentry" doctrine was the lavish, "gentlemanly" way of life.

It was precisely because of its internal contradictions and ambiguities that the "gentry" idea played a formidable part in confusing the new middle classes of Magyar society about the expressions "noble" and "Magyar." While pretending to be exclusive, the "gentry" ideal was not exclusive. In practice it was available to anyone who was willing to assume a certain flamboyant behavior, such as Gejza Moskovitz's. And while pretending to redefine the national ruling class so as to include nobles who had been ruined, it really opened the gates of the ruling class to anyone who had a properly noble facade, and who served the Magyar State.

Revulsion into Science

We will discuss the later doctrinal evolution of Magyar nationalism more fully in subsequent chapters. Here, however, it is more important to turn to the second problem which interests us in this book, the formation of the Hungarian scientific geniuses, and as it happens we can do so conveniently. Gejza Moskovitz spent much of his life on his estate; but with his wife's money he also kept a Budapest salon, which became a major meeting place for the intellectual leaders of "Young Budapest." One may find in this salon the first link in a chain of circumstance which binds the cult of science among those young intellectuals to the cloudy formalism of Magyar "gentry" nationalism.

Other links in this chain appear from the career of Oszkár Jászi the sociologist and radical politician who became Gejza Moskovitz' son-in-law, and whom (perhaps somewhat arbitrarily) we included among the "geniuses"

---

[59] This was Jenő Rákosi's phrase according to Concha, "A gentry," p. 170.

[60] Lippay, *A magyar közbirtokos középosztály*, p. 33, claims that the single unifying characteristic of "gentry" is latent anti-Semitism.

listed at the start of this book. Born in 1875, the son of a Dr. Jakubovits of Nagy Károly (Carea Mare) on the Transylvanian frontier, Jászi grew up in a patriotic, upwardly mobile social environment. [61] Typically, his parents left Judaism when he was a child, so that the stigma of their ancestry might not impede their children's careers. His uncle, Dr. Leó Liebermann of Budapest, who provided him with decisive career guidance, became a noble in 1905 to satisfy family social ambitions. When Jászi completed his studies in law and sociology at the University of Budapest he himself followed the bourgeois conventions of the day to the extent of becoming a bureaucrat in the heavily "gentry" Ministry of Agriculture. And in specific relation to this nationalist milieu from which he emerged Jászi, both as a scholar and as a politician, resorted to "science."

At the turn of the century, for example, Jászi was instrumental in founding a periodical, the *Huszadik Század* [Twentieth Century], whose explicit purpose was to raise Hungary out of the intellectual torpor of her late-nineteenth century nationalism by importing and publicizing the newest cosmopolitan ideas of Western Europe. [62] Prior to the establishment some years later of Lajos Hatvany's *Nyugat*, the *Huszadik Század* was the major and characteristic journal of the renaissance out of which Hungary's scientific geniuses emerged. Next, in 1901 Jászi helped organize the *Társadalomtudományi Társaság* [Social Sciences Society] as a propagandistic organization to abet the *Huszadik Század* in the achievement of its goals. This society was designed to bring leaders of all branches of Magyar Hungary's political, social, and cultural life into communication with one another on a high cosmopolitan intellectual level. Though it split in 1906 into nationalist right- and quasi-socialist left-factions, it was by no means ineffective at deflating the foggy euphoria of Gejza Moskovitz' "gentry" nationalism. Meanwhile in the first few years of the century while still a part-time petty bureaucrat and scholar, Jászi dabbled with the most complex and

---

[61] The best source on Jászi's early career is a series of four autobiographical fragments in *Látóhatár* [Horizon] (Munich), Vol. VI, no. 2 (March—April, 1955), pp. 132—140; Vol. VIII, no. 1—2 (January—April, 1957), pp. 59—70; Vol. VIII, no. 3 (May—June, 1957), pp. 135—139; and Vol. VIII, no. 4 (July—August, 1957), pp. 208—217.

[62] The most extensive published analysis of Jászi's ideas is György Fukász, *A magyarországi polgári radikalizmus történetéhez, 1900—1918*. This volume examines numerous aspects of Jászi's thought as if they were simply divergences from the main tenets of Hungarian Marxism-Leninism as it existed about 1960. The result is a little schematic. Fukász' study is based, however, on very broad reading of Jászi's published works, and on extensive Archive material; and it has the great virtue of quoting *in extenso*. Consequently, it is a valuable source-collection.

esoteric social and political doctrines he could find in Europe of his day. For a time he played with Spencer's positivism, then he turned to neo-Marxism, then he considered anarcho-syndicalism. But when during his country's great political crisis after 1904 he tended to enter politics more seriously, he turned away gradually from non-bourgeois political philosophies and at the climax of his political career, from 1913 until 1918, he was founder and chief of a specifically bourgeois Radical Party.

In founding this party Jászi's basic premises were generally that "Progress" — or as we would call it, "modernization" — was necessary to society; that it could not be achieved without a certain self-conscious, democratic struggle on the part of the "bourgeoisie"; that Hungary's trouble lay in the willingness of its bourgeoisie to act out, both economically and socially, the role of a noble landowner's "servant;" [63] and that the key to the bourgeois failure lay in the ignorance of its Magyar nationalism.

I'm sure that Democracy's struggle with Hungary's medieval authorities,... with the latifundia,... with the gentry county institutions, and with the whole pseudo-culture of the counts and the priests could be won more easily and more certainly if only there did not exist in the bourgeoisie and in the people itself a host of false theories and pointless feelings regarding the past. I think that the prospects of our struggle would be entirely different, if Magyar public opinion and especially bourgeois public opinion were well informed, for example, about our aristocracy's foreign-adventurer and robber-baron past. [64]

For Oszkár Jászi, "science" was specifically rejection of the foggy sort of Magyar nationalism we have been discussing in this chapter.

Jászi's career is especially interesting to our study of Hungary's scientists because it contains hints that their science was not only a revulsion from Magyar nationalism, but also its continuation. Jászi spent his active life in Hungary organizing an intelligentsia, steeped in Western science, which he hoped would act as "vanguard" for the bourgeoisie. [65] This sounds internationalist. Jászi's theatre of operations was not, however, the wide world, but Greater Hungary; and in his view before the war, to be a "scientific" reformer there did not mean to be anti-Magyar, or non-Magyar, but simply to oppose the noble class. In a book of 1912 Jászi radically rejected such Magyar nationalists as Széchenyi in so far as they wanted to modernize the country through a noble elite. But he stood in their footsteps in thinking

---

[63] See the quotation dated 1911 in Fukász, *op. cit.*, p. 384.
[64] See the quotation dated 1911 in Fukász, *op. cit.*, p. 377.
[65] See Fukász, *op. cit.*, pp. 246—249.

that through an elite from another Magyar class multinational Greater Hungary might be saved. [66]

We may detect continuation of Magyar nationalism also in a key episode towards the end of Jászi's political career at home. In 1917 a colleague of his at the *Huszadik Század*, Péter Ágoston, published a sociological study of the role of the Jews in Hungarian society. [67] Ágoston was a socialist. [68] He was under the influence of Werner Sombart's then recently published study *The Jews and Modern Capitalism*. With his book he evidently wanted to attack Budapest capitalism, which, as we will observe in a subsequent chapter, was during the war singularly gross in its profiteering. So heavy-handed was Ágoston's style, however, that the book gave an impression of strong anti-Semitism and roused loud cries of indignation, not only from the capitalist circles which it condemned, but from the entire nationalist-Liberal establishment of Magyar politics. At this point Jászi, though he himself was a convert Jew, stepped into the controversy. Outraged over the vivid contrasts between the luxury of the profiteering, dominantly Jewish, Budapest business world, and the misery of the war-front, [69] he circulated a questionnaire among the leaders of the Budapest intelligentsia asking whether there was a "Jewish question" in Hungary or not; and he then published the decisively affirmative results in the *Huszadik Század*. Momentarily on this occasion Jászi's scientific radicalism revealed a suggestion not only of Magyar new-generational reaction against Magyar "gentry" nationalism but also of Jewish new-generational rejection of assimilationist Judaism. We may sense therefore (albeit no more than sense) from Jászi's career that Hungary's scientific "geniuses" not only

[66] See *A nemzeti államok kialakulása* [The Formation of National States] (Budapest: 1912), a lengthly tract which presumes the Great Hungarian nationalities would Magyarize if only the Magyar regime in Budapest pursued democratic policies.

[67] Péter Ágoston, *A zsidók útja* [The Path of the Jews]; (Nagyvárad: TTT, 1917).

[68] Ágoston was not Jewish, but came from a Swabian family of the Banat, and Magyarized himself in exactly the same way as did many Jewish intellectuals of the day. He became a leading figure in the predominantly Jewish free-thinking intellectual circle at Nagyvárad (Oradea), which played a significant role in Hungary's "second reform generation" (to use Zoltán Horváth's expression). A tacitly Zionist observer in 1917 labeled Ágoston "a masonic, progressive, and therefore quasi-Jewish author." See *Mult és Jövő*, 1917, no. 4, pp. 157—159. See also, *Párttörténeti Közlemények*, no. 2, 1963, pp. 155—156; and Horváth, *Magyar századforduló*, p. 625.

[69] See Jászi's comment on his motives in *Revolution and Counter-Revolution in Hungary* (New York: Howard Fertig, 1969) p. 187ff. Fukász, *op. cit.*, sees fit to omit all mention of this episode. See also my article, "Jews in Revolutions — the Hungariaι. Experience," in *Journal of Social History*, Sept., 1972.

reacted against the Magyar nationalism of the nineteenth century, but continued it along the peculiar "inverse", or rejectionist lines of modern Magyar and Jewish political ideology.

* * *

The career of Georg Lukács, who far more easily than Jászi fits into our collection of international Hungarian scientific geniuses, reveals even more pronounced patterns of revulsion from the dogmatic Magyar nationalism of the late-nineteenth century. Lukács was born in Budapest in 1885, the son of a young bank official who had then only recently moved from Szeged to Pest. [70] His father, József Löwinger, enjoyed a meteoric financial career rising from obscurity in the 1880's to become managing director of a smaller Budapest bank and a noble in 1899, and to attain membership after 1905 on the Board of Directors of the *Hitelbank*, Hungary's most important credit institution. Lukács was precociously intelligent and this intellectual birthright was obviously the main reason why he chose not to follow his father into a career of banking and business. According to his own testimony, however, the mode of his commitment to science and philosophy was not a matter simply of inclination, but a deliberate flight from the crass materialism and nationalist hypocrisy of his father's world.

As is well known, I come from a capitalist, *Lipótváros* family. [The *Lipótváros* is a district in Pest which was then fashionable among the town's richer merchants]... From my childhood I was profoundly discontent with the *Lipótváros* way of life. Since my father, in the course of his business, was regularly in contact with the representatives of the city patriciate and of the bureaucratic gentry, my rejection tended to extend to them too. Thus at a very early age violently oppositional feelings ruled in me against the whole of official Hungary... Of course nowadays I regard it as childishly naive that I uncritically generalized my feelings of revulsion, and extended them to cover the whole of Magyar life, Magyar history, and Magyar literature indiscriminately (save for Petöfi). Nonetheless it is a matter of fact that this attitude dominated my spirit and ideas in those days. And the solid counterweight — the only hard ground on which I then felt I could

---

[70] The most extensive published biographical material on Lukács is in Peter Ludz (ed.), *Georg Lukács. Schriften zur Ideologie und Politik* (Berlin: Hermann Luchterhand, 1967), p. 709ff. This volume reprints Lukacs' autobiographical account, "Mein Weg zu Marx" (1933). A highly tendentious, factually imprecise, but interesting intellectual biography is Victor Zitta, *Georg Lukács' Marxism, Alienation, Dialectics, Revolution* (The Hague: Martinus Nijhoff, 1964). See also the recent George Lichtheim, *Georg Lukacs* (New York: Viking, 1970).

rest my feet — was the modernist foreign literature of the day, with which I became acquainted at the age of about fourteen and fifteen. [71] In order to escape from his environment, of which Magyar "gentry" nationalism was a characteristic feature, Lukacs plunged into science. In this he was like Jászi.

In the aftermath Lukács' career significantly differed from Jászi's. Lukács moved even before the war from one philosophical system to another, from Spencer and Comte to an intense neo-Hegelianism; and he moved from one area of philosophy to another, from aesthetics to social philosophy. This movement of his mind and interest was presumably the result above all of his natural curiosity, of the eclecticism of European thought, and of a tendency to polarization, favorable to sudden intellectual leaps, which was extremely popular among Central European intellectuals of the time. It requires no greatness of imagination, moreover, to find in this "natural" intellectual movement the partial source of the great event of his career: his involvement in politics. In the prewar days Lukács remained far from politics. He wrote neo-Hegelian essays on drama and art, and he became a lecturer in Philosophy at the University of Heidelberg. After the war began he came home to Budapest, turned to social activism and became a Marxist. But it was only in the autumn of 1918 while the Austro-Hungarian Monarchy collapsed, that Lukács precipitantly turned to Bolshevism. [72] Outwardly Lukács found his social mission by a process far more abstract and intellectual than did Jászi. As a result it seems initially difficult to see Lukács as a "continuer", as well as a rejector of traditional Hungarian nationalist trends. Initially his development seems wholly cosmopolitan.

By Lukács' own testimony, however, he first came to grips with the great social questions which tortured his age, and which turned him into a scientific revolutionary, in a framework not just of his "natural" curiosity, but also of Magyar nationalism under the impact of the radicalism of the poet Endre Ady.

> ... an important [new] counterweight entered my life [when] in 1906 Ady published his 'New Verses'. ... In 1910 I made my first attempt at thinking out the meaning of the experience, but it was probably only much later, when I was much more mature, that I really succeeded in grasping the decisive significance of my encounter with

---

[71] See "Utam a magyar kultúrához",

[72] There is an interesting depiction of this conversion in Vol. II of the *roman à cléf* Ervin Sinkó, *Optimisták* [Optimists] (2 vols.; Novi Sad: Forum, 1965).

Ady's verses for my intellectual development. . . . The German philoso-
phers (and not just Kant and his followers among my contemporaries,
but also Hegel, under whose influence I came only some years later),
despite their apparently revolutionary ideological influence, remained
conservatives in the great questions of the development of society and
of History: Reconciliation with Reality *(Versöhnung mit der Wirklich-
keit)* is one of the basic tenets of Hegel's philosophy. Now Ady's
influence on me was decisive precisely because he never, even for a
minute, reconciled himself with Magyar reality, or through it with the
world of his day. From my early youth I had had the dream of such
an ideological stand within me, but I had never been capable of concep-
tualizing it. Despite several readings, I had been unable even to see
how clearly Marx expressed my feelings... But Ady's poetic behavior hit home. From the moment I encountered Ady, irreconcil-
ability was inescapably present in all my ideas, although for a long
time I was still unable fully to appreciate all this. [73]

Georg Lukács' rejection of the world into which he was born was no
more a matter of pure intellectual exploration than was Jászi's. Lukács'
resort to "science" took place in a Hungarian context; and we may hazard
that under scrutiny it may appear far more in the traditions of multinational
Greater Hungary than is generally supposed.

*   *   *

Lukács and Jászi were not the only Hungarian scientific geniuses to
follow a pattern of rejecting Magyar gentry nationalism. Significantly both
the Polányi brothers and also Karl Mannheim developed their scientific
inclinations in an atmosphere of rejection of the prevailing bourgeois ideas
of the day. It may be conceded that many of the scientists in whom we are
particularly interested in this book, the Edward Tellers, the Theodore von
Kármáns, the Georg von Hevesys, and the Leo Szilards, did not become
as politically active as did Jászi, Lukács, the Polányis, and Mannheim.
But if one regards the membership of the famous Galilei Circle, the club
for young radical intellectuals whence eventually came a major spark for
the revolutions of 1918—1919, one may find a truly astounding number of
names which subsequently figured high in the ranks of our century's international cultural elite. [74]

---

[73] See "Utam a magyar kultúrához," p. 1019.
[74] See Márta Tömöry, *Új vízeken járók. A Galilei Kör története* [Sailors on New
Seas. The History of the Galilei Circle] (Budapest: Gondolat, 1960), p. 273—277.

It would be venturesome and even useless in this investigation into the background of Hungary's scientific geniuses to dogmatize about how, alongside the anomalous atmosphere of turn-of-the-century Budapest, and the mobility of the ennobled bourgeoisie there, the nationalistic tendencies in the Westernization process in Hungary were the principal dynamic factors in the formation of the geniuses which Hungary has given the twentieth-century world. We have been construing hypotheses, pointing out parallels, suggesting avenues of approach. We have not been drawing rigid lines. Yet it should be quite clear to the reader that gradually in the course of these opening chapters a suggestive case is emerging. It is not so improbable now as it was at the start of our investigation that the same factors which drew Jewish capitalists into ennoblement, and indeed, their ennoblement itself, contributed also to the formation of the Hungarian scientific geniuses.

PART III

THE ROAD
TO SUCCESS 1860—1905

CHAPTER V

THE PRECONDITIONS FOR ECONOMIC TAKE-OFF

The Hungarian Economy and the Jews in Mid-Century

In 1867 and 1868 Franz Joseph approved legislation affecting both sides of the Leitha that not only freed the Jews and established a generally liberal social order, but also removed from the middle Danubian economy the last of the medieval legal restrictions which had hitherto burdened it. [1] This and the following chapters are first and foremost a narrative of how economic growth took place in Hungary in the aftermath of these reforms.

Franz Joseph's legislation coincided broadly with a galaxy of landmark economic and political events elsewhere in Europe — with the emancipation of the serfs in Russia, with the unifications of Italy and Rumania, with the founding of the Third Republic in France, and with the emergence of the Second *Reich* in Germany. As a result of these events all Europe experienced in the decades after 1867 a great wave of economic development which in Leninist terminology represented the maturity of imperialist capitalism and the extension of its tentacles into the non-western world — into Eastern Europe not least of all. In these chapters, however, we will regard Hungary's economic development not only as a part of that all-European phenomenon, but also as an example of a modernization process, which takes place perhaps according to a common pattern in all countries of the world, but does so in each country separately, and

---

[1] Standard accounts of the economic development of Central Europe in the Dualistic era are H. Benedikt, *Die wirtschaftliche Entwicklung in der Franz-Joseph-Zeit* (Vienna: Herold, 1958); Iván Berend and György Ránki, *Közép-kelet Európa gazdasági fejlődése a 19—20. században* [The Economic Development of Central Eastern Europe in the 19th and 20th Centuries] (Budapest: Közgazdasági és Jógi Könyvkiadó, 1969); and Wolfgang Zorn, "Umrisse des frühen Industrialisierung Südosteuropas im 19. Jahrhundert," *Vierteljahrschrift für Sozial- und Wirtschaftsgeschichte*, Vol. LVII (Dec. 1970), pp. 500—533.

according to individual variants. [2] And this process affords us the opportunity to bring economics into the argument of this book.

In earlier chapters we studied dynamic background factors, notably
mobilization and cultural Westernization, which contributed both to the
ennoblement of the country's nineteenth-century capitalists and to the
formation of her scientific geniuses. Now we will propose that Hungary's
modernization process was a factor which not only contributed to, but
which largely accounts for these two phenomena which we are studying.

* * *

Our account of Hungary's modernization will focus in particular on
the stage of economic development which W. W. Rostow has labeled
"take-off." Since take-off follows only after the achievement of certain
"preconditions," it seems well to begin with a glance at Hungary's condition in the middle of the nineteenth century.

From the point of view of modernization a most conspicuous feature
of the country at that time was its paucity of cities. In 1848 the adminis-
tratively separate towns of Pest, Óbuda, and Buda, with a combined population of about 150,000 persons, comprised Hungary's largest urban conglo-
meration. [3] Apart from them there were a number of walled settlements
in hilly western Hungary and the mountainous North (the *Dunántúl* and
Felvidék in modern Magyar terminology), which had never been captured
by the Turks and therefore retained a resemblance to medieval towns elsewhere in Central Europe. The most important were Pozsony, which as
mentioned elsewhere was for two centuries the capital of Hungary, Kassa
[Košice], and Eperjes [Prešov], bustling trading towns; and Germanic
Bistritz [Banská Bistrica], a northern mining center. There were also the
famous walled "Saxon" towns in distant Transylvania, which had been

---

[2] The theoretical framework used here derives primarily from W. W. Rostow, *The
Process of Economic Growth* (paperback edit.; New York: Norton, 1962); and his *The
Stages of Economic Growth* (London: Cambridge University Press, 1960). This framework has been applied to Hungary's development in a number of recent books and essays,
of which the most original are László Katus, "A keleteurópai iparosodás és az 'önálló
tőkés fejlődés' kérdéséhez" [To the Questions of Eastern Europe's Industrialization, and
"Independent Capital Development"] *Történelmi Szemle* 1967, no. 1, pp. 1—45; and the
essay by Peter Hanák in *Austrian History Yearbook*, Vol. III, Part I, pp. 260—302.

[3] For the following see in general the classic account by Szekfű, *Három nemzedék*,
p. 64ff.; the recent summary in E. Molnár (ed.), *Magyarország története*, Vol. II, p. 21ff.;
and the specialized accounts in M. Futó, *A magyar gyáripar története*, Vol. I; Gyula Mérei,
Magyar iparfejlődés, Part III; and E. Lederer, *Az ipari kapitalizmus kezdetei* [Beginnings
of Industrial Capitalism] (Budapest: Szikra, 1955), Ch. I.

settled by German immigrants in the middle ages and which still thrived on mining and on trade across the Carpathians. In central and southern Hungary, isolated on the broad flat *Alföld*, there were a number of so-called *mezővárosok* [plains towns], or large villages such as Debrecen and Kecskemét. And there were forts and trading posts of the former frontier such as Szeged and Temesvár (Timişoara). But in general mid-nineteenth century Hungary contained only peasant villages; and over 96% of her population lived in settlements of under 20,000 persons. [4]

The country's economic plant mirrored this poverty of towns in the sense that it was overwhelmingly agrarian and non-industrial. A description of Pest as late as 1843 lists only 17 industrial establishments. [5] The largest was a silk factory employing 200 persons, founded late in the eighteenth century, which collapsed in the face of Austrian competition after the removal of the customs frontier in 1851. Of the other establishments, four were textile plants, two processed vegetable oil, two dealt with leather, one with soda, three with iron, and four were small tool and machine firms. To these were added before 1848 a sugar mill, a soap factory, and a medicine and chemical plant. Guilds dominated Pest's economic life until 1848, and influenced it until their final abolition in 1859. Outside Pest Hungary's only important industrial features in mid-century were the iron mines of today's Slovakia and Transylvania, and a distilling industry. The mines were small and scattered. Often they had wholly inadequate transport facilities; and they were restricted by medieval regulation. The distilleries were mainly on great estates.

Far more important than industry in Hungary in mid-century was trade. Pest and Győr both figured as considerable markets for the agricultural produce, particularly grain, from the estates of the hinterland. At Pozsony, as mentioned elsewhere, there was a thriving textile trade. All over the country local trade in produce and goods led to handsome profits. In Pest in 1846 an Association of Traders in Gross had 36 members; there were 246 members of a Citizens' Traders' Association; and 136 members in a Jewish Traders' Association. [6] By 1848 substantial sections of a railroad had been built from Pozsony to Pest, and Széchenyi's famous suspension

---

[4] For precise figures see Kovacsics (ed.), *Magyarország történeti demográfiája*, pp. 199—200.

[5] See Anton Deutsch, *Die Pester Lloyd Gesellschaft, 1853—1903* (Budapest: Pester Lloyd, 1903), p. 25ff.

[6] See Deutsch, *Die Pester Lloyd Gesellschaft*, p. 27; comp. Gyula Szávay, *A Magyar kamarai intézmény és a budapesti kamara története, 1850—1925* [The History of the Hungarian Cameral Institution and of the Budapest Chamber of Commerce] (Budapest: Pesti Könyvnyomda, 1927), p.101ff.

bridge over the Danube at Pest was well begun. Hungary's first savings bank was established at Kronstadt [Braşov] in Transylvania in 1836. The first public commercial bank appeared in 1842, and 36 towns had savings banks by 1848. In the 1840's, moreover, the Magyar political leadership was active in encouraging Hungary's commercial growth.

Even in trade Hungary was weak by Western and Central European standards. In most respects communications were appalling. The roads were so bad that in the 1830's even in good weather it took sometimes three days to get from Pest 120 miles across the *Alföld* to Debrecen. [7] The banks listed above were a poor substitute for a domestic credit system in a land where until the 1860's the courts often lacked the will and the power to make nobles pay their debts. The first domestic insurance company was not established until 1857. The Pest grain exchange was not founded until 1854, and a Stock Exchange did not appear until 1864. [8] Yet two other aspects of her economic structure made Hungary something more than simply an "underdeveloped" land in the middle of the nineteenth century.

One of these was the disruption which had affected traditional agriculture. Prior to 1848 virtually the entire population, whether noble or peasant, had been bound by the system of legal serfdom which had crystallized during the fifteenth and sixteenth centuries. In 1848 this system was abolished. The peasant, of course, in most cases found that his old legal serfdom was replaced by bonds of debt, and that his new legal mobility was useless because there were few cities to which he could escape. But the emancipation affected not only the peasant: it affected the landlords also; and from the point of view of modernization, this was perhaps its most important effect. Whereas prior to the reform the landholding nobility could still virtually abstain from capitalist agriculture, simply living off its estates, after the reform this was no longer possible. Particularly because the Magyar nobility never got to the point of voting itself compensation for the emancipation in 1848—1849, it had afterwards either to enter the international grain market, or starve. Although Hungary remained overwhelmingly agrarian after the great reform, and would be a land of latifundia and great estates well into the twentieth century, it became after 1848 decisively a land of capitalist agriculture, whose agrarian resources were devoted not just to the subsistence of a landlord class, but to the ends of a modern state.

The second structural factor that led to Hungary's development after mid-century was the propinquity of foreign economic, particularly financial,

---

[7] See Kállai, *A 150-éves Goldberger gyár*, pp. 32—33.

[8] See Ágoston Félegyházy, *A Budapesti tözsde története*, Vol. I, pp. 1—30.

institutions. As mentioned in an earlier chapter, such institutions had long played a major role in Hungary. From Maria Theresa's time, for example, until 1851 Vienna had systematically manipulated the customs regime to discourage industrial developments in the Hungarian lands, while encouraging those in Austria. By 1848 the Viennese and Bohemian textile industries were flourishing, even though they could not compete with the industries of western Europe, because they could exploit the Hungarian market. Similarly, the Austrian State Bank, the private bank houses of Vienna, and the Vienna Stock Exchange exerted an overwhelming influence on the finances of nearby Hungary. Viennese and Italian insurance companies found in Hungary a fertile market, and from the 1830's on they were establishing filial offices on this plain, so susceptible to harvest disasters, hail, and floods.

Because of this record of foreign commercial domination many historians have found it useful to think of pre-Dualistic Hungary as virtually a "colonial" land. [9] Yet there is another way of evaluating the presence of these foreign economic institutions. When in the 1850's and 1860's railroad construction got under way in Hungary, its pace was much more rapid than could possibly have occurred had it depended on domestic investment power. The reason was the willingness of Viennese financiers to place their capital in this "colonial" region. Correspondingly, when the railroads stimulated the mining of coal in the Pécs, Esztergom, and Temesvár regions in the sixties, the Danubian Shipping Company and the Austrian State Railroads, both firmly based in Vienna, assumed the lead. A comparable development in iron mining likewise stemmed from Vienna-based investment in the 1850's. Whether the export of profits from these investments outweighed the benefits Hungary derived from them is and will remain a matter for debate. Suffice it here to stress that we do not know what would have happened if Hungary had developed independently; whereas we do know that the availability of foreign capital made

---

[9] This trend, common enough in the more chauvinist historiography of the past, found a new peak in the Marxist-Leninist surveys by Vilmos Sándor, *Nagyipari fejlődés Magyarországon* (1954); and by Iván Berend and György Ránki, *Magyarország gyáripara, 1900—1914* (1955). These authors subsequently modified their views, and, indeed, became advocates of recognizing the benefits of foreign investment. But then the whole question of "foreign" interference in Hungary's development was raised again by György Tolnai, "Az önálló tőkés fejlődés és a nacionalizmus megítélése a mai magyar gazdaságtörténetirásban" [The Development of Independent Capital, and the Evaluation of Nationalism in Contemporary Hungarian Economic Historiography], *Történelmi Szemle* (1966), no. 1, pp. 98—118.

possible the long leap by which Hungary actually plunged into the modern industrial world.

* * *

The preconditions for economic take-off consist not only in the achievement of a base for industry and in the availability of investment capital but also in social factors, and in particular in the development of business classes — the equivalent of what in the West we might call "bourgeoisie." In Hungary in the middle of the nineteenth century these classes fell into two parts defined to a large extent by their culture.

In mid-century Christians, and particularly Germans, dominated the scene and controlled the institutions of almost all the more substantial Hungarian towns. [10] This was particularly true of Pest and Buda, of the Saxon towns of Transylvania, of the mining towns of modern Slovakia, and of the border markets in the West. In all these places German was the language of both business and administration. In Pest and a few other towns, notably Újvidék (Novi Sad), Serbians formed a substantial part of the commercial stratum. There were moreover still some Greeks in the urban population, though they occupied nowhere near the prominent position they had held as a group in the eighteenth century. And of course there were some Magyars. But none of these groups outweighed the Germans.

These Christian elements of the urban population monopolized the industrial sectors of the economy. [11] The mining of iron, for example, was entirely in the hands of Germans, as were most auxiliary industries which used iron. Correspondingly, Christians dominated most urban crafts through the guilds, which survived until 1859. Factories, likewise, were in general Christian-owned.

The other major cultural element in the Hungarian "bourgeoisie" in mid-century was, of course, the Jews. Scattered as they were all over the country, often recently immigrant, the Jews were conspicuously weak in the urban institutions and in the economy's industrial sector. In fact, until the 1840's, when residential restrictions were removed, Jews could not even live in the counties where mining was important. Because until the 1840's Jews were often prohibited from owning real estate, even when they had special dispensation to reside within the walls of a town, they owned few factories. There were exceptions to this last rule. The town of

---

[10] See for the following apart from Szekfű, *Három nemzedék*, p. 64ff.; Kosa, *Pest és Buda elmagyarosodása*, Ch. 6.

[11] The following is based upon an unpublished manuscript by Károly Vörös on the Budapest virilists of 1873 and 1888.

Óbuda, for example, and some towns in the West, were built on the estates of great nobles, who for various reasons saw fit to tolerate Jewish industrial activity. In Óbuda as a result there were a number of Jewish manufacturers, notably some textile bleach-and-dye establishments. At the west Hungarian village of Herend, moreover, there was by mid-century a Jewish-owned porcelain factory. [12] But these exceptions were few.

In commerce, on the other hand, Jews already dominated the scene in mid-century Hungary. In the countryside, for example, Jewish traders had long since replaced the Greeks to the exclusion of almost all other ethnic elements. In provincial towns and villages tavern keepers and moneylenders were often Jewish. Jews often served as managers of noble estates, and they virtually monopolized the business of purchasing the produce of the estates and conveying it to the markets where it was sold. Particularly after reform legislation of 1840 made most residential restrictions on the Jews illegal, Jews settled in the suburbs of Pest and became very important in that town's weekly market and her financial life. The convert and ennobled Jew Samuel Wodianer founded the firm which was transformed in 1842 under distinguished Magyar auspices into the Pest *Kereskedelmi Bank*, one of Hungary's first public commercial institutions. The convert and ennobled Jew Mór Ullmann was a moving spirit behind that transformation, and behind many other major public economic projects as well. Twenty-six of the 36 "traders in gross" who incorporated themselves at Pest in 1846 were Jewish. [13] In addition, because so many of the leading Viennese court bankers had come from Hungary early in the century to the Habsburg capital, Hungary's Jews had special access to Viennese capital all through the latter half of the century.

The economic position of the Jews in Hungary was certainly far from advantageous in mid-century. Though some grew as wealthy as the Wodianers and the Ullmanns, even these were subject to the disasters of bankruptcy, as was, for example, Miksa Falk's father. Most of Hungary's Jews spent their lives tediously eking out pennies to survive. In particular the grain trade, off which perhaps most of them lived, was an exhausting business. [14] Long after mid-century the profits in this trade lay not in any vast difference between the price the traders paid the landlords and the

---

[12] See M. Gelléri, *A magyar ipar úttörői* [Pioneers of Hungarian Industry] (Budapest: Dobrowsky & Frankó, 1887), p. 176ff.

[13] See the essay by A. Deutsch, in Vidor Szirmai (ed.), *A magyar zsidóság almanachja. Védőirat*, p. 144.

[14] See the description of the grain traders and their business by Imre Balassa in the *Pesti Tözsde*, 20 Jan., 5 Feb., 12 Feb., 14 Feb., and 26 Feb., 1925. .

payment they subsequently received from the millers, much less in any cut they extorted from the wagoners who actually transported the grain, but in a fractional commission which they received per measure of produce for arranging the transport. Much in the fashion of modern brokers, it fell to the traders to be skillful in mediating between cunning principals. While modern brokers grow rich by dealing in huge quantities of grain in a world equipped with telephones, insurance, and reliable transportation, in nineteenth-century Hungary the grain traders had no insurance in case the crop a noble landlord offered them in May failed to ripen in July, and they lived in a land still virtually without reliable communications and transport. Only a very few grain-traders could grow rich enough, like the Strassers of Győr, to buy warehouses and wagons of their own. [15] And because so many professions were closed in mid-century to Jews, the grain business was very crowded.

Mid-century Hungary's Christian businessmen had, no doubt, an interest in economic change in the same sense as do all businessmen in countries which are open to capitalism, yet in which the capitalists do not govern. But those Christian burghers were inhibited from pressing for change by their control of the country's traditional urban institutions. The Jews, on the other hand, because of their pariah status had a clear interest in both change and rapid change. This interest was particularly important from the point of view of the preconditions for take-off, because the Jews far more than the Christians had access to the accumulated capital of neighboring Vienna, which, as much as any other basic factor, made economic take-off a realistic possibility in mid-century Hungary.

A Governmental Invitation

A graph (Table 8) of when and how many Jews won nobility in Dualistic Hungary attests another most important precondition of the country's economic take-off. The first peak year of ennoblements on this graph, 1867, was, as mentioned earlier in the chapter, the year of the Austro-Hungarian *Ausgleich* (Compromise) and of an array of great social and economic reform legislation. [16] Between 1882 and 1887, another peak

---

[15] The Strasser family built up the Strasser and König shipping firm, which at the turn of this century was the fifth largest in the world. See the account based on family records in the *Pesti Tözsde*, 2 April, 1932.

[16] Standard accounts of Hungarian political life of the Dualistic Era are Gratz, *A dualizmus kora;* Szekfű, *Három nemzedék;* and the recent survey in Erik Molnár (ed.), *Magyarország története*, Vol. II.

TABLE 8
CHRONOLOGICAL GRAPH.

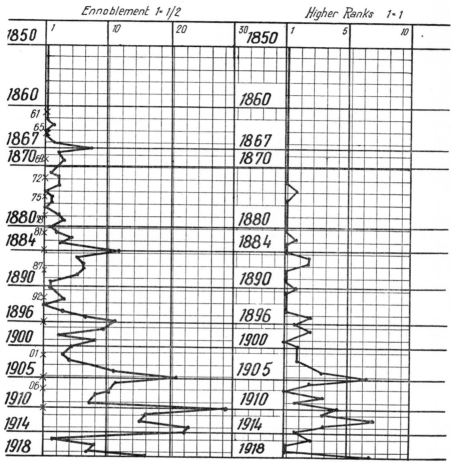

X   Election year.

period on the graph, the Hungarian Prime Minister Kálmán Tisza took
up the defense of the Jews against an emerging anti-Semitic wing of the
oppositional Independence Party and prepared the ground for a civil mari-
age law which would enable Jews to marry outside their faith without
converting. Between 1895 and 1897, the third peak in our graph, the Hungarian Government (often in that day called "mercantilist") organized a
great industrial exhibition to celebrate the country's national Millennium;
and finally established Judaism as a legally "received" religion in Hungary.

In sum, the graph shows that the Jewish capitalists of Hungary sought ennoblement at times when they were particularly aware of benefits the Government extended to them. One may recall here the alliance which had existed in mid-century between reformer Jews and the liberal leadership of the Magyar noble nation. Our graph shows that this alliance was transformed in the 1860's into a *de facto* coalition which favored modernization — a significant precondition for economic take-off. [17]

To probe into the material on which our graph is based is to refine our understanding of nineteenth-century Hungary's coalition for modernization. It soon appears that five out of the ten families which received nobility between 1866 and 1868, the *Ausgleich* years, were linked not with the Magyar Liberals, but with Vienna. [18] The Biedermanns in particular were a great Vienna banking family with hardly any connections left in Hungary, whence they had emigrated early in the century. Moreover, though the other five in this group did have distinctly Hungarian connections, at least three of them also had strong connections in Vienna. [19] Widow Goldberger's husband, for example, had helped the Hungarian cause in 1848, and the family textile firm was one of the few industrial jewels of the Hungarian crown; but she herself had lived for a decade in Vienna prior to the *Ausgleich*, and her social connections there seem to have played a considerable role in the family's ennoblement. [20] Nor did the Viennese imprint on the distribution of Hungarian nobility to Jews end after 1868. Only five of the sixteen ennoblements distributed to Jews in Hungary between 1869 and 1880 went to families whose connections were only in Budapest. All the rest were in one way or another Viennese. [21] Our sample suggests thus that it was not the Magyar Govern-

---

[17] See Rostow, *The stages of Economic Growth*, pp. 28—29; and the much more complex system of Barrington Moore, *Social Origins of Dictatorship and Democracy* (Boston: Beacon Press, 1967), especially Ch. 8.

[18] Gottesmann, Biedermann, *maglódi* Wodianer, Harkányi, and Lévay.

[19] *Farkasházi* Fischer (the Herend china-factory family), Gans, and Goldberger.

[20] It was popular at the turn of the century for Magyars to depict the Goldberger establishment as *ab origine* ardently Magyar: see, for example, the sketch in Mór Gelléri, *A magyar ipar úttörői*, p. 17ff. But the Viennese connections are clear from László Kállai, *A 150 éves Goldberger gyár*, p. 112.

[21] The *gyömrői* Herzfelders, Zombory-Steins, Baronyis, *csengeri* Mayers, and Glücks. Of the other eleven, five went to the Popper, Gutman, Eisenstädter, *p.* Weisz and Baruch families, which were engaged in foreign trade centering in Vienna; two went to Dóczy and Wich, who were Viennese civil servants; two went to the Flesch and Barber families, which had close family ties in Austria; and two went to the Lackós, who figured in the Vienna *Bodenkreditanstalt* directorship, and their in-laws, the Hatvany-Deutsches, who supplied the *K.K.* Army in the Bosnian Campaign of 1878.

ment in post-*Ausgleich* Budapest, but Franz Joseph in Vienna who specified in this early period who would get nobility in Hungary. [22] It follows that in Hungary a coalition for modernization was offered to the business classes not only by the Magyar liberals, but also by the King.

We may approach an explanation of why Franz Joseph participated in this coalition by studying the history of the Schey family. Philipp Schey was born in a ghetto town in today's Burgenland in 1798, made a fortune in textile trading during the Napoleonic wars, and then moved to Vienna, where he became a private banker for the Archduke Albrecht, the wealthiest of the Habsburgs. In the 1830's and 1840's Schey served the Imperial House well. In the revolutionary years, 1848 and 1849, he came out openly on the side of the Habsburg forces in Hungary. Yet he received no reward until 1859 when at the age of 61 he became the equivalent of a Hungarian noble. [23] It is not hard to deduce why the elder Schey received no reward for his services until so late in life. He had remained a religious Jew; and a glance at the record of the Viennese court bankers shows that only during the Napoleonic wars had the Habsburgs allowed unbaptized Jews into the Austrian nobility without reluctance. [24] Prior to 1859 they had allowed none into the Hungarian nobility. One may recall that even the Rothschilds, who gained social acceptance in several Western countries early in the century, had troubles in Austria. Why, then, did the Crown suddenly show its benevolence to the still unconverted Philipp Schey in 1859? This question is all the more puzzling when one learns that in 1859 Schey's much younger nephew, Friedrich, also obtained nobility. This nephew's distinction was not lengthy service to an Archduke, but consolidation of his personal prominence in the Viennese banking world through marriage, in succession, to three heiresses of the tolerated Landauer family. It is easy to resolve this question only when we recall that the year 1859 was a watershed in the history of Habsburg government from Vienna.

From the middle of the eighteenth century until 1859 the Habsburgs had perceived the problems of administrating their far-flung central Euro-

---

[22] For references, see Sándor, *Nagyipari fejlődés*, pp. 314, 372.

[23] Technically Schey received Austrian nobility awarded with a Hungarian predicatum. By all reports, however, Hungarian nobility was intended, but could not be granted because the Hungarian Constitution was not in force at the time. Biographical material on the Schey family has been compiled by Heinrich Benedikt in *Neues österreichisches biographisches Lexikon*, Vol. XVII, p. 130 ff.

[24] For the ennoblement of Vienna Jews prior to 1848, see above Chapter III, ftn. 19. The following is based on the catalogue of Jewish ennoblements in Austria compiled by Hanns Jäger-Sunstenau in *Die geadelten Judenfamilien im vormärzlichen Wien*, p. 88ff.

pean dominions in consistent terms. [25] Whether they had been "enlight-ened," as was Joseph II, or "reactionary," as were Franz I and Franz Joseph in his early years, they had seen their main foe first in provincial anarchy, and later in Liberalism, and had sought to solve their problems with centralism, pushing out the arms of a centralized Viennese bureau-cracy into the multitudinous dominions of their House. In 1848—1849 the Viennese bureaucracy was shaken by revolution. Still it emerged victo-rious; for the dominions, having revolted against it, proceeded to cut each other to pieces. But in 1859 Viennese bureaucratic Absolutism was defeated at Solferino, and Franz Joseph had to recognize that centralism had failed.

That in the late 1850's Franz Joseph bestowed nobility on Philipp and Friedrich Schey without insisting, as in the past, that they convert, recalls that a full decade before the establishment of Dualism with Hungary the Emperor-King had decided ennoblement was a fair means by which to diminish his dependence on his centralized, but now demonstrably fallible, Viennese bureaucracy. Ennobling Jews was, of course, by no means the only or the most important way in which he sought this end. In 1860 and 1861 through Anton von Schmerling he set up a two-house *Reichsrat* (Imperial Council or Parliament) for all his dominions which gave partial satisfaction to his German subjects. Subsequent to his defeat by Prussia in 1866 he reached his *Ausgleich* with the Magyars, gave satisfaction to the Poles, forced a settlement upon the Croats, and made overtures even to the Czechs. But alongside this flurry of constitutional innovations he evidently did decide in principle to use ennoblement as a means of encou-raging businessmen to collaborate, even if they were unconverted Jews. In 1861 he allowed the Rothschilds to assume a place in the Upper House of the *Reichsrat*. In 1863 he made the convert court bankers, the Wodia-ners, barons in Austria. In 1867, as we have seen, he issued a spate of ennoblements to Jews in Hungary. In 1869 he made the Scheys, and two other Jewish banker families, the Todescos and the Königswarters, barons in Austria. And meanwhile he literally deluged lesser figures in the Vienna business community with ranks and titles. In the 1870's by one count he made 100 such awards to Austrian Jews. [26] The coalition for modernization

[25] Recent general histories of the Habsburg Monarchy are C. A. Macartney, *The Habsburg Empire, 1790—1918* and Hugo Hantsch, *Die Geschichte Österreichs* (2 vols.; Graz: Styria Verlag, 1959 and 1962). Both contain extensive bibliographies. There is particular stress on the significance of 1859 as a turning point in Habsburg history in G. Franz, *Der Liberalismus*, p. 125ff.

[26] Jäger-Sunstenau's study does not deal with non-Viennese families or families which settled in Vienna after 1848; and in the post-1867 era it mixes Austrian and Hungarian

between Government and Capitalism which was to characterize Dualistic Hungary began thus in Vienna.

* * *

The ennoblement materials for the 1880's bring to light a relationship between the Magyar Government in Budapest and Hungary's leading businessmen comparable to that we have just seen in Vienna. According to our graph, 1882 was the start of a boom of Jewish ennoblements in Hungary. As it happens the Prime Minister of Hungary Kálmán Tisza, had been in office for seven years by that time and was discovering that the formula by which he had been ruling was in trouble. At risk of over-simplification let us suggest that Tisza had designed this formula originally to meet an age-old question which had frustrated central governments in Hungary: how to control the provinces in the face of an insubordinate nobility entrenched in an administrative system of legally autonomous counties?[27] Tisza, as a noble, had had no desire to solve this problem by diluting noble hegemony over the mass of the population; and indeed, in the earlier *Ausgleich* years perhaps he could not have diluted noble power in the counties, because there was no other social class articulate enough to serve as a base for ruling Hungary against the nobility. Generally speaking, therefore, Tisza had not attacked the noble-dominated counties directly. Instead step by step he had sought to nullify their independence by constructing a centralized administrative bureaucracy extending from Budapest; and he had distracted the nobility from the bureaucracy's intrusions not by encouraging in the provinces a greater spirit of democracy, but by allowing the national Parliament in Budapest to become a main sounding-board of Magyar noble nationalism. This formula entailed, of course, a danger. The Parliament could have become too nationalistic and could have damaged the *Ausgleich* with Austria, by virtue of which alone the King tolerated Hungary's constitutional life. To control Parliament, therefore, Tisza had made his own political party, backed by the national police forces, into an instrument for the fixing of elections. Here lay the catch: elections came every three years, and to "fix" them cost money.

---

ennoblements. Nonetheless, it reveals the following pattern. In the 1840's there were four bestowals of rank to Jews, all to converted families. Between 1850 and 1858 there were 16, all to long-since converted families. In 1859 there were two awards to converted families, and ennoblement for the non-convert, Philipp Schey. In the 1860's, there were 62 bestowals of Austrian nobility to Jews, at least 13 of them to non-converts, with a total of six baronages.

[27] For the following interpretation, see in particular Szekfű, *Három nemzedék*, pp. 373—374.

After the election of 1881 the intense resentment against Tisza's "system" made it obvious that the next campaign, in 1884, would be very expensive. As it happens, Tisza won the election of 1884, and the election of 1887 also. But meanwhile he did not content himself with defending the Jews against anti-Semitism. In 1882 he obtained nobility for the distiller-and-stock-investor *megyeri* Krausz family, and for the grain merchant *domonyi* Brülls, both of whom were leaders of the capitalist community which as we will see later was making Budapest one of the grain-milling centers of the world. [28] Further, in 1884 Tisza obtained nobility for the *dirsztai* Fischls, the *tószeghi* Freunds, the *borsai* Flesches, and the *ilencfalvi* Linzers, in 1886 for the *csetei* Herzogs, and in 1887 for the *zimonyi* Schwartzes, all of the same circle. It seems legitimate, therefore, to deduce that Tisza resolved his financial problems at this time *inter alia* by encouraging a rage for ennoblement among Budapest's newly rich.

Nor is this the only evidence which suggests governmental initiative behind the ennoblement of Jewish capitalists in Pest in the 1880's. In 1884 one of these newly ennobled families, the Krauszes, ran a son for Parliament in support of Tisza in a troublesome district of Pest County. Another, earlier-ennobled Pest grain-trader family, the *erényi* Ullmanns, ran a candidate for Tisza in Transylvania. The recently ennobled Hatvany-Deutsches organized the collection of election funds for Tisza in the Budapest "City." [29] And, it may be noted, at least two rich Tisza Party parliamentary deputies from the provinces got ennobled in this period. [30] All this evidence seems to demonstrate that the governments of Dualistic Hungary offered the new urban capitalists of Budapest a distinctive, albeit limited, place in the political process; and that ennoblement was thus the wherewithall in a not-so-tacit political coalition favorable to economic take-off.

* * *

Franz Joseph, of course, was even after 1880 still the ultimate source of ennoblement in Hungary. If therefore he then began to distribute en-

---

[28] These and the other important families mentioned below will be identified in later chapters. For a commentary dating the cult of ennoblement and other dignities to this time, see Tamás Vécsey, *Tisza Kálmán* (Celldömölk: Dinkgreve Nándor, 1931), p. 184ff.

[29] See the *Egyenlőség*, 29 June, 1884; and Mór Gelléri, *Ipartörténeti vázlatok* [Sketches in Industrial History] (Budapest: 1906), pp. 530—537.

[30] Lajos Máday ennobled in 1884 and Ödön Gajáry, ennobled in 1888, were Tisza-Party deputies. It is relevant that Izidor Rósa, who received nobility in 1883, was one of the Tisza-Party leaders in Szeged; and Károly Sváb, whom Tisza selected to represent the Jews in the Upper House of Parliament in 1886, was a Tisza-Party deputy.

noblements to help Kálmán Tisza, we must deduce he had innovated on the system of 1859, which served primarily his own interests in governing Austria. This change requires further explanation, and explanation, as it happens, is available in terms of a new political crisis Franz Joseph faced just prior to 1880.

From the time of the French Revolution until 1859 the Habsburgs had consistently relied on bureaucratic centralism against the provinces, and against Liberalism, not just because they feared "Revolution," but also because the bureaucrats seemed capable of protecting the power of the Habsburg House and its army, whereas first the provinces, and then Liberalism challenged this power. As we have observed above, Franz Joseph came to terms with Liberalism after 1859, and particularly after the military defeat in 1866 because the bureaucrats had proved incompetent to sustain an effective army. In these same terms Franz Joseph's "system of government" once again broke down in 1878. During the military campaigns in Bosnia in that year the parliamentary liberals of both Vienna and Budapest claimed a right to interfere with military affairs. On an earlier such occasion, in the middle 1860's, Franz Joseph had been able to buy them off with a combination of absolutism and constitutional concessions. Now, however, the Monarch had less room for manoeuver, and the liberals threatened to become regularly a challenge to the freedom of the Army.

In this situation Franz Joseph instituted in Austria the regime known in history as the "Iron Ring." [31] Its strength lay in the ability of its author, Count Taaffe, to maintain a *Reichsrat* majority of liberal Slavic nationalists, on the one hand, and of reactionary aristocrats and clericals, on the other hand. Taaffe kept his majority in part by resting on unprincipled hostility to German Liberalism, but in part also by corrupting friend and foe alike with "tidbit" concessions to their special interests. As a system of government the "Iron Ring" possessed, in a pronounced fashion, all the advantages and none of the faults of Franz Joseph's two earlier experiments. On the one hand, it was not insulated from below, as Prime Minister Schwarzenberg's absolutist bureaucracy had been in the 1850's. Taaffe rested on a public consensus expressed through the *Reichsrat* and could provide the semblance of popular consent necessary for a modern military machine. Taaffe's *Reichsrat* on the other hand, was not autonomous and

---

[31] For the connection between the Army question and the emergence of the Iron Ring, see the recent study by William A. Jenks, *Austria Under the Iron Ring* (Charlottesville: University of Virginia Press, 1965), Ch. 2.

potentially out of control, as Schmerling's had become in the 1870's, and consequently it did not make trouble for the Army.

The Hungarian regime did not undergo any visible change after 1878 comparable to that in Austria. Our ennoblement sample allows us to see, however, that it did in a sense become parallel to the Taaffe system. Perhaps we can generalize that before 1878 no less than afterwards Tisza ruled essentially through manipulation of the Parliament, but that before then he tended to parade illusions that the *Ausgleich* was just a stage on the road to Hungarian independence. [32] Tisza had built his career, for example, on the premise that he was "left-center" — not completely for Hungary's absolute independence from Austria, but not completely for the compromise with the King either. In 1875 he accepted the *Ausgleich* and became Prime Minister after fusing his Party with Ferenc Deák's pro-*Ausgleich* Liberal Party. But then in 1877 he attempted to use the decennial customs union negotiations to extract further concessions to Hungary's independence. No doubt after 1877 also Tisza fought to achieve ever greater concessions for Hungary. But his failure in the negotiations of 1877 prevented him from posing any longer as the champion of independence in the material terms which Magyar politicians were apt to stress. As we have seen in an earlier chapter, even the assimilationist Jew Ferenc Chorin left Tisza's Party in 1877, because he felt that the Prime Minister's failure to extract material concessions represented a "betrayal" of Hungarian interests. Thus by the early 1880's Tisza, as unveiled defender of the *Ausgleich*, needed to strengthen his hand. That Franz Joseph after 1878 allowed Tisza increased discretion in the distribution of ennoblement suggests, therefore, that Tisza now changed his system, subtly, and like Taaffe began to rely ever more heavily on systematic behind-the-scenes corruption of individuals and corporations.

Certainly throughout the 1880's and 1890's the pattern of Jewish ennoblement in Hungary reflects a continuing government invitation to businessmen for accommodation and collaboration. For example, 1892 and 1896 were election years in Hungary. Even though Tisza by then had fallen, and his successors had sought to change his formula for rule, both years show an upturn in the ennoblement graph. One may argue that in 1896 the major increase in ennoblements reflected the numerous honors given out in connection with the Magyar national Millennium; and that the election that was not sharply contested. The record shows, however, that of the eleven ennoblements of 1896, only four were unmistakably inspired

---

[32] For the following, see Gratz, *A dualizmus kora*, Vol. I, Ch. 9.

by a desire to honor distinguished men during the Millennial celebration. [33]
Three, on the other hand, went specifically to commercial families which
were putting up government-party deputies in the parliamentary election. [34]
And it is interesting to note in this connection that of the 62 Jews who
entered the Hungarian Parliament on a Government ticket in the Dualistic
Era, 29 came from ennobled families, and seven others were closely related
to Jewish nobles. [35] Evidently the governmental invitation to the business
classes to enter a coalition for modernization grew stronger as time passed
in Hungary.

* * *

By way of conclusion to this review of the preconditions for economic
take-off in nineteenth-century Hungary let us confront an important problem. In the 1880's and 1890's in Austria there was a great deal of explicit
political anti-Semitism. [36] In Hungary also anti-Semitism reared its head,
though Kálmán Tisza prevented the emergence of a lasting anti-Semite
political party. [37] To recall its importance one has only to mention the
Tiszaeszlár "ritual murder" trial of the early 1880's, which ranks with the
Dreyfus case as one of the most shocking manifestations of official anti-
Semitism in all nineteenth-century Europe. Evidence such as we have cited
in this chapter often led anti-Semites to the conclusion that Dualism in
Hungary rested on a contractual relation between the Habsburgs, Tisza,
and the Jews. As is known, Karl Lueger, the Mayor of turn-of-the-century
Vienna, even referred to Budapest as *Judapest* because of the alleged hege-
mony of Jews and Jewish interests there.

Study of the overall record of whom Franz Joseph and the Hungarian
governments ennobled during the Dualistic Era suggests that the invitation

---

[33] Balázs, Bródy *(Főrend)*, Frigyessi, and Körösy.

[34] Mándi, Mende, and *csepeli* Weisz.

[35] Partial lists of the 103 Jews who became members of parliament in the Dualistic
Era are in *MZsL*, "Törvényhozás"; Schickert, *Die Judenfrage in Ungarn*, pp. 101—103;
the *Egyenlőség*, 29 Jan., and 5 Feb., 1905; and the articles by Ede Vadász, "A magyar
országgyűlés jelenlegi és azelőtti zsidó tagjai" [Former and Present Jewish Members of
the Hungarian Parliament] in *Magyar Zsidó Szemle* [Hungarian Jewish Review], Vol.
22 (1905), pp. 117—118; and Vol. 23 (1906), pp. 252—254.

[36] See Pulzer, *The Rise of Political Anti-Semitism*, Chs. 14—18.

[37] On the history of anti-Semitism in Hungary see the philo-Semite Venetianer,
A magyar zsidóság története, p. 314ff.; and the anti-Semite Schickert, *Die Judenfrage
in Ungarn*, p. 117 ff. An interesting recent account of the anti-Semitic movement in the
1880's is Judit Kubinszky, "Az antiszemita párt megalakulása és részvétele az 1884-es
választásokon" [The Formation of the Anti-Semite Party and Its Participation in the Elections of 1884], *A Legújabbkori Történeti Muzeum évkönyve*, V—VI (1966), pp.107—160.

of which we are speaking was neither made predominantly to the Jews, nor accepted predominantly by them. An exact analysis of the overall ennoblement record has proved impractical: there were well over two thousand ennoblements and, in addition, a large number of reconfirmations of old patents of nobilities, and also a number of awards of higher titles. Yet even cursory counting shows that the great bulk of these new ranks went not to Jews, but to administrators, cultural figures, military personnel, and businessmen with German and Slavic sounding names. Rough calculation indicates that the Jews account at most for 20% of the total. [38] This figure is decidedly higher than their share of the total population of Greater Hungary (which averaged about 4% over these 70 years), but it is not proportionate to their role in Hungary's urban society; and it is decidedly lower than their share in the new commercial world. [39] The records suggest that if any nationality group won a disproportionate number of new nobilities, it was the Germans, who shared with the Jews in the distribution of titles given to businessmen, and who received also a very high proportion of the titles given administrative and military personnel.

In sum, if Jews acquired a large number of ennoblements in Dualistic Hungary, it was probably because the government invited the Hungarian multinational bourgeoisie as a whole to enter a coalition for economic modernization in which part of the wherewithal was ennoblement. Inferentially, Hungary's coalition for modernization was not a compact made as consciously and explicitly as anti-Semites would have it between the Government and the Jews. Yet in rebutting anti-Semitism, let us not deceive ourselves! We have seen earlier in this chapter that the Jews dominated the sector of the mid-century Hungarian economy that was best suited for take-off, and that as a group they were more ready for radical socio-economic change than any other group in the Hungarian business class. It follows that the Governmental overtures to the business class which we have been discussing were, irrespective of their intent, historically significant primarily in so far as they were made to Jews.

---

[38] Out of the final 182 alphabetically consecutive cases of simple ennoblement listed in Gerő, *Királyi könyvek* (letters T—Z) 34 were Jewish civilian, 22 were German civilian, 65 were military personnel (mostly German, only 1 Jewish), 18 seemed Slavic, and 43 were, judging from the names, Magyar.

[39] In 1910 Jews comprised 5% of the population of greater Hungary, 23.1% of the population of Budapest, and 54.1% of the persons engaged in trade and finance in Budapest. See the anti-Semitic, but nonetheless authoritative statistical discussion of Hungarian Jewry in Alajos Kovács, *A zsidóság térfoglalása Magyarországon* Tables 2, 4, 6, 7.

CHAPTER VI

ECONOMIC TAKE-OFF, ENNOBLEMENT, AND GENIUS

Domestic Capital and Ennoblement

The main task of this chapter is to describe how the process of modernization which affected Hungary in the later nineteenth century led both to the large-scale ennoblement of the country's leading capitalists, and to the formation of her scientific geniuses. The history of the Schossberger family of Pest can help us embark on this task. It affords on the one hand a fine illustration of how the first phase of the Hungarian economic take-off contributed to the ennoblement of the business community. On the other hand, it affords a link between economics and our geniuses. As will appear at the end of the chapter, the Schossbergers gave birth to one of the more important scientists of the twentieth century, Georg de Hevesy.

In many ways the Schossbergers seem the typical successors of the Vienna court bankers. [1] Lazar Schossberger, the founder of the family firm, was a trader of "rabbinical" knowledge from Nyitra on the Moravian frontier, who had settled at Pest by the 1830's. He and his son, Simon Vilmos Schossberger, were produce merchants, but neither seems to have been particularly prominent prior to the political upheaval of 1848. [2] Then under Austrian Absolutism after 1850 they emerged as founders of an oil refinery and a biscuit plant, both of which supplied the needs of the Imperial Army. These industrial ventures launched them on the road to significant wealth, and they proceeded apace on the same road when later in the 1850's they became decisively involved in the production and export of tobacco. They had traded in tobacco even before this, but the key to their success was

---

[1] The following account of the Schossbergers derives from the *Egyenlőség*, 23 March 1890, pp. 3—5; OL. K-26 Min. Eln. 1889, IX 2310; and OL. K-26 1906, IX 82; Emma Lederer, *Az ipari kapitalizmus kezdetei*, pp. 51—52; Zsigmond Groszmann, *A magyar zsidók a XIX század közepén, 1849—1870*, p. 20ff.; and Simon Krausz, *Életem*, p. 30ff.

[2] For example, the family does not figure in a famous list of Pest's large merchants in 1846; for which see the account by A. Deutsch in Szirmai, *Védőirat*, p. 144.

the establishment in 1851 of a government tobacco monopoly. In the reorganization of the tobacco trade entailed by this reform, the Schossbergers so deployed their influence in official places as to make their fortunes. [3] Subsequently, between 1861 and 1863, Simon Vilmos Schossberger showed political preferences by serving as Kaiser-appointed Chairman of the wealthy Pest Israelite Community. As such he made sure that Pest's assimilee Jews did not swing their weight too violently in favor of the Magyars. Meanwhile, he grew extremely prominent in railroad financing — an area of economic growth which in Hungary no less than elsewhere in Europe brought vast profits to those who knew how to abuse the public confidence. In 1863, typifying his intimate relation with the Vienna authorities, S. V. Schossberger became the first unconverted Jew since the Middle Ages to become a Magyar noble. [4]

In the early years of the *Ausgleich* the Schossbergers were among the wealthiest traders of Pest, and among the leading investors in domestic industrial establishments. In the 1880's, as we will see, they figured among the founders of a prosperous new Hungarian sugar-refining industry and lent their huge estates to a broad range of industrial and semi-industrial ends. [5] But in all this they both continued to maintain their links with Vienna and established new associations with the Magyar regime in Budapest. In 1868 S. V. Schossberger was a leading moderate at the Hungarian Jewish Congress, swinging his weight as usual against radical reforms which might displease the Government. In 1885 one of his sons, Zsigmond, was considered suitable to become President of the Traders' and Industrialists' Association of Budapest. In 1890 the same son had a sufficiently clean record of government service and sufficiently influential government contacts to become Hungary's first non-convert Jewish baron.

Hungary's leap into the modern industrial world began with the emergence after the revolution of 1848 of a small but significant body of domestic capitalists, interested in industrial investment. Many of these capitalists

---

[3] See Futó, *A magyar gyáripar története*, Vol. I, p. 294; and Lederer, *Az ipari kapitalizmus kezdetei*, p. 237ff.

[4] It is sometimes claimed that the Schey family, ennobled in 1859, was the first Jewish family to receive nobility in nineteenth-century Hungary. As mentioned in a previous chapter, however, the Scheys received an Austrian nobility with a Hungarian predicatum.

[5] According to Lörintey's list of 1893, Zsigmond Schossberger owned 26,000 holds of land at Tura in 1890, and his brother Henrik owned almost 16,000 holds at Aszód. Among the Jewish nobles their holdings were matched then only by the two Albert Wodianers, who held 30,700 and 25,600 holds respectively, and by the Barons Popper, who shared an estate of 47,000 holds.

made their fortunes as the Schossbergers did through close collaboration with Vienna, where the tradition of the court banker was strong. The Hungarian take-off began in this fashion because Hungary did not have to enter upon the path of industrialization simply through her own efforts or through her own skill and resources, as had the lands of the first European industrial revolutions on the Atlantic shores. Hungary, quite naturally, and one may add, "normally" for a "backward" land, could and did draw on the earlier experience of the West, and on the earlier accumulated capital of the West. And the consequence of this "normal" development was that, among the capitalists whom that process first thrust to wealth and influence were men whose business interests entailed compliance with the social traditions of Vienna.

*　*　*

The history of the Sváb family illustrates another of the most important ways in which the first accumulation of domestic capital took place in Hungary. [6] The earliest Sváb we know of was born about 1800 in southern Hungary, and began his career, as had the Ullmanns and the Wodianers, as a trader on the *Alföld*. By the 1840's he possessed a certain wealth and in 1844, when the Diet removed the ban on Jewish leasing of noble land, Sváb leased one of Count István Károlyi's larger estates on a long-term basis, and undertook to manage it with more on an eye for efficiency and profit than Count Károlyi, a typically extravagant and spendthrift Magyar magnate, was capable. Sváb was one of the first Jews to take advantage of the new legislation (though by no means the last), and his undertaking proved lucrative. [7] Subsequently, he sent his sons to agricultural schools in Budapest and abroad, so that they might assist him in the business of overseeing, and might rent further estates on their own. Through the profits this elder Sváb derived from renting (and later buying) estates a younger Sváb, Károly by name, became a capitalist in the 1870's and 1880's, active in Budapest's investment world.

The story of the Kohner family confirms the structural importance of estate management in the development of take-off capitalism in Hungary.

---

[6] For the Sváb family history see the *Egyenlőség*, 5 July, 1885.

[7] The major work on this subject is Béla Polyák, *Zsidók a magyar mezőgazdaságban* [Jews in Hungarian Agriculture] (Budapest: 1928). See also Géza Petrassevich, *Zsidó földbirtokosok és bérlők Magyarországon* [Jewish Landowners and Land-renters in Hungary] (Budapest: Stephaneum, 1904) , which on pp. 16—18 gives a scurrilous, but entertaining, contemporary account of how Jewish renters worked the land, instead of treating it "decently," and then gradually with hard bargains drove the Christian noble Magyars off their estates.

The Kohners came to Pest from Leipzig via Bohemia before 1840 as poor feather and wool traders. [8] In the following decades they speculated widely; and Adolf Kohner and his sons Zsigmond, Károly, and Ágoston, emerged from the great international financial crash of 1873 with a dominant interest in a flour mill in Pest. Thereafter they became decidedly rich. Zsigmond Kohner, the most prominent member of the family, married a Schossberger, sat on the Board of the Austro-Hungarian Bank in the 1870's and with his brother figured prominently in the Pest *Kereskedelmi Bank* in the 1880's and 1890's. For years he was Chairman of the *Pester Lloyd Society*, the mother of Budapest's late nineteenth-century commercial institutions. At the end of the century he became chairman of Pest's Neolog Jewish Community, by far the largest in Hungary. By then the Kohner family's investments ranged from flour-milling, sugar, and distilling to railroads and Rumanian oil. Nonetheless, from the start the Kohners leaned heavily on land as a source of capital, and owed their fortune, in no small part, to the difficulties into which the political defeat of 1849 and a prevailing grain-price decline after 1873 cast Hungary's traditional land-owner class. In 1893 Zsigmond Kohner and his son Károly (who handled the firm's agricultural interests) owned 20,000 holds of land between them, and both were among Hungary's 300 largest landholders. By 1911 these holdings had disappeared, but the family firm was renting some 40,000 holds of land from the Counts Schönborn in Bereg County (Carpathian region). At one time the firm is supposed to have controlled 130,000 holds.

Hungary's take-off process focused significantly upon the commercialization of agriculture made possible by the abolition of legal feudalism in 1848. In the West European modernization models, commercial land-management played a significant part in the emergence of capital in the seventeenth and eighteenth centuries; but by the nineteenth century it no longer did. [9] Further, in the West even before the nineteenth century the urban commercial classes had sufficient political strength to forge their own way to industrial wealth. In Hungary only on the very eve of the industrial take-off did the modernization of agriculture become possible, and considerable profit was still available there when the take-off era arrived.

---

[8] For the Kohner family history, see the *Pester Lloyd*, 27 May, 1928; the *Egyenlőség*, 18 Oct., 1896; Sándor, *Nagyipari fejlődés, passim;* Vilmos Balla, *A Vadember* [The Savage] (Budapest: Légrády, 1923), p. 265ff.; and A. Zichy (ed.), *Magyar zsidók a millenniumon* [Hungarian Jews at the Millennium] (Budapest: 1906) p. 117ff.

[9] For background on the role of commercialized agriculture in the modernization process of the West, see Barrington Moore, *Social Origins of Dictatorship and Democracy* (Boston: Beacon Press, 1966), esp. Chs. 1 and 2.

Further, in Hungary the urban classes lacked political strength, whereas great landowning magnates remained well into the twentieth century both politically dominant and consistently protective of their own economic interests. Characteristically, the Hungarian magnates were able to specify by political means that much of the foreign capital invested in the country in the 1850's and 1860's went into their estates; and that the initial railroad network served the grain-growing *Alföld* as opposed to the mining and industrial areas of the north. [10] Under these circumstances, businessmen who went into estate management could both get rich quick, and benefit from the magnates' protection.

Here once again the evidence is strong that the modernization process in Hungary thrust to the fore businessmen who by the nature of their profession were particularly susceptible to ennoblement. Károly Sváb was one of the first two unconverted Jews to be admitted to the Upper House of the Hungarian Parliament. The Kohners held back from ennoblement for as long as the *pater familias*, Zsigmond Kohner, was alive, probably because of his religious scruples. But they showed the pressures they felt to ennoble in 1912, when just after their father's death the whole clan both ennobled and acquired baronage in the same year. But the most effective evidence of the pressure the Jewish land managers of the early *Ausgleich* era felt in favor of ennoblement is visible in a professional profile of Hungary's Jewish nobility (Table 9).

Thirty-one Jews obtained nobility in Hungary prior to 1876. In terms of original profession, one was a doctor, one was a journalist, one was a soldier, four were in banking and insurance, three were "industrialists," 19 were "traders," and two lived off their estates. In terms of the profession in which they ended their careers, the pattern is not too different. The main changes were a shift from "trading" into "banking" and related activities, and an increase of five in the number of families living off their estates. The important change, however, appears in the way these people were "styling" themselves. In public documents of the 1880's no less than 21 of these 31 new nobles were styling themselves "landowners,"and 12 actually possessed estates large enough to qualify them as "large landholders." [11] In the Western past businessmen had wanted nobility to sanctify their wealth, and had

---

[10] A scandalized account of the role of the magnates in the economic development of Hungary during the sixties and seventies is in Lederer, *Az ipari kapitalizmus kezdetei*, Ch. 2.

[11] The sources for these statements are the Budapest virilist list of 1888 and Lörintey's estate-holder list of 1893.

TABLE 9 —

	A. Original Profession				B. Eventual main profession			
I. 1820—1899	1. 1820—1876 31 nobles	2. 1878—1889 50 nobles	3. 1890—1899 45 nobles	4. 1820—1899 126 nobles	1. 1820—1876 31 nobles	2. 1878—1889 50 nobles	3. 1890—1899 45 nobles	4. 1820—1899 126 nobles
Public Admin. (and Affairs)	—	1	—	1	—	3	6	9
RR. Admin.	—	1	2	3	—	1	3	4
Shipping Admin.	—	—	—	—	—	—	—	—
Public Instit.	—	—	—	—	—	—	—	—
(Totals)	(—)	(2)	(2)	(4)	(—)	(4)	(9)	(13)
Military	1	—	—	1	1	—	—	1
Medical	1	3	3	7	1	3	3	7
Lawyer	—	4	4	8	—	1	—	1
Judge	—	—	—	—	—	2	—	2
Archit.-Arts	—	—	—	—	—	—	—	—
Writer-Journal.	1	1	2	4	—	—	—	—
Academic	—	1	3	4	—	1	1	2
(Totals)	(3)	(9)	(12)	(24)	(2)	(7)	(4)	(13)
Insurance	1	—	3	4	1	—	4	5
Bank: Budapest	3	1	4	8	7	4	4	15
Bank: Province & Vienna	—	1	3	4	3	3	2	8
(Totals)	(4)	(2)	(10)	(16)	(11)	(7)	(10)	(28)
Industry: Gen'l.	—	2	—	2	—	3	1	4
Publishing	—	1	1	2	1	2	2	5
Goldsm.-China	1	—	1	2	1	—	—	1
Construction	—	—	—	—	—	—	—	—
Coal	—	—	1	1	—	—	1	1
Iron	—	—	—	—	—	1	1	2
Oil	—	—	—	—	—	—	—	—
Milling	1	1	—	2	1	4	—	5
Leatherg	—	—	—	—	—	—	—	—
Distillin	—	4	1	5	—	3	2	5
Sugar	—	—	1	1	—	1	1	2
Textiles	1	—	—	1	1	—	1	2
Chemicals	—	—	—	—	—	—	—	—
Machine	—	—	—	—	—	—	1	1
(Totals)	(3)	(8)	(5)	(16)	(4)	(14)	(10)	(28)
Trade: Gen'l.	8	13	3	24	5	2	1	8
Shipping	—	—	1	1	—	—	—	—
Textile	—	—	1	1	—	—	—	—
Iron	—	1	—	1	—	—	—	—
Produce	7	3	3	13	—	—	—	—
Wood	2	5	2	9	1	4	1	6
Wine	—	1	—	1	—	1	—	1
Tobacco	2	1	—	3	—	—	—	—
(Totals)	(19)	(24)	(10)	(53)	(6)	(7)	(2)	(15)
Capitalist (stockholder)	—	—	—	—	1	6	4	11
	—	—	—	—	(1)	(6)	(4)	(11)
Land: owner	1	1	5	7	6	3	5	14
renter	1	4	1	6	1	2	1	4
(Totals)	(2)	(5)	(6)	(13)	(7)	(5)	(6)	(18)

Professional Make-up

| | II. 1900—1918 | | | | | | | | | | III. Totals | | |
| | A Original profession | | | | | B. Eventual main profession | | | | | | | |
	1. 1900—1906 60 nobles	2. 1907—1909 25 nobles	3. 1910—1914 105 nobles	4. 1915—1918 30 nobles	5. 1900—1918 220 nobles	1. 1900—1906 60 nobles	2. 1907—1909 25 nobles	3. 1910—1914 105 nobles	4. 1915—1918 30 nobles	5. 1900—1918 220 nobles	A. Original profession	B. Eventual profession	
3	2	2	3	10	5	4	3	6	18	11	27	Public Admin. (and Affairs)
2	2	—	—	4	1	2	—	—	3	7	7	RR. Admin.
—	1	1	—	2	—	2	2	—	4	2	4	Shipping Admin.
1	—	—	—	1	1	—	—	—	1	1	1	Public Instit.
(6)	(5)	(3)	(3)	(17)	(7)	(8)	(5)	(6)	(26)	(21)	(39)	(Totals)
1	1	1	8	11	—	1	1	8	10	12	11	Military
7	3	12	1	23	7	3	12	1	23	30	30	Medical
6	2	8	7	23	—	1	4	2	7	31	8	Lawyer
—	—	—	—	—	—	—	2	1	3	—	5	Judge
2	—	5	—	7	2	—	5	—	7	7	7	Archit.-Arts
1	2	2	1	6	—	—	—	—	—	10	—	Writer-Journal.
1	1	—	2	4	1	1	1	1	4	8	6	Academic
(18)	(9)	(28)	(19)	(74)	(10)	(6)	(25)	(13)	(54)	(98)	(67)	(Totals)
—	1	1	—	2	2	1	1	—	4	6	9	Insurance
7	3	10	4	24	11	3	10	4	28	32	43	Bank: Budapest
2	—	8	—	10	6	1	11	1	19	14	27	Bank: Province & Vienna
(9)	(4)	(19)	(4)	(36)	(19)	(5)	(22)	(5)	(51)	(52)	(79)	(Totals)
—	1	1	—	2	1	2	1	1	4	4	8	Industry: Gen'l.
1	—	1	—	2	1	—	3	1	5	4	10	Publishing
1	—	—	—	1	—	—	—	—	—	3	1	Goldsm.-China
—	1	3	—	4	—	1	4	—	5	4	5	Construction
—	—	—	—	—	1	—	—	—	1	1	2	Coal
1	—	—	—	1	1	—	—	—	1	1	3	Iron
—	—	1	—	1	1	—	1	—	2	1	2	Oil
—	—	3	—	3	—	—	2	—	2	5	7	Milling
2	—	1	1	4	2	—	1	1	4	4	4	Leather
1	—	2	—	3	1	—	2	—	3	8	8	Distilling
—	—	2	1	3	—	—	1	1	2	4	4	Sugar
1	—	1	—	2	1	—	2	—	3	3	5	Textiles
—	—	1	—	1	—	—	1	—	1	1	1	Chemicals
—	—	3	1	4	—	—	4	1	5	4	6	Machine
(7)	(2)	(19)	(3)	(31)	(9)	(3)	(22)	(5)	(39)	(48)	(67)	(Totals)
4	3	14	1	22	—	—	8	1	9	46	17	Trade: Gen' 1.
2	1	2	—	5	2	1	2	—	5	6	5	Shipping
—	—	2	—	2	—	—	2	—	2	3	2	Textile
1	—	—	—	1	1	—	—	—	1	2	1	Iron
6	1	2	—	9	1	—	1	—	2	22	2	Produce
3	—	1	—	4	1	—	1	—	2	13	8	Wood
—	—	1	—	1	—	—	—	—	—	2	1	Wine
—	—	1	—	1	—	—	1	—	1	4	1	Tobacco
(16)	(5)	(23)	(1)	(45)	(5)	(1)	(15)	(1)	(22)	(98)	(37)	(Totals)
—	—	—	—	—	6	2	5	1	14	—	25	Capitalist (stockholder)
—	—	—	—	—	(6)	(2)	(5)	(1)	(14)	—	(25)	
2	—	6	—	8	2	—	5	—	7	15	21	Land: owner
2	—	7	—	9	2	—	6	—	8	15	13	renter
(4)	(—)	(13)	(—)	(17)	(4)	(—)	(11)	(—)	(15)	(30)	(34)	(Totals)

retired onto the land when they got it. This group of Hungarian new nobles contains businessmen who acquired land and nobility, but who did not retire. Only three families in this group disappeared from Hungary's commercial world because of their acquisition of land and nobility.

* * *

The meteoric career of Lipót Popper illustrates another way in which domestic capital emerged in the first phase of Hungary's take-off. Popper came to Pest from northern Hungary in the 1830's as a penniless boy selling faggots. [12] Through what his descendents called "skillful, clean, and honorable speculation" he managed to accumulate some capital. He fought as a lieutenant for Kossuth in 1849. He then rented some forest land, established a steam-run sawmill, and became exceedingly rich.

The reason Lipót Popper managed to make such a splash was that lumber, a natural product with which Hungary's then virgin mountainous periphery was still well supplied, became during the construction of railroads in the 1860's and 1870's one of "backward" Hungary's major exports. [13] The lumber industry fed, of course, on the construction boom in Budapest, and (since coal was expensive and hard to get) on the fuel needs of some domestic industries. But it was directed also to the requirements of the huge city of Vienna; and then later in the century to the demand in the timberless Middle East, where Popper's mills played a role in the construction of the Suez Canal. By the time of his death in 1888 Popper was playing a major role in the export of Central European lumber; his firm had branches in Vienna and Paris as well as Budapest; and his family figured in the *Wiener Bankverein*, one of Austria's greatest banks. [14]

Lumber, like land management, was one of the opportunity areas in Hungary's economy when the take-off process began; and lumber, like land, made businessmen singularly susceptible to ennoblement. The lumber business involved extensive dealings with the great magnates and aristocratic

---

[12] For the Popper family history, see Mór Gelléri, *A magyar ipar úttörői*, pp. 109—112; the account in the *Egyenlőség*, 26 Feb., 1927; and the biography of the deputy Ármin Popper in the *Egyenlőség*, 10 June. 1892.

[13] For brief accounts of this industry, see Eckhardt, *A magyar közgazdaság*, pp. 70 and 111; and Sándor, *Nagyipari fejlődés*, pp. 178ff. and 427ff. The lumber boom was a passing phenomenon, because Hungary (and even Transylvania) was not heavily wooded, and because scientific forestry was on the whole not practiced. While her supplies lasted, however, Hungary was a major exporter of lumber.

[14] Several directors of the *Wiener Bankverein* bore Popper's name. Adolf Schenk, who was President of that Bank for many decades, was not Popper's son-in-law, Adolf *Ledec*, Schenk, it should be noted.

institutions which owned the great timber tracts in the Carpathian foothills. To approach these owners, men such as Lipót Popper could well have found it more and more convenient as they grew wealthy to acquire rank and title of their own. No less than thirteen families in the Hungarian Jewish nobility derived their fortunes originally from trading in lumber. Lipót Popper himself became a noble in Hungary as early as 1869, and he became a baron in Austria in 1882. Moreover, he lived in a *Ringstrasse* palace, and of his eight children, one became a French countess, two became baronesses by marriage, and the rest all married nobles.

Distilling also was an agricultural industry, important in the development of Hungary's capitalism, which like land-renting and lumber often led mid-nineteenth-century businessmen in Hungary to sudden wealth. A most conspicuous case was that of the Mayer Krausz family. [15] The founder of this clan was in Pest by the mid-1840's. By the 1860's he directed one of the city's large produce-trading counters. Then in 1869—1870, just after the Jewish emancipation, he and his son Lajos managed to acquire the major interest in a large distillery. Throughout agrarian Eastern Europe in modern times distilling has been a major source of private gain and government income. The grains to make the mash and the fields for the disposal of waste were easily available, and spirits were the one product which even in a poor agrarian economy the peasants could be counted on to buy. Inevitably in Hungary as the economy began to grow rapidly, capitalists found in distilling a profitable field of enterprise. [16] Within a decade after 1870 the Krausz' distillery had brought them such wealth that they could construct, privately, the "Gizella" flour mill, one of the largest in Budapest. Lajos Krausz subsequently became a member of Parliament, and a leader of the *Pester Lloyd Society* and of the Stock Exchange. A second son, Izidor, acquired large estates by marrying the daughter of Pest's leading banker, Mór Wahrmann.

Precisely in proportion as distilling became their major source of profits the distillers could have found it convenient to ennoble. They were wholly dependent on the produce of Hungary's great estates, many of which remained in noble hands and all of which involved their owners in the landlord-

---

[15] See Zichy (ed.), *Magyar zsidók a millenniumon,* p. 34; the *Egyenlőség,* 20 Jan., 1889 and 18 July, 1890; and Sándor, *Nagyipari fejlődés,* pp. 93, 218, and 497.

[16] For survey accounts of this industry in Hungary, see Eckhardt, *A magyar közgazdaság,* pp. 40, 82—83, and 132—134; and Sándor, *Nagyipari fejlődés,* pp. 89—95, 355—358, and 499—502. The distilling industry in Hungary enjoyed its greatest prosperity in the 1860's and 1870's, after the introduction of steam-run equipment. In that period 53% of the distilleries in the Monarchy were in Hungary, although much of the refining took place in Austria.

peasant social world of the countryside. For this reason alone ennoble-ment could have seemed interesting to the wealthier distillers. And besides, the distillers of Budapest had a vital business interest in minimizing anta-gonisms between themselves and the nobility, which was sufficiently powerful in the Parliament to legislate favors to distilleries on rural estates. The Krausz family acquired nobility in 1882. This ennoblement was, moreover, contagious. Mayer Krausz's six daughters all married into leading families in the Budapest commercial world. By the turn of the century three of the sons-in-law were also in the Jewish nobility. [17] His granddaughter became a Princess of Thurn and Taxis. In all, eight families in the Jewish nobility gained their wealth originally through distilling. The meaning of this record seems again to be that the Hungarian take-off process hurled to wealth and prominence businessmen who were by the nature of their profession particularly susceptible to ennoblement.

* * *

It would not be just to claim that all the areas of business in which do-mestic capital was accumulated in the early part of the take-off in Hungary were "conducive" to ennoblement. One may point out, for example, that one of the major areas in which new wealth appeared was Budapest real estate; yet there was a striking dearth of ennoblement, at least among Jews, in this sector. The tools for measuring this finding are of a somewhat later date, but they are clear enough. In the list of Budapest taxpayers for 1888, sixteen Jews paid very high taxes on real-estate holdings. [18] In this group, five ranked among Hungary's largest land-holders, and of these four joined the Jewish nobility. Of the remaining eleven Budapest real-estate tax-payers, however, none joined the nobility. It follows that real-estate in Buda-pest was not "conducive" to ennoblement, save insofar as it was joined with an interest in great estates. Comparably, one can correlate the 180 Jews in the banker-industrialist elite described above in Chapter II with the Buda-pest tax list of 1888. It turns out that of the 69 who paid high taxes and also acquired nobility, 39 (56%) owned estates, whereas of the 26 who paid high taxes and did not acquire nobility only four (15%) owned estates. A case history confirms the role of Budapest real-estate in inhibiting businessman ennoblement in late nineteenth-century Hungary. In the early 1880's a Pest trader named Adolf Tafler, who made a large fortune in railroad

---

[17] They married into the Schwartz, Fürst, Brüll, Egger, Basch, and Gutmann fami-lies. The Fürsts, Brülls, and Gutmanns acquired nobility.

[18] The following is based on the card file compiled by Károly Vörös.

construction and who owned large estates, requested nobility. He died, however, before the King granted his petition, and his children neglected to carry the matter further. A radical change in the family's investment pattern suggests the reason. By the end of the century the family ceased to figure among Hungary's largest estate holders; yet after 1900, Tafler's son, Kálmán, became for almost two decades Budapest's largest real-estate taxpayer. [19]

As we proceed through the other profit-making sectors of the Hungarian take-off economy, we increasingly gain the impression that not all led to ennoblement. An important early industrial sector in which Jews were well represented, for example, was leather processing. Out of the three most important Jewish families in this industry in Budapest in 1888, two are conspicuously absent from the Jewish nobility, and the third acquired nobility only well after the turn of the century for special reasons to be discussed in another chapter. [20] Construction was another vitally profitable sector in the Hungarian economy all through the latter half of the nineteenth century. Here there was a virtual dearth in Budapest in 1888 of important families which ennobled. Particularly conspicuous in its absence from the Jewish noble group were the partners in the Haas and Deutsch construction and real-estate firm, of whom it was quipped in the 1890's that they had hung a sign on the frontier reading "Haas and Deutsch, formerly Hungary." [21]

This record notwithstanding, further probing confirms unmistakably that the emergence of domestic capital in the early phases of take-off in Hungary affected an extremely significant number of men whose professions made them susceptible to ennoblement. The most important sector of capital accumulation of all in the Hungarian take-off was the grain trade. Judging from our professional chart of the Jewish nobility (Table 9), the grain trade, quite as much as land-involvement, lumber trading, and distilling, inclined businessmen to accept the invitation which the governments of Austria and Hungary extended them after 1859 to collaborate. Nineteen families in the Jewish nobility were originally grain brokers, while 46 others, the second largest single contingent in our sample, were originally "traders in gross," which in nineteenth-century Hungary usually meant dealing in

---

[19] See OL K-148, B-Min Eln. 1882, I B 1013.

[20] The three families were the Mauthners, the Neuschlosses, and the Wolfners. Only the last ennobled.

[21] See the two long articles on Haas and Deutsch in the *Pesti Tözsde*, 1 August, 1924, and 11 February, 1926; and the rather garbled account in Balla, *A Niebelungok*, p. 31. The joke about the Haas and Deutsch firm reportedly originated with the journalist Miklós Bartha.

grain. Nor is it difficult to understand why so many grain traders acquired nobility. The grain trade was dependent on the agricultural base of the Hungarian economy. The traders had to deal directly with the noble estate-owners, from whom they obtained the produce. The traders, indeed, were in many respects at the mercy of the estate-owner who could pick the trader to whom he sold his crops, and boycott those he disliked.

Once again we may sense that the particular businessmen whom Hungary's take-off process lifted out of obscurity to wealth were by the nature of their professions peculiarly liable to collaborate with the regime through ennoblement.

The Milling Boom

In the West the industrial revolution began as a rule with an internal accumulation of capital, with the making of machines, and with the factory production of goods such as textiles for mass consumption. [2] In "backward" Hungary, even in the late nineteenth century, the internal capital and the internal markets for reproducing such a development were only just developing. Capital, however, could be borrowed from the West; machines could be imported from abroad; and markets could be found in the West. One may estimate, therefore, that for the emergence of industrialism in Hungary, all that was really necessary was mechanization in some sector of the economy and high profits which could be used for further industrial investment. The grain business offered itself for such mechanization.

Until the 1860's most of Hungary's grain went to Vienna for milling. [23] With the advent of railroads in the 1850's, however, and with the abolition of the old customs frontier which had inhibited investment in Hungarian industry, it began to seem logical to develop a milling industry at home. The times were by no means unfavorable to such an enterprise. Europe's cities were growing and affording a constantly growing demand for flour. In the period of Absolutism there were increasingly large sums of investment capital available; and a new official tolerance of stock companies made

---

[22] The following theses were developed by Vilmos Sándor in various works published during the later 1950's and have been expounded recently in the essays by László Katus and Péter Hanák cited in Ch. V, footnote 2 above; and in Iván T. Berend, *Közép-kelet Európa gazdasági fejlődése*, passim.

[23] See Sándor, "A Budapest nagymalomipar kialakulása," p. 363ff.; and A. Félegyházy, *A Budapesti tözsde története*, Vol. I, pp. 1—30.

it simpler than ever before for merchants to pool their resources in industrial foundations. Further, an element of competition entered the picture. In the 1850's and 1860's the Hungarian grain trade focused on two towns, not only Pest, but also Győr; and though Pest was nearer the producers of the Great Plain, Győr was nearer the Austrian markets. Faced with this combination of opportunity and challenge, the newly rich capitalists of Pest became exceedingly active. By the middle 1860's they had established grain and stock exchanges in their own city to beat down their rivals at Győr. Meanwhile, they began forming stock companies to encourage industry locally, and during the decade before the *Ausgleich* they founded numerous small mills and seven great mills equipped with the most modern steam-run machinery.

These mills became what we may label the main take-off sector in the industrialization of Hungary. By the late 1870's Pest had become because of her mills, not only the grain emporium of the whole mid-Danubian basin, but the flour-milling center of much of Southeastern Europe.

* * *

The history of the Hatvany-Deutsch family indicates that it was by no means easy to get on the crest of the wavelike development of the Hungarian milling industry. [24] The founder of this famous clan was Ignác Deutsch, of whose origins little is known save that he was born near Temesvár, that he founded a grocery shop at Arad about 1820, and that sometime after that he was prosperous enough to marry a girl from the wealthy Adelsberg family of Pest. In the course of time Ignác Deutsch became *házi zsidó* (house Jew — a common expression signifying "jack-of-all-trades" and money lender) to various aristocratic families of the Arad region [25] and pioneered in the insurance business. [26] This gained him a certain wealth; and then a turning point in his career came in 1848—1849. A descendant remarks: "One hates to think what he did"; but in 1850 Ignác Deutsch won admission to citizenship in Arad, the scene of General Haynau's retribution against the Hungarian rebels. This could only have been possible with Austrian backing. From 1853 until 1865, moreover, he was Chairman of the

---

[24] The following account reflects, in addition to the general sources mentioned in the Bibliographical Appendix below, an interview with a surviving member of the family, Bertalan Hatvany of Paris, in September, 1969.

[25] Robert Zelénski, *Emlékeim* [My Memories] (Budapest: Pallas, 1930), pp. 16—17.

[26] See *A Triesti Általános Bistosító Társulat 100 éves története Magyarországon, 1831—1931* [The History of the Trieste *Assicurazioni Generali*'s 100 years in Hungary] (Budapest: Atheneum, 1931), p. 63.

wealthy Arad Israelite Community. Again Austrian patronage must be supposed. In 1852, presumably confident in the opportunities of the Austrian centralist regime, he sent his sons, Bernát and József, [27] to Pest, to participate in its grain trade. Yet there they discovered how dangerous business could be.

The grain trade was irregular. Harvests might be bad, competition was enormous, men were fickle, and even for these relatively well-off merchants from Arad bankruptcy threatened at every corner. Because of the risks the Deutsch brothers tended to diversify their interests. In addition to grain, they dealt in insurance, they invested in railroad construction, they experimented in banking. In the 1860's they were among the Pest traders in gross who pooled resources to establish industrial joint-stock companies; and it was thus that they first entered the flour-milling business. But the deeper they became involved in such enterprises, the greater became the perils, for now they became dependent on the Pest Stock Market. This was a healthy, profitable institution as long as business retained its confidence. But as in many other smaller financial communities of the day a loss of business confidence could result in disaster for all concerned.

If a panic once did start, there would be virtually no buyers on this small exchange and consequently no bottom. [28] Traders who were even slightly overextended, therefore, could in such panics be forced to sell anything and everything they posessed for a fractional price in order to obtain cash. The key to the Deutsch family's final rise to flour-milling wealth was precisely such a panic. In 1873 the family firm started to play the stock market *à la baisse*. As it happens the game worked. A great crash arrived in June of that year. The Deutsches' wealth was liquid when most of Pest had to sell. They had a world to gain and gained it. But a descendant has recorded that, for six months until the great crash arrived, the family lived in unadulterated terror that it might not come. [29] Such was the life of those who tried to ride the crest of the great Hungarian milling boom.

The history of this family indicates not only the perils of getting into the milling industry but also what this take-off sector of the economy did for

---

[27] Along with Bernát and József, a Simon Deutsch is mentioned in Sándor, *Nagyipari fejlődés*, p. 70, and in Gelléri, *Ipartörténeti vázlatok*, pp. 570—571. A Simon Deutsch also figured prominently in the Hatvany-Deutsch controlled "Concordia" Mill throughout the 1880's. This Simon Deutsch was probably a member of one of the numerous other Deutsch families in Budapest.

[28] There is a good latter-day account of the perils of the Pest Stock Exchange in Krausz, *Életem*, p. 44ff.

[29] This legend is incorporated in Lajos Hatvany's novel, *Urak és emberek*, Vol. I, although that romance does not pretend to reflect the author's family history precisely.

those businessmen who succceded in it. The Deutsches emerged from the crash of 1873 with almost complete stock ownership of one of the largest flour mills in Pest, the "Concordia." [30] And once they were thus on top of the milling industry, their perilous speculations paid off. The later 1870's, the 1880's, and the 1890's were a period of hugely growing demand in Western Europe's cities for flour. Hungary's steam-run mills, with their new equipment, could command the best prices in the market. That was a period also in which the appearance of North American and Russian grains in Europe was driving down the price of grain received by the producers; but the millers not only were immune to the price fall, they were able to take advantage of it. Even during the crisis of 1873, for example, the Deutsches combined with other mill-investors in a price-fixing operation which undercut and nearly destroyed the grain exchange, but which made the participants handsome profits. [31] On another occasion the Hatvany-Deutsches combined with other millers in a milling recess to keep the flour prices up while the grain cost dropped. [32]

Meanwhile, the Budapest millers as a group enjoyed the formidable advantages of the so-called "milling-traffic." [33] This arose thanks to a provision of the Dual-Monarchy's protective grain tariff whereby grain could be freely imported for purposes of milling, provided it was exported again within a certain time limit. The millers recognized that no one could tell at the time of "re-export" which flour came from imported grain and which came from domestic grain. Consequently, they would import huge quantities of cheap wheat and corn from the Balkans and Rumania, using it to drive internal grain prices down, and would later "re-export" a suitable quantity of flour when the external price was high. [34]

During the 1870's, moreover, which were years of depression for the Central European economy, the Deutsches availed themselves of opportunities to invest outside the mills. They bought land. They built up their railroad interests. They emerged on the Board of the Austro-Hungarian Bank. In 1881 in combination with the Brüll and Kohner families they purchased the sugar refinery at Nagysurányi in modern Slovakia. [35] In 1882 in combination with those same families, and also with the Schoss-

---

[30] See Sándor, *Nagyipari fejlődés*, pp. 495—498.

[31] See Félegyházy, *A Budapest tözsde története*, Vol. 1, p. 31ff.

[32] See Sándor, *Nagyipari fejlődés*, p. 329.

[33] See *ibid.*, p. 495ff.; and for a general survey of the milling industry, Heinrich Benedikt, *Die wirtschaftliche Entwicklung in der Franz-Joseph-Zeit*, p. 18ff.

[34] The "milling traffic" was limited by agrarian political pressures in 1896 and suppressed in 1900. See Eckhardt, *A magyar közgazdaság*, p. 131ff.

[35] Sándor, *Nagyipari fejlődés*, p. 329—330.

bergers, they took over distilleries at Szeged and Temesvár and established a starch plant in the latter town. By then the Deutsches were among the richest families of all Hungary, borne to enormous heights by the economic take-off.

The continuation of the Hatvany-Deutsch history is even more dazzling. In 1881 when, as mentioned above, the Deutsches invested in the sugar refinery at Nagysurányi, the sugar industry was very far from the most important in Hungary; [36] and the Deutsches seem to have entered it because that refinery was available at a bargain price. There was room in Hungary, however, for another take-off industry based on agricultural production; and, more important, there were modern organizational devices for developing such an industry. The results were impressive.

Legend has it that the Hungarian sugar boom began when József, the energetic elder son of old Ignác Deutsch, announced in 1882, at the age of 57, that one should not rest on one's laurels. Bored perhaps with the now prosaic profits of flour-milling, he began dabbling with the family's new sugar factory. With his equally energetic son, Sándor, [37] József read up on new production techniques, applied them at Nagysurányi and later at a refinery on the family estate at Hatvan, and then deployed his connections in the Ministries at Budapest. By the middle 1880's the Hungarian Government began to subsidize a massive expansion of the sugar industry.

In the customs negotiation with Austria in 1886, moreover, Budapest obtained a revision, favorable to Hungarian producers, of the Monarchy's sugar tax system. [38] Meanwhile the Hungarian refiners, led by the Deut-

---

[36] For reviews of the development of this industry, see Eckhardt, *A magyar közgazdaság*, p. 134ff.; Sándor, *Nagyipari fejlődés*, p. 448ff.; and Benedikt, *Wirtschaftliche Entwicklung*, p. 11ff.

[37] Research into the business history of late nineteenth century Hungary is impeded by the existence of two Sándor Deutsches. The second was not only about the same age as Sándor Hatvany-Deutsch but also headed a grain-trading, flour-milling firm (Gábor and Jószef Deutsch, Inc.), also figured in the Austro-Hungarian Bank, as did the Hatvanys, and was also related to the Schossberger family by marriage. This second Sándor Deutsch acquired nobility with the predicatum *halmi* in 1902. To distinguish these gentlemen from one another must have been difficult even for their contemporaries.

[38] Prior to 1888 the Dual Monarchy's sugar consumption tax was applied at the place of production, which gave the Austrians, naturally, virtually 90% of it, since theirs was by far the larger production. The burden of compensating manufacturers who exported their sugar was, however, distributed according to the *quota*, which made the Hungarians pay out 31.4% in cash. When in the seventies the Monarchy's sugar exports started soaring, the Hungarian treasury began running a heavy deficit. The Reform of 1888 placed the whole sugar tax in proportion to production percentile and thus gave the Hungarians a clear interest in increasing production. The authority on this subject is Moszko Wiener, *A magyar cukoripar fejlődése* [The Development of Hungary's Sugar Industry] (2 vols.; Budapest: 1902).

sches, developed a cartel which gave them bargaining strength against their Austrian colleagues and reduced competition at home. Within fifteen years Hungary was producing one fifth of the Monarchy's sugar and enjoyed substantial export markets in Turkey, India, and, of all places, Japan. [39] Because of the cartel, the enormous profits of this growth were concentrated in the hands of a very few investors. About one fifth of the whole went to the Austrian Patzenhofer and Schöller sugar dynasties. Well over a third went to a consortium of Austrian, German, and Hungarian banks; but the remaining 27% went to the now patriotically Magyar Hatvany-Deutsches and to their relatives, the Schossbergers, the *dirsztai* Fischls, and the Brülls.

A new generation took over the Hatvany-Deutsch family firm in the 1890's, but the change by no means brought on a slackening of its race for wealth. To the contrary, Sándor Hatvany-Deutsch, the son of old József and the leading figure of this new generation, began his career by cementing an alliance with his first cousins József, Károly, and Béla Hatvany-Deutsch by marrying their sister Emma; and in close partnership these four men pursued the family's mighty venture into sugar refining even after the elder József died. By the start of the new century their joint holdings were so large that they required banking assistance. They obtained it primarily by buying into the *Hazai Bank* [Fatherland Bank] which had been founded by an older Budapest savings bank in 1895 to handle its commercial business. But their splendor was such that one bank could not suffice them. By 1904 it had become suddenly observable that there was a Hatvany-Deutsch in the directorship of almost all the great Budapest banks. Only strong intervention by other bankers prevented the Hatvany-Deutsches from consolidating a family bank-cartel in Hungary. [40]

* * *

The professional profile of the Jewish nobility (Table 9) suggests that flour-milling was, like the grain trade, "conducive" to ennoblement: in all 16 Jewish mill-founder families, including the Hatvany-Deutsches, acquired nobility before the end of the *Ausgleich* era. [41] Yet one can argue, when one thinks of it, that grain milling led less directly to ennoblement than grain trading. The millers, for example, did not have so much direct contact with the noble estate-owners. To deal with the owners was the role of the grain traders; and the millers were, if anything, immune from dependence on the

[39] Sándor, *Nagyipari fejlődés*, pp. 453—456.

[40] See József Radnóti, *Kornfeld Zsigmond* (Budapest: Révai, 193—), pp. 84ff.

[41] The list is compiled on the basis of data from Sándor, "A Budapesti nagymalomiar kialakulása," and from the *Magyar Compass* for 1872— 1873.

great estates. The estate-owners could hardly go about boycotting and thus ruining a mill as they could one or another petty trader.

Certainly in the Hatvany-Deutsch case there is little evidence of a direct interest deriving from the milling business in ennoblement. The Deutsches probably had some inclination to ennoblement even before coming to Pest and investing in its mills. The Adelsberg family, into which old Ignác Deutsch had married, had changed its name to Nemeshegyi, converted, and acquired nobility in 1834, and the Adelsbergs had married into the family of Mór (Szitányi)-Ullmann, who had converted and ennobled in 1825. Here was a good family tradition for the Hatvany-Deutsches to follow after they won their wealth. The Deutsches received nobility officially in 1879, moreover, not for their contribution to Hungarian milling, but for the services they rendered the *K.K.* Army during the Bosnian Campaign of 1878. [42]

The milling boom nonetheless made indirectly a real contribution to a readiness among Hungary's businesmen all through the *Ausgleich* era to accept the ennoblement which their government was tendering them. In this boom the economic force of the Hungarian take-off process hurled a very few families to a truly legendary prominence and wealth. These few families became, so to speak, the Horatio Algers of Hungarian capitalism. Their triumph served as a beacon for their whole class, confirming that all the risks were worth while, and that enormous success could crown any Hungarian capitalist's struggle. The very fact, therefore, that several of these families, and most particularly the Hatvany-Deutsch family, the most successful of all, acquired nobility had a decided effect on the behavioral style of their whole community. Regardless of precisely why these families ennobled, Hungary's Horatio Alger may be said because of them to have crowned his career with ennoblement. After the flour-milling boom, businessman ennoblement in Hungary connoted career success.

High Finance and Ennoblement

The career of Zsigmond Kornfeld illustrates a third major peculiarity of the Hungarian economic take-off. Kornfeld was born in Bohemia in 1852, the son of a reputable but impoverished distiller. [43] At the age of eleven he had to enter a Prague bank as a clerk in order to support himself. Essen-

---

[42] Interview with Bertalan Hatvany, Paris, September, 1969.

[43] The following is based on the extensive, although perhaps overly laudatory, biography of Kornfeld by József Radnóti cited in footnote 40 above.

tially he was still a minor functionary with no knowledge of Magyar when he came to Budapest in 1878 to manage the *Magyar Általános Hitelbank* [Hungarian General Credit Bank]; and that bank had just then been rescued from insolvency through the intervention of the House of Rothschild, which Kornfeld represented. Yet this functionary was able even in the first years after his arrival to acquire a major economic and political importance in Hungary. Nor did he succeed, as had the Schossbergers and the Hatvany-Deutsches, through conspicuous business risks and through accident of the fickle market. Kornfeld succeeded because the prosaic regularity of modern banking had a major role to play in the Hungarian take-off process.

Kornfeld owed his initial success to the deplorable financial condition of the then still-young Hungarian State, which for a decade before his arrival had hovered on the brink of insolvency. Late in 1878 it was in need of 150 million crowns. Kornfeld with the help of the Rothschilds obtained a loan abroad; and three years later he arranged the conversion of the entire State debt at a discount which was considered quite favorable for a country whose finances were so precarious. Kornfeld's price for these transactions was not high, considering what was at stake. But it included the installation of a Hungarian magnate, the Marquis Pallavicini, as figurehead President of the *Hitelbank* and recognition for the bank itself as *de facto* Hungarian State bank. And these concessions opened the door for him to a great deal of business.

Kornfeld arranged new debt conversions for the State in 1888 and 1892, each time at a better rate. He also managed a currency reform in 1894. But meanwhile with the profits from these formidable operations his bank found its way into a series of industrial enterprises. First, as was almost natural in that age of railroad constuction, it lent its prestige to a number of new lines. Then it took up the cause, favored by its governmental customers, of developing the "Hungarian" port of Fiume, and became major backer of a new rice-processing plant there, and of an oil refinery. [44] Next it moved into the Ganz Works, an iron and machinery establishment in Pest which was having difficulties, but which by the end of the century acquired a European reputation for producing electrical equipment and, especially, locomotive engines. Meanwhile the bank took over a bankrupt flour-mill and got involved in the rapidly booming sugar industry. Under Kornfeld's management, thus, the *Hitelbank* assumed the role of an industrial entrepreneur.

---

[44] See Benedikt, *Wirtschaftliche Entwicklung*, p. 154ff.; and Sándor, *Nagyipari fejlődés*, p. 483ff. for details of this oil business.

Zsigmond Kornfeld's career acquired another aspect when in 1891, as a result of his bank's industrial prominence, he entered the governing council of the Budapest Stock Exchange. In the following decades he became one of the most important figures in the commercial life of the city. In so doing he departed perhaps a little from the bureaucratic sobriety one often associates with banking. In 1895, for example, he seems to have created an artificial panic by manipulating the *Hitelbank* dividend. This made him temporarily so unpopular that he saw fit to go on vacation abroad. But he explained it away in terms of paternal concern for the welfare of the entire economy. His bank's industrial prominence was by then sufficiently great that the excuse sounded probable. Soon he returned home, whereupon in the later 1890's, having learned Magyar and bought a small estate, Kornfeld came forward with a plan for Magyarizing the Stock Exchange, which until then had conducted its business in German. In 1899, on this "reform" platform, he had himself elected President of the Exchange.

Through such dealings Kornfeld step by step built up to the climax of his career, which came at the turn of the century. Then at last he discontinued his bank's formal affiliation with the Rothschilds; and coincidentally he discontinued his personal dependence on the Marquis Pallavicini. In 1902, President in name as well as in fact of the *Hitelbank*, Kornfeld demonstrated the power the take-off process had brought this Magyar institution by independently arranging a new conversion of the Hungarian state debt.

In the lands on the Atlantic shore where industrialization first occurred in world history, banks were an important factor in the take-off process, but were only one of the factors conspicuously active in it; alongside them were entrepreneurial private industrialists, who bit by bit built up through manufacturing enough capital to invest in further factories. In Germany banks played a larger role in the economic take-off; for in Germany industrialization began considerably later than on the English Channel, at a time when the science of banking was considerably more developed than it had been in Napoleonic England, and when through large-scale banking various shortcuts to industrialization could be followed. Yet even in Germany an historic division of forces divided high finance from industrial capital in the industrialization process. In Hungary a modern industrial economy developed late, and on a backward base, at a time when European banking was leaping to new peaks of technical sophistication. In Hungary, accordingly, the new industrial economy, dependent in its infancy on the nearby international banking center at Vienna, shifted its dependence in its maturity to a precocious new financial establishment staffed by westernized professional bankers such as Kornfeld, but centered at Budapest. This was the third major peculiarity of the economic take-off process in Hungary.

* * *

Zsigmond Kornfeld had much within him of the typical German school teacher. On the one hand his private life was soulful. He took his vacations studying art in Venice and the Umbrian hill towns, avoiding the fashionable spas at Karlsbad, Gastein, and Ostende which his business colleagues frequented. His friends were historians and educators such as Ignác Goldzieher, the orientalist; Henrik Marczali, the annalist of eighteenth-century Hungary; and Mór Kármán, the educator-father of one of our geniuses. On the other hand, in characteristic Teutonic contrast with this private existence, his public life was methodical, puritan, and pedantic. For Kornfeld bankruptcy was Sin; and he was formalistically religious, prominent in the affairs of the Neolog Pest Israelite Community. It may seem surprising, therefore, that Kornfeld accepted in 1901, at the climax of his career, the worldly dignity of membership in the Hungarian House of Lords; and that in 1909, mortally ill, he requested and obtained a baronage.

In all, 70 of the families in the Hungarian Jewish nobility were involved in banking — the largest single professional contingent in the group (see Table 9). In the light of this fact, it appears logical enough to explain Kornfeld's ennoblement by recalling the strength of the court banker tradition in Vienna. The Budapest bankers, who grew up in the shadow of Vienna, could naturally have adopted this tradition. Zsigmond Kornfeld, who in many senses actually was Viennese, could have accepted the tradition particularly easily. From external appearance, thus, we may judge that insofar as the Hungarian take-off dynamically threw the Budapest bankers to the fore, it once again afforded prominence to men whose profession made them particularly susceptible to the Government's invitation to ennoble.

The victories which economic take-off brought bankers in Hungary did not always lead to their ennoblement, however, and an anecdote about the banker Mór Wahrmann can suggest why. [45] Wahrmann was born in Pest in 1832 into a distinguished rabbinical family and became after 1867 the most important private banker in Hungary. Because of his rabbinical

---

[45] An extensive biography of Wahrmann appeared in the *Egyenlőség*, 30 Oct., 1891. The following anecdote has been widely repeated and is printed in the Miksa Falk biography in Halász, *Országgyülési almanach, 1886*, p. 48.

background he played a prominent role from an early date in his career in the affairs of the Neolog Pest Community and he figured largely at the Jewish Congress of 1868. He was also a lawyer and an articulate political journalist. Because of this versatility he became in 1869, alongside Miksa Falk, a leading candidate for the position of Liberal-Party parliamentary representative of the *Lipótváros* [Leopoldstadt], the suburb of Pest along the Danube where the most wealthy businessmen then resided. The story has it that neither Wahrmann nor Falk would agree to cede to the other, and that consequently Ferenc Deák, the leader of the Party, was called in to decide the issue. Deák decided in favor of Wahrmann, because the latter, as a "real Jew," outwardly unassimilated, would be far more representative of the constituency than Falk, a convert who though not ennobled had many Magyar and noble connections.

This anecdote recalls that, despite the grain merchants, the estate-renters, the distillers, the flour-millers, and the lumber and sugar magnates, Budapest businessmen were not in the 1870's universally addicted to ennoblement. To the contrary, most of Budapest was still modest and humble; most of her businessmen were still "traders" as opposed to "merchants"; and on the tax-lists householders, butchers, bakers and iron-mongers still figured with dignity among the "factory-owners" and "men of property" who would later crowd them out. [46] It was only fitting that both the parliamentary representatives of this city and its bankers should conform in externals to its spirit. And, indeed, Wahrmann never did ennoble, despite the formidable wealth and prominence his banking business brought him. Further, the professional profile of the Jewish nobility shows that of the 70 bankers who acquired nobility in the sample, only 23 did so before 1900, and that of these 23, eight were Viennese (see Table 9).

Zsigmond Kornfeld's ennoblement at the climax of his career thus raises a real question. Budapest's bankers were not susceptible to the Hungarian Government's offers of ennoblement just because of court banker traditions inherited from Vienna, but became susceptible after the turn of the century. One must inquire why banker attitudes thus changed about 1900.

* * *

The history of the *csetei* Herzog family suggests one reason why Budapest banker attitudes towards ennoblement changed at about the turn of

---

[46] This evaluation derives from Károly Vörös' unpublished study of the Budapest virilists of 1873 and 1888.

the century. [47] Adolf Herzog, the founder of this family's wool and tobacco consignment firm, came to Pest from southeastern Baranya county about 1836 but achieved no great success apart from remaining solvent through tempestuous times. His son Péter, however, took over the firm in 1862 and rose to dizzy heights. Péter Herzog's first killing was in the investment fever of the later 1860's. He emerged from the crash of 1873 as prime shareholder in the "Viktoria" flour mill, one of Pest's largest; and he received nobility in 1886. The Herzog firm did not rest on the laurels of its mill acquisition, however. Like his rivals, the Schossbergers, Péter Herzog continued to work the tobacco trade, and by the turn of the century he had become a major Central European handler of Balkan and Turkish tobaccos. Like his sons-in-law, the Hatvany-Deutsches, moreover, Herzog invested significantly in flour mills other than his own and waxed wealthy on the milling traffic. Further, his firm dabbled in the Hungarian coal and chemical industries, which were not unprofitable; and after the Austrian occupation of Bosnia, the Herzogs won the Emperor's gratitude by establishing two ammonia factories and otherwise investing there. This variety of enterprises was of course difficult to control. Consequently the Herzog firm participated in the 1890's in the foundation of an institution for the financing of Hungarian foreign trade, and shortly after 1900 the Herzogs developed this institution into an important commercial bank. [48]

Such was the dynamism of the Hungarian take-off economy, in sum, that the Herzogs, originally grain traders, became bankers. And when, as heads of their bank, Peter Herzog and his son-in-law, a Constantinople merchant-turned-Hungarian-estate-owner, [49] became in 1904 and 1905

---

[47] For data about the Herzogs, see OL. K-19, KK 1886, 1913; and Gelléri, *Ipartör téneti vázlatok*, pp. 568—569. Sándor's assertion that the Herzog firm was founded after 1855 is incorrect: see his "Nagymalomipar," p. 366. Probably the firm was simply enlarged then. There is an account of the Herzog's tobacco business in Mihály Habar, *A Wekerle-Kossuth kormány panamai. Adatok a koaliciós kormány erkőlcsrajzához* [The Wekerle-Kossuth Government's Panamas. Contributions to a Portrayal of the Coalition Government's Morality] (Budapest: Világosság Könyvny. Rt., nd), pp. 70—71. The account presented here of the Herzog firms' turn-of-the-century development is based on OL. K-19, KK 1904, 3.

[48] This company was originally entitled *Magyar Kereskedelem Rt.* [Hungarian Trade Inc.] but later became the *Magyar Bank és Kereskedelem* [Hungarian Bank and Trade Inc.], and eventually after the War became the *Angol-Magyar Bank* [British-Hungarian Bank]. Its history, which is helpful to an understanding of the whole period after 1900 in Budapest, is contained in Imre Balassa, "Elek Pál regénye" [The Romance of Pál Elek], which appeared in 14 installments in the *Pesti Tözsde* beginning on 18 September, 1924, and continuing weekly till the end of that year.

[49] The son-in-law was Fülöp Orosdy.

barons, they symbolized the degree to which Budapest banking was being challenged towards the turn of the century by the flashy, new-noble *nouveaux riches* of the commercial world. Perhaps one may estimate that this challenge stimulated the Budapest bankers to play into the Government's hands by seeking ennoblement.

Another important factor in the change of mind among Budapest bankers towards ennoblement around the turn of the century was, as will appear in the following chapter, politics. But by far the most convincing explanation of the change in style emerges from the career of Zsigmond Kornfeld's great rival inside the banking world, Leó Lánczy. [50] Born, like Kornfeld, in 1852, Lánczy was the son of a Moravian named Lazarsfeld, who had come to Pest as a tanner's apprentice in 1843, converted to Protestantism, entered the drug and distilling business, and modestly prospered. Leó Lánczy attended trade school in Budapest, then went to work in one of the numerous small banks founded in the boom years after the *Ausgleich*, and before he was 30 became Managing Director of the *Pesti Magyar Kereskedelmi Bank*, which had been founded in the 1840's, but had not thrived. Where Kornfeld was religiously Jewish, Lánczy was Lutheran and worldly, married to a divorced woman. Where Kornfeld was ascetic and artistic, Lánczy was fat and fashionable, constantly appearing in the lounges of the great Austrian resorts. While Kornfeld would at least shake hands, humanly, with a bankrupt who had finally paid his debts, Lánczy kept the dirt of his business at an arm's length, employing Fülöp Weisz and Ferenc Vas, [51] dry and heartless bureaucrats, to act as hatchetmen. But like Kornfeld, Lánczy was a brilliant organizer; and with the aid of his team of assistants and the backing of the *Wiener Bankverein* in Vienna, Lánczy converted the *Kereskedelmi Bank* from relative insignificance not only into Hungary's leading commercial banking institution [52] but also into a major industrial bank.

---

[50] The following is based on the biographical essay on Lánczy by Ernő Makkai, *Huszonöt év a magyar közgazdaság terén* [Twenty-five Years in the Hungarian Economy] (Budapest: Grafikai Intézet, 1907); on the notices in the *Pester Lloyd*, 26 Jan., 1921 and the *Pesti Tözsde*, 21 Dec., 1922; and on anecdotal material in Radnóti, *Kornfeld* and Simon Krausz, *Életem*.

[51] There are sketches of both Fülöp Weisz and Ferenc Vas in József Radnóti, *Pesti pénzoligarchák* [Pest Financial Oligarchs] (Budapest: May János, 1929).

[52] The distinctions between various kinds of banking were not strictly observed over the years by either the *Kereskedelmi Bank* or the *Hitelbank*. Generally speaking, however, prior to 1900 the *Hitelbank* concentrated on state banking and larger industrial foundations, while the *Kereskedelmi Bank* laid out an extensive network of provincial branches and specialized in smaller enterprises, local railroads and the like. The parallelism

The interesting aspect of Lánczy's career from our point of view is its illustration of how, through their financial expertise, bankers in Hungary penetrated and "took over" important sectors of the economy which in mid-century had been wholly closed to them. One such area was iron mining, which it may be remembered was in 1850 largely German in complexion and closed to Jews. [53] During the railroad building boom in the 1850's and 1860's the traditional mining and smelting interests of Slovakia and Transylvania enjoyed a certain prosperity. But then they encountered trouble. Hungary was not rich in iron ore, the known beds were nowhere conveniently close to the beds of hard coal required in modern founding, and the miners were unable in these early decades to obtain railroad construction to the mining districts. Further, there was an older and more developed iron industry in the Austrian lands, which preferred to import Hungary's ore to Austria, than to see it processed in Hungary. Consequently, the financial crash of 1873 that interrupted railroad construction, brought the traditional mining interests to their knees. At this point the trader-capitalists of Pest stepped in for the first time, and bought out one of the bankrupt smelting companies, reorganizing it as a stock company. After a number of mergers the control of this company fell in 1881 to the *Wiener Bankverein*, which made Leó Lánczy's brother-in-law, Ármin Brüll-Bíró, a director. Hitherto, in general terms, the ownership of the iron mining business had not differed greatly from what it had been. Under banker management, however, this *Rimamurányi-Salgótarján Iron Works* underwent a rapid modernization and expansion. Brüll-Bíró, with Lánczy's backing, rose to be Commercial Director and then Managing Director. By 1913 the company controlled 57% of Hungary's 6 million quintals annual production of pig-iron; and 56% of the country's 8 million quintals of steel. In barely a generation, thus, a new bank-backed management acquired the decisive role in this essential sector of the industrializing Hungarian economy.

Coal was another vital area of the Hungarian economy which experienced a major change in ownership as a result of the intrusion of Lánczy's

---

between the two was then mainly in the area of stockbroking. After 1900, however, as Kornfeld grew old the *Hitelbank* suffered from lack of energy, whereas Lánczy's *Kereskedelmi Bank* reached the peak of its activity. Consequently the *Kereskedelmi Bank* began to acquire important large-industrial interests, and even to do some of the State's businesss. The parallelism was increased after Kornfeld's death in 1909, when his successor, Adolf Ullmann, decided to establish a network of *Hitelbank* provincial affiliates. See on this subject the useful review in the *Pesti Tözsde*, 25 Jan., 1923.

[53] For the development of the iron industry in Hungary, see Eckhardt, *A magyar közgazdaság*, Part II; Sándor, *Nagyipari fejlődés*, pp. 139—177 and 418—427; and Berend and Ránki *Magyarország gyáripara 1900—1914*, p. 189ff.

bank. [54] Like the iron industry, Hungarian coal production experienced a minor boom during the railroad building era after 1850. A new industry, exploited from the start by Austrian transport interests, hampered by surviving medieval regulations which gave noble estate owners special mining rights, and limited by Hungary's shortage of hard black coal, it experienced difficulties, and by the 1870's it had grown stagnant. At this point, as in the iron industry, the traders of Pest made their first intrusion by purchasing a bankrupt mine and reorganizing it as a joint-stock company. By the 1880's the key figure in this *Salgótarján Hard Coal Company* (it actually produced soft brown coal) was Ferenc Chorin, the liberal politician whom we have encountered elsewhere in another connection. As a parliamentary deputy Chorin offered the company a screen for various unpopular protectionist policies which were necessary for its survival in the face of foreign competition. The money behind Chorin, however, was from Leó Lánczy and the Vienna's Länderbank; and the effect of the combination of new money and new management techniques was similar to what happened in the iron industry. By the 1890's, when Chorin became president of the company, it was responsible for 40% of 1.6 million quintals of brown coal mined annually in Hungary and for 31% of the country's total coal production. In 1913 there was a change in this pattern. The country's coal production was up 44% but Chorin's company produced only 27% of the whole. The reason was, however, not some driving back of bank-backed control over this industry, but the intrusion of Kornfeld's *Hitelbank* into the field. Kornfeld had developed a company to rival Chorin's, tempted perhaps by the fact that this cartelized industry could offer its shareholders dividends, sometimes, of 106%. In 1913 these two bank-backed Hungarian coal companies produced 56% of Hungarian coal.

By the eve of the war, Leó Lánczy and his colleagues were present in virtually every one of Hungary's new industries, and particularly in the cartels which by then dominated many areas of the economy. In 1910 Lánczy and four other executives at the *Kereskedelmi Bank* possessed between them 150 directorships in different firms — a huge number when one considers how relatively few stock companies there still were in Hungary. [55] This was an achievement of which these bankers could quite reasonably be proud. And it was, moreover, only one of their achievements.

---

[54] On the Hungarian coal industry, see Eckhart, *A magyar közgazdaság*, Part III; Sándor, *Nagyipari fejlődés*, pp. 118—138 and 403—418; Berend and Ránki, *Magyarország gyáripara 1900—1914*, p. 174ff.; and Jenő Varga, *A magyar kartellek*, p. 17ff.

[55] The four colleagues were Henrik Fellner, Miksa Fehér, Fülöp Weisz, and Mór Mezei.

Perhaps the greatest, which was yet to come at the turn of the century, was a dramatic change which overtook the country's whole economic relation with the outside world. All through the nineteenth century Hungary had developed under the wing of foreign, primarily Austrian, capital. This had been an age of colonialism, and Hungary had unmistakably stood in colonial relationship to Vienna's banks. In 1900 41% of Hungary's industrial plant was entirely in foreign hands. [56] Through the coordinated action of the Budapest banks, however, and particularly through the efforts of Kornfeld and Lánczy, this situation was after the turn of the century decisively altered. By 1913 only 28.9 per cent of Hungary's industrial plant was entirely in foreign hands; and the foreign share in mixed-ownership joint-stock companies had fallen from 60.1% in 1900 to 36% in 1913. What is more, in 1900 the Austrian banks had still been the overwhelmingly great foreign investors in Hungary, whereas by 1913 there was an equitable distribution as between Austrian, German, and even English, French, and American capital. In this decade, when in every other part of Eastern Europe, including Russia, foreign capital flooded in, and when in the Balkan lands European capital threatened to "take over" many state functions, the Hungarian bankers managed to mitigate their dependence on outside capital, and, one may insert, even to send Hungarian capital abroad. In effect the Kornfelds and the Lánczys made Hungary in this decade a part of "imperial" Europe and took her out of the colonial world. This was a unique achievement.

Even visually Budapest by the end of the nineteenth century was reflecting formidable economic victories for which her bankers could hold themselves largely responsible. It was only in the 1880's that Budapest had acquired a modern Opera House and had opened to traffic her famous imitation of Vienna's *Ringstrasse*, and her *Andrássy-út*. Yet by 1900 Budapest was building a Parliament on the Danube embankment which even today is architecturally among the most pompous in the world. At the same time Budapest was doubling the size of her Royal Castle, perched grandiosely on a hill across the stately broad river from the Parliament. She who had built one of the world's first suspension bridges was now constructing her third and greatest such bridge. She had dug the Continent's first subway, and she was decorating herself with commercial and residential palaces as grand as any in Europe. [57]

---

[56] For the following figures, see Berend and Ránki, *Magyarország gyáripara 1900—1914*, p. 130.

[57] One may get impressive intimations of the change in Budapest during the *Ausgleich* Era from Gábor Preisich, *Budapest városépítésének története* [The History of the Construction of Budapest] (2 vols.; Budapest: Müszaki Könyvkiadó, 1960, 1964), Vol. II.

Leó Lánczy was a leading figure in a new banking community which had expropriated control of large areas of Hungary's booming industrial economy from its former possessors. He could remember Budapest as she had been before 1867, divided into three administratively-separate old-fashioned towns, with only one narrow bridge across the Danube to bind them. Though he did not ennoble, he did in 1905 join Zsigmond Kornfeld, Ferenc Chorin, and Sándor Hatvany-Deutsch in the House of Lords; and he did in 1912 accept from Franz Joseph the rank of Veritable Privy Councilor of the Hungarian Crown, one of the highest honors which the King was able to bestow. One may suppose that he did so because these ranks seemed appropriate to the astounding accomplishments which his lifetime had witnessed in Hungary, and for which he could hold himself responsible.

Perhaps we may generalize from this example that an exuberant pride in their accomplishments was responsible for the change in attitude towards ennoblement among the Hungarian bankers after 1900 into which we are inquiring. No doubt this was a false pride. Today we can surmise it was not the bankers themselves, but the process of economic take-off which was responsible for these accomplishments. We can surmise that they were thrust into power and prominence because of the peculiar importance in the take-off process of banking. And we can point out that the new businessmen-nobles in Hungary after 1900 were overwhelmingly employee-managers — far more cogs in a system than even Leó Lánczy was, and far less justified in claiming for themselves the miracles that their system had accomplished. Yet even today we can recognize that the accomplishments were enormous — that in the process of take-off the whole world of Budapest business was transformed — and that no matter who or what was actually responsible, there was apparently firm ground in the "Queen City of the Danube" around 1900 for confidence in the power of Man, through system, to overcome any obstacle. This conceit, generated by the take-off, was presumably responsible for the ennoblement of Hungarian bankers in the following years.

The Optimism of the Scientific Geniuses

The central event in George de Hevesy's scientific career suggests a linkage between the economic developments of nineteenth-century Hungary and the formation of her scientific geniuses. Hevesy was born in 1885 to a "gentry" new-noble industrial-manager and his Schossberger wife. [58] Educated at the Piarist Gymnasium in Budapest and then trained in chemistry at the universities of Berlin and Freiburg, he became assistant to Fritz Haber at Karlsruhe and moved in 1911 to Manchester to work with Ernest Rutherford. [59] As it happened Rutherford was just then discovering the atomic nucleus, and (as Hevesy expresses it) "devising, carrying out, and interpreting" experiments of epic significance for the history of physics. In the course of these experiments he needed a strong radium D sample. He possessed one, but it was imbedded in hundreds of kilograms of lead presented to him by the owner of the Joachimsthal mines, the Austrian Government. He assigned Hevesy the task of separating the radium by chemical means from the lead.

After a year of work, Hevesy decided that his assignment was impossible. Yet instead of surrendering, he put his essentially negative finding to work. Since radium D was evidently inseparable by chemical means from lead, Hevesy decided that by adding radium D (which is measurable) to any substance containing lead, one might trace the lead through various chemical changes. Hevesy has described what resulted from this experimental idea. He tells that one day he was drinking tea with a colleague, who exclaimed: "George, this is very bad tea! Tell me, how long it will take my body to get rid of it?" This was a question which at that time seemed even less soluable than the separation of radium D from lead. Yet Hevesy decided to tackle it, driven as he claims by an optimism of his youth. [60] By working first with radioactive lead as a tracer, later by

---

[58] Hevesy's father was Lajos Bischitz, the old-age child of a Pest merchant who had grown rich in mid-century by leasing one of the larger Esterházy estates. Lajos Bischitz' mother was from the Herend-China Fischer family. She was a founder of the Jewish Ladies' Society of the Pest Community, and well-known for her Jewish charities. The whole clan acquired nobility in 1895, a few years after Lajos Bischitz' Schossberger fatherin-law became a baron. Lajos Bischitz was the managing director of one of the Schossberger mining enterprises, sat on numerous bank, insurance, and railroad boards, and controlled large estates. The family hyphenated its name to Hevesy-Bischitz in 1904 and became Hevesy alone in 1917. For background, see the *Egyenlőség*, 21 June, 1895, supplement; and 7 February, 1897, p. 9.

[59] Hevesy wrote an autobiographical sketch for Dwight J. Ingle (ed.), *A Dozen Doctors* (Chicago: University of Chicago Press, 1963), pp. 65—85, but weak editing made it unintelligible. More helpful are: the Nobel Prize citation printed in Eduard Ferber (ed.), *Nobel Prize Winners in Chemistry* (London: Abelard Schumann, 1953), pp. 176—180; the material in *Current Biography*, 1959, p. 186ff.; and the interview by Roberta Silman in the *Saturday Review*, 7 March, 1959, pp. 56—57; in all of which the following anecdote appears.

[60] See *A Dozen Doctors*, p. 69.

identifying what are now called "isotopes," and eventually by developing other tracers, Hevesy for the first time made it possible to trace tea and other substances in living beings. In the process he revolutionized research in physiological and organic chemistry.

Hevesy's work illustrates the essential role of optimism in scientific work. Evidently a scientist's burning interest in what can be done through application of scientific methods may run cool when searches go vainly on for years with no results. Without overstressing the connection, one may hazard that the optimism necessary to their work was reinforced in budding scientists of turn-of-the century Budapest by the city's recent and on-going economic miracle, which was at the same time encouraging their banker fathers to ennoble.

Franz Alexander, one of the most influential of the several pioneering Hungarian psychoanalysts who came to this country between the wars, has suggested a way apart from the economic boom in which late nineteenth-century Hungary may have inspired optimism in the intellectuals with whom we are concerned. [61] In his autobiography he begins by emphasizing (as Hevesy does) the greatness of the challenge which intellectuals of the turn of the century had to face. He recalls that a "revolution in modern art, literature, science and philosophy preceded the military and economic events" of 1914 and after.

It is most revealing that in theoretical physics, in the area of the most precise reasoning of which the human mind has been capable, the mechanistic-materialistic orientation was in the process of yielding to a dynamic orientation. The unit of the universe was no longer the solid particle, but the 'event.'... In all [other] fields of human thought and creativity [likewise] the naive materialistic-mechanistic preoccupation with the immediate, the visible and the tangible yield[ed] to a preoccupation with connections, relations, tendencies, forces.... [62] Man, in his common sense outlook on the world until the last fifty years, dealt mainly with the man-sized world which appeared to him as a space populated with tangible and visible objects. Our current cognitive categories are consequently patterned after this... conception... Access to phenomena of different dimensions, [however, requires new categories] which are not based on the visible and the tangible, but abstract constructs.... For such concepts [Man] has

---

[61] For a discussion of the entire group, see Laura Fermi, *Illustrious Immigrants*, Ch. 6.

[62] See the intellectual autobiography, Franz Alexander, *The Western Mind in Transition* (New York: Random House, 1960), pp. 68—69.

only... symbols, although he is constantly struggling to find a verbal translation of them. [63]

To meet this challenge optimism and immense confidence were necessary. And Alexander makes clear that in his own case he got his optimism directly from nineteenth-century philosophy.

Franz Alexander was born in Pest in 1890, the son of Bernát Alexander, a university professor of philosophy who was among the more prominent professional intellectuals of late nineteenth-century Budapest. The elder Alexander evidently radiated confidence.

> My father's generation could without any doubts devote their lives to the realization of a progressive, enlightened national culture dedicated to fostering the spiritual qualities of the citizen, the Platonic Utopia of a society led by the intellectual elite. This was something they believed in without inner conflict.... They absorbed in a harmonious way the prevailing trends of that creative century, a firm belief in the power of reason and in the unlimited possibilities of knowledge and, above all, a high regard for the individual's creative self-expression. [64]

Alexander reflects the impact of his father's confidence upon his development when he opens his autobiography with a calm identification of Father with the Kaiser, the Sun, and God as "benevolent rulers beyond criticism" of his boyhood. Young Alexander admits that when in 1908 he chose a medical profession he was in certain respects revolting against his father, who wanted him to become an archeologist. But he admits also that he inherited from his father certain basic outlooks:

> In the conservative atmosphere of my home every rebellion had a distasteful connotation. Minorities always believe that they are chosen people, become suspicious, withdrawn, provocative, narrow-minded.... Science cannot be well pursued in a sectarian attitude. Clinical psychiatry may have been in a blind alley, but there were the great accomplishments of modern physiology which could not be suddenly ignored, no matter how ingenious and fundamental the new approach appeared to be. [65]

Because of the deep-rooted academic rationalism of his father, in sum, young Alexander rejected until 1919 the new and revolutionary developments in psychoanalysis.

---

[63] *Ibid.*, p. 69.
[64] *Ibid.*, p. 44.
[65] *Ibid.*, pp. 54—55.

In 1919 Alexander changed front. Demobilized by the end of the war and displaced by the revolutions in Budapest (which had resulted in his father's dismissal from the University), young Alexander finally did embrace Freudianism. He moved to republican Berlin and became the first student at the new Psychoanalytic Institute there. In the following years by his own confession he grew thoroughly sectarian.

> We [psychoanalists] all knew each other personally.... We were all members of a militant group. ...We had no doubt that psychoanalysis would gradually change the outlook of contemporary man and reform all those sciences concerned with man, not only with medicine and biology but the social sciences as well. [66]

Yet even in his revolutionary scientific activity Alexander claims he was inspired by the ideals and confidence of his father's era.

> During those chaotic postwar years, ...the psychoanalytic movement offered me an opportunity to continue where I had left off at the outbreak of the war six years earlier. It was for me the road back to a life in which I could devote myself to a cause which appeared to me of the greatest possible importance. No matter how revolutionary the method and theory of psychoanalysis was, it represented to me the continuation of the same rationalistic approach to knowledge, which was the strongest tradition of my life. [67]

Franz Alexander did important research in the area of criminal psychology; and as head of the Chicago Institute for Psychoanalysis for nearly 25 years after 1932 he made a major contribution to the development of psychoanalysis in America. But he confesses that all through this career of accomplishment his major objective was to bring psychoanalysis into the fold of nineteenth-century knowledge. And he confesses it was one of the happiest moments of his life when his father, late in the 1920's, accepted the validity of Freud's teaching, lending a nineteenth-century sanction to the revolutionary work of his son. [68]

Franz Alexander did not derive his scientific optimism directly from witnessing the accomplishments of the late nineteenth-century Hungarian economy. To the contrary, he premises that neither he nor his father was even susceptible to any sort of economic optimism, because of their profound belief, characteristic of the academic atmosphere of the time, that man followed his mind, not his stomach — that the individual was essentially

---

[66] *Ibid.*, p. 81.
[67] *Ibid.*, pp. 81—82, comp. p. 16.
[68] *Ibid.*, p. 56.

free. [69] In this he was not alone among our scientific geniuses. Theodore von Kármán, for example, like Alexander the son of an eminent university professor, professed a great ideological debt to his father's generation. As a result of his father's philosophy, he states he never saw any conflict between science and religion, and though he accepted Poincaré's relativistic attitude towards scientific laws, he remained positivist enough to reject Ernst Mach. [70] Further, Leó Szilard, perhaps the most flexible, adventurous, and innovative philosophically of the Hungarian atom scientists, assigned a critical influence in his career to the famous Faustian drama of Imre Madách, *The Tragedy of Man*. [71] That pivotal contribution to the late nineteenth-century Hungarian mentality contains one magnificently pessimistic scene where Lucifer shows Adam that Man's ultimate future is a world over-populated with Eskimos, who are reduced to human sacrifice and to complaining about the paucity of seals. But it ends with a satisfying note of confidence in Man's capacity for regeneration, for enjoying his time on earth, and for hoping — and it was to this that Szilard referred.

Such evidence suggests that the optimism of our scientists derived not from Hungary's economic take-off so much as from nineteenth-century cultural self-confidence, which is quite a different thing. Yet despite this evidence, our thesis seems valid. Even Alexander makes it clear that in his boyhood — which is when his optimism was formed — economic security and philosophical confidence mingled inextricably. He grouped Father, with the Kaiser, the Sun, and God because all seemed equally secure and infallible in a highly material sense. [72] Correspondingly Szilard claims that the economic security of turn-of-the-century Hungary was one of the main reasons for the emergence of the country's scientific geniuses. [73] Obviously he could not have meant the sort of absence of economic danger to the individual which today we associate with the Welfare State and which simply did not exist then in Hungary; so he must have meant the overwhelmingly prevalent feeling, that despite the frequent individual bank-

---

[69] *Ibid.*, p. 47.

[70] See Theodore von Kármán with Lee Edson, *The Wind and Beyond* (Boston: Little, Brown, 1970), pp. 23—24.

[71] See his interview with the *New York Post*, in 1946 as quoted in *Current Biography*, 1947, p. 622. Indicative of the influence of Madách on our whole galaxy of scientists is von Kármán's epitomization of his father's wisdom in terms which paraphrase the closing line of the *Tragedy of Man*: see *The Wind and Beyond*, p. 23.

[72] See Alexander, *Western Mind in Transition*, Ch. 1, and particularly p. 38.

[73] See Alice K. Smith, "The Elusive Dr. Szilard," *Harpers*, July, 1960, p. 78.

ruptcies, and despite the misery of the lower classes, the economic miracle since 1867 had been so great that nothing really seriously could go wrong.

In the career of Edward Teller, Szilard's opposite number among the atom scientists, moreover, there is clear and explicit evidence that the economic conditions of the turn-of-the-century underlay the scientists' optimism in the revolutionary discoveries of our time. [74] Teller was born in Budapest in 1908, the son of a prosperous lawyer. As a child he revealed precocious abilities in mathematics. He recollects that one reason he embarked early on a scientific career was his father's encouragement of his natural penchants. An important second factor was the political evolution of Hungary. Whether or not at the age of eleven he was personally affected by the Communist episode of 1919 is never quite clear; but the anti-Semitism of the political restoration after 1919 deeply influenced him. His father, he recalls, literally "dinned" it into him that because of this anti-Semitism he, as a Jew, had to excel just to keep abreast; that because of it he would have one day to emigrate to a country where conditions were more favorable to minorities; and that from anti-Semitism a sure escape was science, an international discipline. [75]

The third factor which pressed Edward Teller into science, however, was a thoroughly materialist optimism. Looking back he writes:

> As a boy, I enjoyed science fiction. I read Jules Verne. His words carried me into an exciting world. The possibilities of man's improvement seemed unlimited. The achievements of science were fantastic, and they were good. [76]

Verne's dreams were not too far, in Teller's youthful view, from the "revolution of rising material expectation" which characterized the start of the century. [77] And in another context he has specified that he was by no means filled with such hatred of society and the "system" as inspired Georg Lukács and other turn-of-the-century radicals. In his youth, he claims,

---

[74] There are numerous journalistic sketches in print about Teller, but most of them reflect the controversy about his political activities in the 1950's, and he has published no serious effort at an autobiography. The most balanced of the biographical essays seems to be in Norman Moss, *Men Who Play God* (London: Victor Gollianz, 1968), Ch. 3; but see also *Current Biography*, 1954, p. 598ff. There are autobiographical anecdotes in E. Teller and Alan Brown, *The Legacy of Hiroshima* (Garden City: Doubleday, 1962), *passim*.

[75] See Teller and Brown, *Legacy of Hiroshima*, pp. 160—161; and *Life*, 13 Dec., 1963, p. 89.

[76] See Teller and Brown, *Legacy of Hiroshima*, p. 81.

[77] *Ibid.*, p. 80.

he was a "square," and liked chess, hiking, poetry, music, swimming and the material comforts of the day. [78]

A critical turning point came in Teller's development when the Nazis acquired power in Germany in 1933. He had to leave Göttingen and migrate first to Copenhagen, then to George Washington University in Washington, D. C. Perhaps because he was deprived of his laboratory by this move, he became decisively in these years a theoretical physicist. Further, he now progressed from quantum mechanics, which had fascinated him earlier, into molecular and atomic physics. By the late thirties he was sufficiently involved in nuclear experimentation to become one of the three Hungarian scientists who precipitated the start of America's program of atomic fission. In 1941 he joined the Manhattan Project at Columbia University. In 1943 he moved to Los Alamos to participate in the making of the first atomic bomb. And in these years after 1933, also, he made a determining political choice. He not only rejected both the Nazi and Soviet experiments, but also opted with "convert" fervor (as he has recounted) for the United States. That country with its material wealth and liberal traditions became now the focus of Edward Teller's intense optimism. [79]

Faced with the destructive spectacle of the atom bomb in 1945, many atom scientists (notably Szilard) sheered away from it in horror. Not so Teller: the peculiarity of Teller is that he kept on going, though he admits he gave up science fiction now, because the visions its writers conjured up became too grim. Teller's regular and consistent explanation of his dogged pursuit of bigger and bigger bombs has been a vision of ever greater material benefit to mankind from science and scientific discovery. In 1962 he even wrote an apologium entitled "The Legacy of Hiroshima," in which he conjured up images of abundant nuclear power, interstellar traffic, the delving of great new harbors, and infinite new knowledge as the fruit of the bombs he had created. [80] Edward Teller placed this vision squarely in the framework of the materially affluent Hungary into which he had been born:

> Compare the twentieth century with the age of our grandparents' grandparents. In the time they required to visit friends in neighboring states, we can travel to any place on the earth and return home. ...Before 1845 many people suffered unbearable pain and multitudes died of diseases which no one could explain. By 1945, we had con-

[78] See *Time*, 18 Nov., 1957, p. 22.

[79] See *Life*, 13 Dec., 1963, p. 99ff.; and frequent passages in *Legacy of Hiroshima* for example, pp. 80, 95, and 300ff.

[80] See Teller and Brown, *Legacy of Hiroshima*, Ch. 5.

quered infectious disease and had learned how to eliminate pain.
We can be cut up and sewed together again and benefit from the
experience. [81]
In this context Teller proceeded to give America a dire warning about
the perils of disarmament, and of weakness and doubt in the mortal
battle with Communism. He admitted that the struggle would be difficult
to win. But an unquenchable faith in science guided him to feel that hope
still shone for the West, just as it had seemed to shine in the prosperous,
all-conquering capitalist Budapest into which he was born.

* * *

It would be ridiculous to "prove" that the "same" material accomplishments which led Teller's father's generation of Budapest bankers and businessmen to acquire Hungarian nobility determined the emergence of great
scientists among their sons. We can admit, however, that the social atmosphere in certain times and places significantly affects a broad variety of
behavior. In such terms it seems valid to observe that the economic growth
which hurled such capitalists as the Schossbergers, the Hatvany-Deutsches,
the Kornfelds, and the Lánczys onto the path of ennoblement encouraged
an optimism among the young Budapest scientists of 1900 which underlay
their revolutionary discoveries.

---

[81] *Ibid.*, pp. 306—308.

PART IV

THE GREAT CRISIS
1900 — 1918

CHAPTER VII

THE POLITICAL CRISIS

Governmental Insistence

In 1898 British colonial imperialism found its limits when the Boers of South Africa resisted it. Just afterwards the French at Fashoda, the Germans at Algeciras, and the Russians at Port Arthur encountered similar limits. Meanwhile the Dreyfus affair in France and the Badeni crisis in Austria symptomized the end of the social compromises which had governed Europe for three decades. In 1903 the assassination of the Serbian King marked the beginning of a new eruption of the Balkan Question, an eruption which would bring all Europe to war a decade later. Then in 1905 a vast popular upheaval in Russia revealed the new temper of Europe's social questions and foreshadowed the greater upheaval, which after 1917 would change the political shape of the Continent.

Behind these outward signs that Europe was in crisis in the years after 1900 lay dynamic changes of a social and economic character. Population pressures were growing apace. The new metropoli of the later nineteenth century were generating demands for ever greater industrialization. New industries in new places were feeding the rivalries among the Powers. And there was also a crisis of the spirit. Just in these years Europe's intellectuals plunged beyond the limits placed on Reason by the Enlightenment two centuries earlier. Scientists broke with Newton's laws. Psychologists probed systematically into the unconscious. Poets and painters plunged beyond Impressionism into the Surreal.

This and the following chapter are concerned with how this European crisis was manifest in Hungary. We will discuss above all how on various levels the new limits to human political endeavor, the new economic and social frustrations, and the new intellectual horizons made themselves known in the small East European world we have been studying. But we hope to find in the course of this narrative the final keys to the problems of why so many of Hungary's capitalist elite sought nobility and collaborated with the old regime and why a galaxy of scientific geniuses emerged from this same elite.

∗

The primary visible feature of Hungary's participation in the turn-of-the-century European crisis was the collapse of the political system described above in Chapter V.[1] One may recall that from its beginnings in 1867 this system had had many and visible flaws. Designed originally to keep Hungary free of Viennese centralism, it was perfected by Kálmán Tisza as a means for imposing Budapest's bureaucratic centralism upon the noble-dominated Hungarian counties. It rested on expensive election-manipulation, which as early as the 1880's was taxing the Government's purse, and which as it turned out, was not only expensive, but unnecessary: for the nobles in the counties proved willing, in the long run, to surrender their power to central government, provided it ruled in their favor against the peasants and the national minorities. In the end Tisza's election manipulation led not to orderly central government but to tumultuous opposition by precisely the Magyar noble elements whom Tisza designed to protect. Kálmán Tisza himself fell from the prime ministry in 1890. His successors attempted first to appease political opposition with soft measures, and then to suppress it with police brutality. Neither tactic worked, perhaps largely because the Government Party had become a bureaucratic institution unable to abolish itself, and too hide-bound and self-interested to share power with the opposition. Meanwhile a vital cog in the system broke when the great land-owning aristocrats, pressed by changing agricultural conditions into seeking customs protection which the Government found it hard to grant, began to defect to the opposition.

The final crisis began in 1903 when the nationalists in the Hungarian Parliament obstructed passage of a new Austro-Hungarian Army bill demanding *inter alia* the introduction of Magyar as a language of military command for Hungarian units. Their stand amounted to frontal assault on the whole delicate relationship between Hungary and Austria which had been worked out in 1867. Further, the demand for a Magyar language of command struck Franz Joseph, the Kaiser-King, at a most sensitive point. During his whole long reign he had made it a matter of principle to keep his army unified and immune from political interference. Franz Joseph

---

[1] For turn-of-the-century Hungarian politics see the standard accounts in Macartney, *Habsburg Empire*, Ch. 17; Gratz, *A dualizmus kora*, Vol. II; and Molnár (ed.), *Magyarország története*, Vol. II, Pt. 6; and the analytical approach in Andrew János, "Decline of the Oligarchy." See also the important memoirs of József Kristóffy, *Magyarország kálváriája* [Hungary's Calvary] (Budapest: F. Wodianer, 1927).

responded to this nationalist obstruction by placing the Hungarian prime ministry in the hands of Kálmán Tisza's son, István, who promised to bring order. Within a year young Tisza brought complete disorder because he roughly attacked the right of unlimited debate in parliament. His tactics provoked into life a fantastic Coalition of landless nobles, who with rabid nationalism demanded loosening Hungary's ties with Austria; of moderate constitutional liberals who demanded law and order; of urban "democrats" who demanded electoral reform; of great landowning magnates who demanded agricultural protectionism; and of non-Magyar nationality elements who demanded a place in the sun. [2] When early in 1905 Tisza managed to lose an election to this Coalition, his King had to confront an anti-Austrian groundswell in Hungary as if the nearly forty years of *Ausgleich* had not taken place.

This political breakdown in Hungary was particularly serious from the King's point of view, because in Austria also he was having trouble. In 1893, little over a decade after its establishment, Count Taaffe's "Iron Ring" had disintegrated in a trivial squabble over one of the political "tidbits" with which it was supposed to keep order. Bedlam had thereupon broken loose in the *Reichsrat* and in the provincial diets as the nationalities, grown accustomed under Taaffe to sell their silence for political rewards, made ever more noisy and selfish demands. By 1903 a certain equilibrium had emerged in Austria's politics by general recognition that rioting in the *Reichsrat* got no one anywhere; and by tacit acceptance of extra-parliamentary government by bureaucrats. But the political situation remained uneasy. When, therefore, the Hungarian political opposition took aim at the Army, Franz Joseph had fair reason to beware.

For the first few months after Tisza's election defeat of January 1905, Franz Joseph procrastinated, leaving Tisza in office while rejecting compromise with the Coalition. The Coalition-dominated Parliament objected violently to this unconstitutional behavior. Thereupon in June, 1905, Franz Joseph tried a new solution. He installed a general, Baron Géza Fejérváry, as non-party Prime Minister of Hungary. This led to massive and active popular resistance which ran from noisy demonstration to evasion of taxes. Franz Joseph and Fejérváry guessed, correctly as it turned out, that if they stood firm and threatened to institute a democratic electoral reform in

---

[2] Recent studies of the emergence of the Coalition are in István Dolmányos, *A magyar parlamenti ellenzék történetéből* [From the History of the Hungarian Parliamentary Opposition] (Budapest: Akademia, 1963); and Ferenc Mucsi, *A Kristóffy-Garami paktum* [The Kristóffy-Garami Pact] (Budapest: Kossuth, 1970).

Hungary, the Coalition's Magyar nobles would eventually give in to self-interest and might promise to respect the *Ausgleich*. But in the meanwhile the Government was unable to pay its bureaucrats because of the tax-payer strike and, early in 1906, felt obliged to close the Parliament by force of arms. With this, Hungary's political crisis came to its first climax.

Our chronological graph of Jewish ennoblements in Hungary (Table 8 on page 121 above) shows that this political drama is relevant to the subject of this book. The graph shows that between 1904 and 1906 the Hungarian Government fostered a step-up in ennoblements which we may interpret as a change in policy not just towards the Jews, but, as we have seen elsewhere, towards the whole multinational business community of Budapest. In this period of less than three years the Government issued 41 new patents of Hungarian nobility to Jewish families, approximately equalling its average distribution of ennoblements to Jews for each of the past two decades. Most of these new patents of nobility went to Budapest businessmen. Our graph shows, moreover, that behind this quantitative change of Government policy towards the business community lay a qualitative change. During the nineteenth century Franz Joseph had become liberal enough in giving out Hungarian nobility, but he had remained very sparing in his distribution of higher ranks to Jews. In 1874 and 1886, respectively, he had, of course, awarded Hungarian baronages to the Wodianer brothers, important Vienna bankers who had long since become Catholics. In 1890, as we have seen elsewhere, he gave a baronage to Zsigmond Schossberger, who had not converted but was a great landowner and had lofty aristocratic connections. But generally speaking baronage went to Jews in Hungary prior to 1904 only if they possessed strong Viennese and Catholic connections. [3] In 1904, however, Hungarian baronage went not only to the Catholicized Kuffners, a brewer family of Vienna, but to the lumber merchant Gutmanns of Nagykanizsa, and to the *csetei* Herzogs of Pest, who were still of Jewish faith. Further, in 1905, baronage went to Herzog's son-in-

---

[3] In 1895 baronage went to the Harkányi family, long Catholicized, closely related to the Wodianers, and involved in Vienna banking. In 1897 baronage went to the insurance magnate Henrik Lévay, a close associate of the Harkányi's who coincidentally became a Catholic. See the *Egyenlőség*, 10 July, 1896. In 1897 a baronage went also to Hermann Königswarter, the heir of a famous Viennese banking house, who like Lévay had recently converted. See Kempelen, *Zsidó Családok*, Vol. II, pp. 18—19. In 1902 baronage went to Rudolf Biedermann, a member of another great Viennese banking family who like Königswarter had close connections with the Papacy. See Kempelen, *Zsidó családok*, Vol. I, p. 50ff. The only other Jewish Hungarian baronage of this period was that of Lajos Dóczy, awarded in 1900. Dóczy was a talented literary figure, long since converted, who was then retiring from a long service in the *K.u.K.* Foreign Ministry.

law;[4] to the remainder of the Schossberger family, and even to old Zsigmond Schossberger's brother-in-law's family;[5] to the insurance magnate, Henrik Lévay's family; and to the *nouveau-riche* lumber-merchant Groedel family.[6] Most of these were still religious Jews.

The connection between the great political crisis of 1903—1906 and this change in ennoblement policy is finally demonstrated by two further facts. First, the surviving archival materials relating to ennoblement demonstrate that on the eve of his fall Fejérváry was preparing a large-scale distribution of Hungarian nobility to Vienna businessmen who had no connection whatever with Hungary.[7] Secondly, Franz Joseph signed the last of the 41 patents of new nobility which Tisza and Fejérváry obtained for Jewish Hungarians on 8 April, 1906.[8] This was the day on which the Coalition leadership completed a secret agreement to abandon its challenge to the *Ausgleich*. From such facts we may deduce that, because of the political crisis in Hungary after 1903, the Government raised the standing invitation it had for some decades extended to Budapest business to collaborate. No longer did the Government simply leave the door open for businessmen to collaborate, if they so desired, in exchange for ennoblement. Now the Government appealed to Budapest businessmen for collaboration from a position of obvious need and in effect sold patents of nobility to cement the bargain. The invitation had become, to say the least, insistent; and the role of the business community in the Magyar political system was, by implication, significantly enlarged.

* * *

This first phase of the great Hungarian political crisis culminated with a touch of comic opera. During 1903 Franz Joseph allowed his underlings

---

[4] Fülöp Orosdy was the son of a major in the Hungarian army of 1848—1849, who had fled to Constantinople and, in partnership with a member of the Back family, made a fortune trading there. The younger Orosdy returned to Hungary in 1895, bought estates, and married Péter Herzog's daughter, Margit, with whom he converted; and after the First World War he entered the Hungarian Parliament on a Christian rightist program. OL K-128, B-Min. Eln. 1905, II 3719.

[5] The Dirsztai-Fischl family, grain merchants of Pest.

[6] The Groedels were lumber tycoons who immigrated to Transylvania from Germany in the middle 1870's and acquired citizenship in 1890. See the *Egyenlőség*, 26 Sept., 1890, p. 17; and Gelléri, *Ipartörténeti vázlatok*, pp. 576—578.

[7] See the files on OL K-26, Min. Eln. 1906, XI 1310 (Reichmann); 1906, XI 1253 (Thalberg-Kohn); and 1911, XI 370 (Krieser).

[8] The King signed Nándor Beck's baronage and one patent of nobility (Kramer), on 7 April, 1906. He signed two further patents (Horváth and Keppich) on 8 April. On that same day he dismissed Fejérváry and installed Wekerle as Prime Minister. There were no later Jewish nobles in that year by my record.

to drop public hints that he would resolve the crisis through an appeal to the general public in the form of a broad suffrage. Had the Kaiser-King acted according to these hints, Hungary might have followed the path towards ever greater ostensible public participation in the affairs of state which has characterized most other European countries in our century. But Franz Joseph did not force through a new suffrage in Hungary. Instead, as noted above, in April, 1906, he corrupted the Coalition leaders, extracting from them promises that they would not in practice attack the *Ausgleich* institutions, as they had sworn to their public they would; and then he installed them in power. Just as in 1867, Franz Joseph marched out for the *finale* of the political comedy in Hungary hand in hand with the Magyar nobles who all through the play had been his determined foes. He gave once more his blessing to the happy union of noble Hungary and princely Austria, while causing the ugly sisters and wicked aunts, who had seemed to have his favor, to flee to the wings. The difference was that the bridal couple of 1867 had still looked young, whereas now both partners were visibly decayed. Further, in 1867 Franz Joseph was weak and had little alternative: in 1867, the Czechs were the only implacable "ugly sister" with any political strength. Now the "ugly sisters" included nearly everyone in the Monarchy save the Magyar nobles and their Austrian court allies.

The consequences of this finale were not long in appearing. Before it, all through the nineteenth century the Magyar political community had been armed with high morale. This was no doubt an artificial morale, resting on the peculiar oppositional political status, noted elsewhere, which Kálmán Tisza had afforded the Magyar nobles. Nonetheless, the bright-sounding slogans and optimistic self-righteousness of early nineteenth-century Liberalism had remained surprisingly alive in the country's ruling class. In an underdeveloped country such optimism is not an undesirable quality of public life, no matter what the corruption that lies behind it. Now, however, after the secret *pactum* between the Coalition and the Crown, all the high hopes and lofty slogans of the preceding era were deflated. The patriotic Magyar politicians came to power and then neglected to obtain Magyar as a language of military command, neglected to obtain an independent Magyar bank, and neglected to obtain major revisions of the economic *Ausgleich* with Austria. All they did was avoid electoral reform and pass a repressive educational measure against the nationalities. No external enemy could be blamed for this pitiful record, as had been possible, for example, in 1849. The Magyar political community was compelled to recognize that the duplicity and failure of its record stemmed somehow from within itself. Rot spread apace. In the end, late in 1909, the Coalition Government broke into pieces, unable even to obtain a parliamentary majority for the coming year's budget.

From the King's point of view, the disillusionment and factionalization of the Hungarian Coalition was particularly serious because of developments in Austria and abroad. In Austria for a generation prior to 1905 a regime of limited suffrage had brought only the leading classes of the many nationalities into the *Reichsrat*. Experience had shown that appeasement of one of these classes only made the others howl louder, and it had come to seem logical to seek peace by weighting the Parliament with "supranational" representatives of the lower classes. Franz Joseph had, therefore, in 1907 pushed a universal suffrage law through the *Reichsrat*. The results were, from his point of view, disappointing. The first election under the new law seemed simply to add more factions to the already numerous parties in the Parliament, without reducing any of their selfishness or any of their ability to obstruct orderly proceedings. Meanwhile in foreign affairs, also, Franz Joseph's situation was deteriorating. By 1910 the Dual Monarchy was in quasi-permanent conflict with Serbia because of South-Slav nationalist agitation in Bosnia and Hercegovina. The situation was the worse, because a revolutionary process had begun within the Ottoman State, which afforded wonderful opportunities for renewed Russian meddling in the Balkans. And in the background Europe's great system of alliances was rigidifying, raising a perennial threat that some minor conflict could lead to continental war. Under these circumstances Franz Joseph could positively not afford disorders in Hungary.

Early in 1910, with the Government technically beyond the Law because of the absence of a parliament-approved budget, Franz Joseph turned, therefore, once again to István Tisza; and the latter went to work as if the basic political problem in Hungary were still, as in his father's day, simply what to do with a misguided Parliament of gentry deputies. [9] Tisza re-established his father's political Party and backed a prime minister who was willing to stand firm against a hostile House. In the spring of 1910 the opposition leaders happily took up the challenge by returning to the game of screaming down Government speakers and throwing ink at their parliamentary foes. The King thereupon dissolved the Parliament. In an election Tisza's Party won a resounding success. Thereupon, Tisza consolidated as if the old political system had simply been restored.

---

[9] For the details of the Tisza's return, see Ferenc Pölöskei, *A koalíció felbomlása és a Nemzeti Munkapárt megalakulása, 1909—1910* [The Collapse of the Coalition and the Formation of the Party of National Work] (Budapest: Akadémia, 1963).

Of course in reality, as Tisza well knew, his problem now was quite different from what it had been, and he acted accordingly. During his first prime ministry, between 1903 and 1905, Tisza had been able to count on Vienna; now he could not. Then perhaps his problem had been simply to induce his Magyar noble nation to acquiesce to a Dualistic system which was constructed essentially to sustain that nation's supremacy. He had not had to worry that Franz Joseph might side with the Hungarian nationalities, or that Franz Joseph might encourage Hungarian social reform. Time had passed, however, the King was old, and after 1910, Tisza knew that Franz Joseph might at any moment die, giving way to the Archduke Franz Ferdinand, who was notoriously hostile to the Magyar noble cause; who had political advisors from among the Hungarian nationalities; and who was bound by no oath of honor to defend Hungary's constitution. Tisza could no longer even depend on the Magyar aristocrats, the Andrássys and the Apponyis, who had in the past been pillars of the Government and the Throne. They had all revolted by 1905; and though they had failed miserably in their efforts to rule without him, they were no longer anxious to let him rule for them. Finally Tisza now had truly to reckon with the lower classes and the nationalities. Prior to 1905 Magyar Liberalism had been able to placate these elements (and its own conscience) by blaming Vienna for obstructing the broad suffrage which a Liberal platform called for. By 1910 this was no longer possible. As Liberals both Tisza and the noble opposition were still stuck with a commitment to suffrage reform. But workers, peasants, and nationalities were not only more experienced at politics than before the great crisis, but from the behaviour of the Throne could clearly see that only the Magyar Liberals obstructed reform.

Under these circumstances Tisza could hardly afford to stop with simple restoration of his father's system, and he did not do so. Faced with modern problems, he developed modern tools. Prior to 1900 one spoke in Hungary of Kálmán Tisza's "mamelukes" in very much the same fashion one referred in Italy to Crispi's *trasformismo*. One recognized that the political regime depended on a strong man and on his political party; that elections were "rigged"; that sections of the population were not represented at all; and that other sections were fairly regularly repressed. But one recognized also a certain innocence in the ruling "machine." This was imperfect constitutionalism, but it was not dictatorship, and for all its deliberate "illegalities" it left intact the cardinal Liberal principle of free speech. Already under the Coalition, however, steps were taken to enlarge the state bureaucracy and to legislate away the civic rights of the nationalities. István Tisza carried on from here. He constructed a machine enormously bigger and smoother in its operations than anything his father had possessed. He vigorously buttressed the regime against all cries for extensive suffrage reform. And then he attacked the principle of free speech. In 1912 he returned to the Parliament the military reform to which it had been objecting since 1903. Faced with massive obstruction both from the nationalist opposition and from socialists in the street, Tisza took on his own shoulders the office of Speaker of the Parliament and then used force to change the parliamentary rules to eliminate obstruction. Whereas his father had simply sought order, István Tisza called for silence. [10]

The chronological graph of Jewish ennoblement in Hungary shows, moreover, that in this denouement of the country's political crisis Government policy towards the business community shifted once again, and did so now far more decisively than in 1904—1906 (Table 8). The graph shows that during the years between April, 1906, and January, 1910, while the Coalition attempted to rule Hungary, there was a general moratorium in large-scale ennoblement of Jews. Of the 24 Jewish ennoblements of the Coalition Era, ten were of a clearly honorary character, and went to intellectuals, soldiers, and politicians. [11] Three others went to Catholicized gentlemen who had married into old Hungarian noble families. [12] At least two of the others seem to have been hangovers from the Fejérváry period. [13] The Khuen-Héderváry ministry, which Tisza and Franz Joseph installed in 1910, ended this moratorium. During the two years it held office this ministry distributed no fewer than 43 new nobilities and four higher ranks to Jewish families in Hungary. Further, the László Lukács cabinet, which Tisza installed in preparation for the confrontation of 1912, and Tisza's

---

[10] In comparison to latter-day twentieth-century dictatorships, the regime which ruled in Hungary after 1910 can seem extremely liberal. In such features as personality cult, party supremacy, manipulated elections, and use of the mass media, however, one may estimate that as a "system" it now adumbrated the dictatorships of interwar Eastern Europe.

[11] Kárman, Halász, Telkes, Hédervári, Kotányi, Szalárdy, Kornhaber, Horváth, Rosenberg, and Szterényi. The moratorium on ennoblement under the Coalition was in some part probably a healthy revulsion in Budapest against the excesses of the Fejérváry Regime; and Franz Joseph was probably happy enough not to have to put himself out for the sake of the Kossuthists who had caused him so much trouble in the past. The moratorium was not, however, absolute. In 1908, baronage was awarded to the Hatvany-Deutsch and Korányi families of Budapest. Both were by then peerlessly *salonähig*, but one may wonder particularly in the Hatvany case whether the Coalition Government did not have some ulterior political motives.

[12] Altmann-Hahn, Brükler, and Eidlitz.

[13] Fábri and Back.

own cabinet of 1913 distributed in two short years 58 new nobilities and eight higher ranks to Jews. [14] Evidence from the archives makes it clear that this massive distribution of nobility was in part a reflection of the formidable pecuniary requirements of reconstructing Tisza's political party, and of winning the election of 1910.[15] Such things could not be done in Hungary without funds, and practice had shown that Jewish businessmen had the money. Analytical evidence tells, however, that money was not the whole story.

In previous distributions of nobilities, the Government had solicited support form a rather narrow stratum of Budapest merchants and bankers. In 1905, for example, one could suspect that the *csetei* Herzog and Schossberger families exercised inordinate power over selection of businessmen to be ennobled. [16] After 1910 Tisza abandoned this narrow approach to the commercial world. Some of the new honors, to be sure, went still to the great Budapest capitalists: for example, in 1910, Adolf Ullmann, who had just succeeded Zsigmond Kornfeld as head of the great *Hitelbank*, entered the House of Lords; and in 1911 and 1912 those members of the *madarasi* Beck family who had not won baronage earlier did so, as did the Kohner family. But far more characteristic of the new trend was the installation of Ferenc Heltai as Mayor of Budapest in 1913 and his coincident promotion

---

[14] Indications of Tisza's abuse of his right to recommend ennoblement in this period are the ennoblement of Zsigmond Leitner, his banker, in 1913; of Ferenc Schwartz, his estate-manager, in 1911; and of Mark Konrad, his father's personal physician, in 1914.

[15] See in particular the bizarre conditions revealed in OL K-26, Min. Eln. 1911, XI 214, which contains correspondence regarding a rumor that Tisza's party was offering nobility to two apparently very corrupt Jewish businessmen of Arad. Although legally a *Főispán* was supposed to be the initiator of any ennoblement in his county, the Arad *Főispán* was so convinced that the Party now had virtually complete discretion in such matters that, on the basis simply of the rumor, he tried to forestall the ennoblements. He accepted testimonials from prominent local institutions about how disastrously such ennoblements would affect local public opinion; and he sent these to the Minister of the Interior in Budapest, who legally should have had central control over all ennoblement processes. The Minister also, however, evidently felt that the Party was the real influence now in such matters; for he in his turn, simply on the basis of the rumor, forwarded all the material received to the Prime Minister.

[16] By my findings, the following ennoblements may be associated with the Herzog firm: Hoffmann, 1904, Vajda, 1904, Bachruch, 1905, Landauer, 1905, Keppich, 1906, Wix, 1906, and Fábri, 1907. There is circumstantial evidence that the Schossberger firm enjoyed patronage in the Dirsztay baronage in 1905; and that the Groedel firm enjoyed patronage in the Vécsey ennoblement in 1905. The Herzogs were pivotal also in the *Magyar Bank* which in 1905 lent the Government Party considerable backing, and did so again even more forcefully in 1910, in exchange for renewal of a contract on the Government's salt mines. This transaction resulted in the scandal which caused László Lukács' resignation as Prime Minister in 1913. For details, see Imre Balassa, "Elek Pál regénye," Installation V, in the *Pesti Tözsde*, 16 October, 1924, p. 9.

from the Lower to the Upper House of Parliament. [17] Heltai had made his career as a representative of the Budapest lesser capitalists. And the bulk of the new nobles of these years were second-level Budapest bankers, industrial managers, or provincial bankers, who could bring a much broader business-class support than before to Tisza's assistance. [18]

The suggestion of these facts is that Tisza approached the Hungarian business community after 1910 not just with an insistent invitation to collaborate, but more broadly, with an offer of political alliance. His approach was not haphazard but systematic and sophisticated. This suggestion seems confirmed, moreover, by the presence of Jews now in the Hungarian cabinet. First in 1910 Baron Samu Hazai became Minister for Defense. Next in 1912 János Teleszky became Minister of Finance; and in 1913 Baron János Harkányi, the scion of one of the oldest and most important Jewish noble families in Pest, became Minister of Trade. All three remained in office until mid-1917 when Tisza finally fell from office. If we may judge from the presence of Jews, the business community was represented even more heavily in the lower reaches of the national cabinet. [19] Such facts make Tisza's new regime not entirely unworthy of being labeled "dictatorship of the bourgeoisie," albeit this "bourgeoisie" was ennobled.

Tisza's consolidation was so effective by 1913 that only splinters of the opposition remained vocal thereafter. Typically, when war threatened in 1914, Tisza himself had qualms, but since he suppressed them in public, the rest of Hungary's politicians responded virtually as one body with wholly uncritical rejoicing and entered a *Burgfrieden*-like moratorium on political conflict, which enabled Tisza to keep his Parliament open for the duration without continuing the flow of ennoblements. Only in 1917, six months after the death of Franz Joseph, did Tisza's system begin to crack. [20]

---

[17] Heltai was Budapest's only Jewish *Főpolgármester*. He died within a few months of the appointment. Evil rumor had it that the King appointed him knowing that he would not live long.

[18] For example, of the 100 ennoblements between 1910 and August, 1914, 17 went to persons resident outside Budapest and listed in the *Magyar Compass* for 1913 as directors of banks outside Budapest.

[19] Lipót Vadász, for example, became State Secretary (Deputy Minister) in the Justice Ministry in 1913; Elemér Hantos became State Secretary in the Trade Ministry in 1916; Imre Neményi assumed the same office in the Cultural Ministry in 1917; Lajos Beck became State Secretary for Justice in 1917; László Fejér became State Secretary, apparently attached to the Prime Minister, in 1917; and Samu Fejér, Artur Gáspár, Bertalan Kallós, Dezső Pap, Géza Pap all seem to have become deputy state secretaries before the end of the Monarchy, largely because of services rendered in the Tisza period.

[20] A recent study of Hungary during the war is József Galantai, *Magyarország az első világháborúban* [Hungary in the First World War] (Budapest: Gondolat, 1964).

In 1917, under the impact of the Russian Revolution and the strain of the prolonged war, strikes broke out in Hungary, and political calls for a real electoral reform grew loud. In June, at the request of the new King Karl, Tisza resigned the prime ministry, and men connected with the old opposition returned to power. Now it was their turn to recognize the realities of ruling Hungary, and almost immediately they did as Tisza had done. They renewed the ennoblement of Jewish businessmen, and they invited a well-known Jewish "democratic" politician, Vilmos Vázsonyi, whom we will encounter at length in the next chapter, to work out a new suffrage law. Unfortunately it was too late for such changes to save the day. International developments were moving too fast. *Status quo* forces in the Parliament made legislative reform hopelessly slow. In May, 1918, Vázsonyi resigned from the Cabinet because he felt that even as a minister he could achieve nothing within the system. Coincidentally, King Karl turned one last time to the Budapest business world. He attempted to appoint as Prime Minister József Szterényi, a distinguished Jewish economist whom we will encounter again. Yet although Szterényi was already a Privy Councilor, and had hovered near the centers of governmental power for over a decade, virtually all the Old Regime politicians expressed horror at the idea of a Jewish prime minister. Thereupon Karl apparently surrrendered. In his last months as King he simply turned once again to the Budapest businessmen. He made Vázsonyi a Privy Councilor even without conversion, a unique honor. He made Szterényi a baron. And in a small orgy, perhaps of despair, he issued 15 new nobilities to Jewish Hungarians, mainly from Pest, and gave baronages to the banker Adolf Ullmann, to the munitions king Manfréd Weisz, and to the leather magnate Tivadar Wolfner, all war-profiteers.

The Social Crisis

The evidence just recited suggests that the political crisis in Hungary after 1903 forced the Government step by step to implore assistance from the business world of Pest, which we have been studying in this book. Towards the end some members of that business world were actually admitted to the seats of power. Nonetheless, it seems fairly evident that up to the last minute, despite its need, the Government got the support it wanted less by real concessions of power than by grants of ranks and titles. The bargain on the surface was thus cheap; and one must wonder why, if the regime's need was really great, the business world did not hold out for more.

The answers lie in study of the background. Let us recall, for example, that in 1890, just after the establishment of the Second Socialist International, Marxists in Budapest founded a Hungarian Social-Democratic Party.[21] At the start this party grew slowly. Until 1903, because of Government repression, it was outshone by various unionist organizations. But after the great Magyar political crisis began, it grew apace. In 1903 for the first time the Party construed a political program. In 1905 for the first time it participated in the legal political process by entering an arrangement with the Fejérváry Government against the Coalition. In 1907 it called with some success for a general strike. In 1912 again it precipitated massive political strike movements. Meanwhile, whereas in 1902 there were only 10,099 trade union members in Hungary, by 1908 there were 102,054; and outside the framework of Marxism other socialist movements appeared. [22] Between 1894 and 1904, for example, there was a wave of agrarian strikes, which brought into being in 1897 and again in 1905 radical peasant parties. So popular were these parties that even under the restricted franchise of the day they managed to return deputies to the Parliament, a feat the SDP never achieved in Old Hungary. Further, in the first years of the century intellectuals in Budapest began to examine the theories of socialism and came to play an important role as "conscience" to the Worker Movement. In 1913 these intellectuals established a "bourgeois" Radical Party, and in general by that time it was evident that behind Hungary's great political crisis lay a social crisis of dramatic proportions.

As the history of the well-known Goldberger textile works at Óbuda attests, the emergence of a socialist movement spelled trouble for the business community of Budapest which we have been studying. In 1903 the female workers on which this factory depended were affected for the first time by agitation of a union. [23] In 1904 a major railroad strike, and in 1905 frequent worker riots interrupted the factory's operations, as did the general strike of 1907. Legislation in 1906 brought no betterment of the unrest, and in 1908, for the first time in its 124 years of operation, the factory was

---

[21] Recent reviews of the beginnings of the worker movement in Hungary are Rudolf Tőkés, *Béla Kun and the Hungarian Soviet Republic* (New York: Praeger, 1967), Ch. 1; Edit S. Vincze, *A Magyarországi Szocialdemokrata Párt, 1890—1896* [The Hungarian Social Democratic Party] (Budapest: Szikra, 1961); and more generally, Süle, *Sozialdemokratie in Ungarn* (Cologne; Böhlau, 1967), Part I.

[22] For these figures, see Gyula Rézler, *A magyar nagyipari munkásság kialakulása, 1867—1914* [The Formation of the Hungarian Industrial Proletariat] (Budapest: Rekord, 1938), pp. 168, 178.

[23] For the following, see Kállai, *A 150-éves Goldberger gyár*, p. 151ff.

closed down by a strike of its own, and the management had to evict the strikers by force. In effect socialism, which centered on Budapest, the seat of the country's largest industries, mobilized the workers against the primitive and cruel labor conditions on which Budapest capitalism had build its prosperity. The socialist movement put an end to the old "patriarchal relations" in the factories which had kept labor cheap in Hungary; and it thus threatened the easiness of Budapest's capitalist profits.

The emergence of a socialist movement was only one symptom, more over, that behind Hungary's political crisis lay a considerable social crisis, and it was by no means the only such symptom which gave the Budapest business elite cause for alarm. Another was the ramification of Hungary's "bourgeoisie."

Even in the Magyar-speaking community it was recognizable in the two decades before the war that a new provincial commercial stratum was developing outside Budapest in the provinces. Some of its representatives entered the Jewish nobility.In 1903, for example, a family named Neumann from Arad acquired nobility; and in 1913 it received a baronage. This family owned a complex of industrial establishments in the Arad region, including a textile plant, a distillery, a cement plant, several construction firms, and banking interests. Correspondingly, at Pécs the ennobled *jánosi* Engel family had a small empire by 1900 in lumber, coal, and banking interests. Both these families were exceptional, however, in the sense that they had marriage connections with the Budapest business elite and entered its sphere. Much of the new provincial Magyar-speaking commercial stratum seems to have striven, not to collaborate with Budapest capitalism, but to resist it. Despite the enormous weight of the Budapest banks and cartels, the Hungarian Industrialists Association, which Ferenc Chorin and Sándor Hatvany-Deutsch founded in 1903, had to enlarge its membership and alter its organizational structure just a few years later to accommodate the demands of provincial Magyar-speaking industrialists. [24]

Ultimately more challenging than the emergence of this Magyar-speaking provincial bourgeoisie was the threat to the Budapest commercial world posed by the emergence of commercial strata among the subject nationalities of Greater Hungary. [25] This development assumed different forms. In

---

[24] Comp. Berend and Ránki, *Magyarország gyáripara 1900-tól 1914-ig*, p. 42ff.

[25] For following see L. Katus, "Über die wirtschaftlichen und gesellschaftlichen Grundlagen der Nationalitätenfrage in Ungarn vor dem ersten Weltkrieg," in Peter Hanák (ed.), *Die nationale Frage in der Österreichisch-Ungarischen Monarchie 1900—1918* (Budapest: Akademia, 1966), pp. 149—216; and I. Berend and Gy. Ránki, "Economic Factors in Nationalism," in *Austrian History Yearbook*, Vol. III, pt. III (1967), pp. 163—186.

the Slovak-speaking regions of northern Hungary, for example, there was relatively little development of Slovak-owned commercial institutions. But in this region before the war was 27% of all Hungary's iron production, 54% of her paper production, and 34% of her textiles, most of this being produced by foreign-owned firms. And among the Slovaks between 1880 and 1900 alone literacy rose from 32.9% to 50.1%. In the Slovak areas thus a broad base was being laid for the development of a sub-bourgeoisie or educated worker stratum of society beyond Magyar control. In Transylvania, on the other hand, though literacy was only 20.4% in 1900 among the Rumanian population, there was a remarkable growth (fed from the Rumanian Kingdom) of Rumanian-owned local credit institutions. Whereas in all Hungary in 1890 there were only 30 banks owned by national minorities, by 1914 there were 200, of which 150 were in Rumanian hands. A third situation developed in Croatia. Literacy there reached 52% in 1900, as in Slovakia, while commercial and industrial development lagged. But in Croatia, of course, there were tolerated national political institutions, entirely denied the Slovaks and Rumanians, which encouraged the development of a national bourgeoisie.

As a result of these developments, there existed in Hungary before the war a situation not dissimilar to that within the Habsburg Monarchy as a whole in the years prior to 1848. The Budapest commercial world wholly dominated Greater Hungary in 1900 and grew fat by exploiting the whole country, just as before 1848 Vienna had entirely dominated the whole Monarchy and had grown fat through exploitation. But in the Great Hungarian provinces after 1900 new economic "compartments" with social elites independent of Budapest were beginning to emerge, just as Hungary and Bohemia had begun to challenge Vienna prior to 1848. And if the development of Hungary in 1910 was by no means inevitably headed in the direction of Trianon, the capitalists of Hungary faced real competition now just as the capitalists of Vienna had around 1848. A phase in Central Europe's development was, in a word, drawing to a close after 1900, and Budapest business was beginning to feel the squeeze.

Here again the history of the Goldberger firm can afford us an insight into developments. Textile production was very undeveloped in nineteenth-century Hungary, but this firm, the oldest in the country, grew comfortably despite many carelessnesses on the part of its owners, and despite many vicissitudes, until after 1900. Then abruptly an end seemed near. [26] The cause in part was the increased tempo of cheap textile production elsewhere in the world,

---

[26] See Kállai, *A 150-éves Goldberger gyár,* p. 156ff.

which threatened to drive the Goldbergers out of their established markets. In part also, however, the squeeze resulted because of a dramatic increase in the competition even within Hungary. Whereas in 1898 there were only 110 textile producers in the country, by 1906 there were 234. [27] In 1905 the Goldbergers were compelled to go public to meet their obligations. From 1908 for several years they could not afford even to pay dividends. Such was the effect of the new competition on one of the more undeveloped branches of Hungary's industry.

Perhaps the gravest threat which the turn-of-the-century social crisis posed the Budapest capitalists stemmed neither from the emergence of socialism, nor from the development of new bourgeoisies in the provinces, but from the condition of the country's ruling class. The economic situation of the Magyar nobility had been difficult all through the nineteenth century; and particularly so since the emancipation of the serfs in 1848. Only towards 1900, however, did the combination of rising prices and falling agricultural income begin to drive the nobles off the land altogether. One calculation indicates that whereas 194,000 estates changed hands in Hungary in 1875, 549,000 did so in 1901. [28] Perhaps one fourth of these transfers were testamentary conveyances within families. The remainder were sales. Presumbly the greater number were sales by nobles to persons with capital, which means there was a steady rise in the number of Magyar nobles who were sufficiently indigent that they had to seek paid employment. [29] Tradition ensured that most of these people entered the county bureaucracies. But by the turn of the century the counties were unable to absorb the overflow from the land; and one of the social forces behind the Coalition of 1904 was gentry desire for an enlargement of the central state apparatus. Once again figures tell the story best. In 1867 in the entire realm of Saint Stephen there were only 30,000 state employees including the railroad and postal services; and of these only 2,000 were in Budapest. [30]

In 1900, however, there were 160,000 state employees in all of Hungary, not including the railroad and postal services; and 6,000 were in Budapest. In 1912, moreover, there were 233,000 state employees in all, without the

---

[27] *Ibid.*, p. 150.

[28] See Petrassevich, *Zsidó földbirtokosok és bérlők Magyarországon*, p. 11.

[29] See for the following Lippay, *A magyar birtokos középosztály és a közélet*, Ch. 3.

[30] The following figures were provided me by Károly Vörös and derive from his long study of the subject. There are comparable figures in János, "Decline of Oligarchy," p. 51; and in the extensive study of the administrative classes by Dezső Buday, "Magyarország honoratior osztályai" in the *Budapesti Szemle*, Vol. 165, no. 470 (1916), pp. 228—249

post and railroads; and 13,500 were in Budapest. And one must note that the growth of the bureaucracy was most startling at the top; in 1913 there were 28,543 "qualified" civil servants in all of Great-Hungary; by 1923/24 there were 33,883 in Trianon Hungary alone. [31] Even this formidable growth of the bureaucracy was, as it turned out, insufficient to relieve the pressure from the indigent nobles. By the eve of the war it was noticeable in Budapest that a few members of the old nobility were at last sacrificing their "gentry respectability" and entering "trade."

This economic transformation in the Magyar nobility had serious consequences for the Budapest business world, because it upset the firm division of spoils on which the society of Dualistic Hungary had hitherto rested. Until 1900 the Magyar nobility and the ethnic business communities of Pest had simply not bumped into each other on the professional level. The Magyar nobles had been predominantly rural, and under no conditions engaged in commerce. Businessmen, on the other hand, and particularly Jewish businessmen, had been predominantly urban and had eschewed any claim to a place in the state service. In 1883 there were only some ten Jews in the entire ministerial aparatus in the Hungarian capital, and there were none in the county administrative system. [32] After 1900, however, as the Magyar nobles moved off the land and into the national capital, Jews began to enter public life. The last two elections under the Monarchy brought the number of Jews who had been parliamentary deputies up to 102. [33] Further, in the judicial system and in the educational, commercial, and legal branches of the State administration Jews became prominent at every level. By 1910 unconverted Jews formed 5.2% of the country's administrators. [34]

To this picture of increasing professional competition between the old nobility and the commercial communities, we must add one aggravating detail. The creditors to whom the nobles owed their debts, and the new possessors of the nobles' land were on the whole Jews. Prior to 1900 this fact was perhaps less than observable, because no statistics were available. By 1904, however, anti-Semitic tracts were appearing for the first time since the 1880's, and in 1904 one of the more important of them demonstrated,

---

[31] See István Weisz, *A mai magyar társadalom* [Hungary's Society Today] (Budapest: Magyar Szemle Társaság, 1930), p. 223.

[32] The *Egyenlőség*, 11 February, 1883, pp. 2—5; 18 February, pp. 2—5; and 25 February, pp. 2—5. There is a comparable survey in the *Egyenlőség*, 23 January, 1887, p. 4; and 30 January 1887, pp. 2—3.

[33] This count is based on several partial lists cited in Chapter V. footnote 35 above.

[34] See A. Kovács, *A zsidóság térfoglalása Magyarországon*, p. 43.

with the aid of the most recent census, that Jews now owned no less that 37.5% of Hungary's arable land. [35]

* * *

With this we can approach the point of our argument, which is that because of the social crisis of turn-of-the-century Hungary the Budapest business elite had serious and good reasons, not only for accepting the reinforced invitation to collaborate which István Tisza was proffering, but for going overboard into the sea of collaboration. In the abstract, perhaps one might argue, this elite had attained a position of such considerable power by 1905 that it could dispense with collaboration. The Budapest banks and cartels which belonged to this elite were in almost absolute command of a booming new industrial economy. The members of this elite were participating in the management of the State and were eligible to be ministers. Theoretically, therefore, the elite should have been able to abandon the craven humility it assumed all through the nineteenth century and should have been able to set its own terms to the old regime, in the style of West European bourgeoisie. A Marxist might cry that this elite should now have fought for "bourgeois democracy" instead of collaborating in the perpetuation of aristocratic "feudalism." In practice, however, this elite faced concrete problems which militated against any such democratic option. Had this elite turned democratic in 1905 and after, it would have had to tolerate and even encourage the socialists, who were threatening the economic pillars of Budapest's prosperity. Moreover, to have been democratic would have meant relying, not only on the new Magyar provincial bourgeoisie, but also on the nationalities, and the latter were simply not reliable allies for Budapest's business. And to have been democratic would have meant taking on the rivalry of the ruined and now competitive Magyar noble class, to which, one must recall, even István Tisza lost a major battle in 1905 and had to cede power. In the social circumstances of turn-of-the-century Hungary, in a word, one may estimate that the Budapest commercial elite chose very well when it allied itself to István Tisza. With such a defender, that commercial elite had far better chances of survival than by itself.

* * *

To this one must add that from such an alliance specific profits were to be gained, as we may intimate from the record of the *csepeli* Weisz family,

---

[35] See Petrassevich, *Zsidó földbirtokosok és bérlők*, p. 26ff.

which, in two brief decades after its acquisition of nobility in 1896, constructed one of Europe's greater industrial empires. [36]

The first of the Weiszes was a humble maker of smoking articles *(Pfeifenbeschlager)* in the outskirts of Pest in the 1820's. His son Adolf was a
traveling grain trader, who also dealt in slivovitz, but who managed in
midcentury to establish a firm of his own in the Lipótváros after marrying
into the prosperous Kánitz family of Óbuda. In the 1860's this Adolf Weisz
invested in the flour mills. Yet, though he survived the crash of 1873 and
though he could afford thereafter to send his youngest son (romantically
named Manfréd) to a German university, he was neither notably prominent
nor notably successful. The Weiszes became important only after 1882,
when Adolf's elder son Berchtold established Hungary's first meat-canning
plant outside Pest; and after 1885 when Berchtold and Manfréd Weisz
won their first contract for supplying Hungary's percentage of the *K.u.K.*
Army's canned gulyas consumption. They became important when they
started working for the State.

By the 1890's, Berchtold and Manfréd Weisz had progressed from filling
tin cans with stew for the Army to making the cans, and then to making
cartridge cases for the Army. Meanwhile, both had married rich women
from Vienna and had become intensely aware, not only of the profitablity
of Army contracting, but of the tax-free status the Hungarian Government
offered newly-founded factories. Consequently, they decided to start filling
the cartridges too; and to this end, in 1892, they established a gunpowder
plant in the open fields of the Csepel Island in the Danube just south of
Budapest. Their enterprise was so successful that it soon required a division
of responsibilities. In 1896 Berchtold handed over the cartridge factory to
Manfréd and turned his attention to family interests in the textile business
(in one factory they made tents for the Army) and to the Grain and Stock
Exchanges. Meanwhile, Manfréd founded a metal-works in order to free
himself from dependence on foreign producers of sheet metal. As it happens,
in this crucial year, 1896, Manfréd Weisz obtained Magyar nobility, and
Berchtold won a seat in Parliament. From the coincidence one may judge
again that they clearly anticipated future profits from the State.

By the early years of the twentieth century, when the great European
weapons competition began, Manfréd Weisz was regularly supplying a

---

[36] The most extensive scholarly account of the Weisz family history is I. Berend
and Gy. Ránki in *Csepel története* [The History of Csepel] (Budapest: Kossuth, 1965),
p. 33ff. See also Balla, *A Vadember*, p. 67ff.; Nándor Kozma, *Hadimilliomosok* [War
Millionaires] (Budapest: Béla Muskát, 1918), p. 9ff.; the *Egyenlőség*, 30 December,
1922, pp. 2—3; and the *Pesti Tözsde*, 7 December, 1922, p. 4.

quarter of the Austro-Hungarian Army's cartridge cases. By playing Army
Headquarters in Vienna against his major rival within Hungary, the State
Steel Works, moreover, Manfréd Weisz had grabbed half of Hungary's
quota to grenade and shrapnel contracts. And he was rapidly opening shops
for the production of long lists of other war materiel. In 1911 he proceeded
from iron and copper processing into steel production. By then he was doing
an active business supplying not just Austria but the Balkan states with
weapons, and he was strong enough to negotiate a private agreement divid-
ing bullet markets with the Rothschilds' great Witkowitz Works in Silesia.

By the middle of the war, Manfréd Weisz was one of the wealthiest
men in Hungary, simply on the basis of his munitions business with the
State. In addition, he was Deputy Chairman of Chorin's GYOSz, a director
of Leó Lánczy's *Kereskedelmi Bank*, a director of a complex of Budapest
machine factories, and a director of one of Budapest's most spectacular
real-estate enterprises. He had just bought a huge estate. His brother Berchtold, who died in 1916, was until then a key figure in the growing textile
industry. One of Manfréd's daughters and one of his sons had married
heirs of Zsigmond Kornfeld and had considerable power, thus, in the
Hitelbank's industrial empire. Another of his daughters had married
the son and heir of Ferenc Chorin and possessed key influence in the country's
coal industry; and he still had a second son to marry off. [37] It was then that
King Karl made Manfréd Weisz a baron.

One must exert caution in deducing at this point that István Tisza's
regime after 1910 was based on profits given to business magnates by the
state. Hungary's economy remained until 1944 a "private enterprise"
economy. The directness with which the *csepeli* Weiszes made their wealth
off the State was until 1914 very exceptional. Indeed, prior to 1905 the Hungarian State simply lacked the income to subsidize the county's industries
The *csepeli* Weisz case does, however, illustrate a trend; and through one
final career story we may discover how important this trend became in obtaining the collaboration of Budapest business for István Tisza's political regime.

János Teleszky was born in 1868 in Nagyvárad, [38] the son of a distinguished lawyer who was for years one of Kálmán Tisza's most faithful parliamentary deputies, and who late in the 1880's became State Secretary in the
Ministry of Justice. János Teleszky studied law as had his father, but then

---

[37] After the war this son married the daughter of Baron Péter *csetei* Herzog, the
tobacco and banking millionaire.

[38] See the useful biographical sketch of Teleszky in Radnóti, *Pesti pénzoligarchák*,
p. 251ff.; and the obituaries in the *Pester Lloyd*, 15 June, 1939; and the *Pesti Tözsde*,
15 June, 1939.

entered the Ministry of Finance and became a professional bureaucrat. By 1903 his skill brought him to the head of the Ministry's budget department, and it was there that he attracted the attention of Sándor Wekerle, who as a member of the Government Party had been Prime Minister for a while in the middle 1890's, and who would paradoxically resume that office in 1906 as representative of the anti-Tisza Coalition. Wekerle raised Teleszky to heights of responsibility and in 1909, in the final months of the Coalition regime, made him State Secretary (Deputy Minister).

Under Wekerle Teleszky was a tax expert, Hungary's major authority on the customs relation with Austria. When, early in 1910, Wekerle and the Coalition regime disappeared, Teleszky stayed on as State Secretary for Finance, and in 1912 he became Minister of Finances, which office he retained until István Tisza resigned the Prime Ministry in May, 1917. As State Secretary and Minister he zealously decried the excesses of unrestrained capitalism, called for heavy taxation of the rich, and succeeded, just before the war, in instituting a regular annual property tax along Prussian lines. This approximated the modern income tax. Then, when the war broke out, Teleszky designed the financial institution which crystallized Hungary's regime of subsidies into a Government-managed war economy. [39] It was he who managed the system of war loans which was meant to pay for the war. Teleszky's efforts sound initially as if they could have destroyed any atmosphere of intimacy between private industry and Tisza's regime. The contrary, however, was true.

Even before the war Teleszky's finance ministry was a leading example of how business was achieving a sort of "personal union" with the state apparatus. [40] When the war broke out, finding Austria-Hungary economically wholly unprepared, Tisza allowed Teleszky to design a war economy and then placed it directly in the hands of precisely those leaders of free capitalism whom it was meant to restrain. Teleszky, a professional deflationist, was the author of a deliberately inflationist economic regime, while prominent manufacturers managed the Hungarian State's allotment of raw mate-

---

[39] On the industrial aspects of the war economy, the authority is Szterényi and Ladányi, *A magyar ipar a világháborúban* [Hungarian Industry in the World War] (Budapest: 1931).

[40] The most extensive account of the post-1905 extension of the relationship between state and industry is in Berend and Ránki, *Magyarország gyáripara 1900—1914*, p. 167ff. While recognizing the biases and schematism of that account (which its authors have since modified in other published essays), for our present purposes it seems an adequate and useful source. Two important contemporary criticisms of the system are: Varga, *A magyar kartellek;* and József Pogány, *A Munkapárt bünei* [The Crimes of the Work Party] (Budapest: Népszava, 1917).

rials to their own private firms. Hungary's economy in the war era bore
a surface resemblance to the nearly-planned economy of the German *Reich*
in the same era. But whereas in Germany the State increasingly was the
dominant element, in Hungary the State became very considerably the
tool of business. There is universal agreement among the historians of the
subject that "state capitalism," as it emerged in Hungary under Tisza and
Teleszky, proved the happiest of hunting grounds for business profiteers. [41]

* * *

    The business world of turn-of-the-century Budapest accepted the offers
of collaboration with the Tisza regime, not only because of the concrete
social problems it faced in Greater Hungary's social crisis, but also because
a new economic era was beginning. In this new era the unregulated individual capitalism of the nineteenth century would become obsolete. Wars
and international competition would dry up the easy profits of the past.
Capitalism could hardly survive now without the State. The Tisza regime
sweetened the transition into this new era for Budapest business. Yet
even with this perspective one must stop short of judging that the collaboration of the Budapest business world with Tisza was "just for profit."
    The gun traffic in which the *csepeli* Weiszes made their fortunes recalls
the martial atmosphere which characterized European civilization before
the war, and which pitted country against country in mortal combat in
1914. This atmosphere, quite as much as the domestic social problems of
Hungary, was a concrete problem which anyone who wished to rule that
country had to face even though Vienna was technically responsible for all
matters of defense and foreign policy. When in the light of this problem
one asks whether Budapest's capitalists had an alternative to collaboration
with Tisza in the early years of this century, again the answer seems "no!."
These capitalists were revolutionaries of a sort in matters pertaining to
economics, but in politics they were little men, conscious to excess of the
strictures of conventional wisdom and practicality. For them to have taken
on not only the problems of ruling Hungary by themselves, but also the
problems of sustaining the country's good name in a warlike world, would
have been at the start of this century beyond their capacities.

---

[41] See for example, Jászi's comment in *Revolution and Counter-Revolution in Hungary*
(New Edition; New York: Howard Fertig, 1969), p. 41ff. Details about the war profiteering are available in Kozma, *Hadimilliomosok, passim.*

CHAPTER VIII

THE MORAL CRISIS[1]

The Magyar Road

Astute though our capitalists may have been after 1905, their continued collaboration with the Habsburgs and István Tisza compounded the moral disaster which was then cracking the image and crunching the ideals of the Magyar world. Such disasters were bound to have repercussions in an age of such fundamental optimism as the European early twentieth century in a seat of such great material accomplishment as was turn-of-the-century Hungary. Among the repercussions was the emergence on the world stage of the Hungarian scientific geniuses whom we have been studying in this book.

* * *

Let us approach this subject by reciting the career of József Szterényi, the convert Jew who nearly became Hungary's prime minister in 1918;[2] for this career illustrates the moral degradation which overtook even leading members of Hungary's urban classes during and after the coalition crisis. Szterényi was born in 1861, the son of a Dunántúl rabbi named Stern. In his childhood he was exposed to the divisive ideological dilemma which the Enlightenment had imposed on Jews in Hungary. His grandfather, Hirsch Fassel, a rabbi of Nagykanizsa, was one of Hungary's best-known Germanizer Jews. His father, on the other hand, became an extreme Magyarizer, a change of identity which seems in the end to have led to mental derangement.[3] The first we know of Szterényi himself, however,

---

[1] Part of the material in this chapter has appeard in different form in the *Journal of Social History*, Sept. 1972.

[2] Szterényi's political career is recorded in his *Régmult idők emlékei* [Memories of Times Past] (Budapest: Pesti Könyvnyomda, 1925).

[3] See the biographies in *MZsL*, and the obituaries in the *Egyenlőség*, 30 Dec., 1883, p. 7; and 6 June, 1886, p.l.

is a decision to evade such spiritual complexities and to secularize his existence. As a youth he became a Catholic, abandoning Judaism altogether.
By profession he became an economist, and as such his career was at the
start exuberantly successful. In the 1880's he settled at Kronstadt (Braşov)
in Transylvania, as the secretary of a Transylvanian trade and industry
association. He made a name for himself encouraging provincial Hungarian industry. His views won him favor with the political opposition, which
was increasingly taking stands then on points of economic nationalism; [4]
but they do not seem to have embroiled him with the Government. To
the contrary, he soon won a place at the Ministry of Trade in Budapest
and at the turn of the century was one of that ministry's leading technical
experts.

The great political crisis of 1905 threw Szterényi's career decisively off
course. After the formation of the patriotic coalition against István Tisza
late in 1904 there were not many distinguished Magyars in Hungary who
were willing to expose themselves to the ignominy of serving the King against
the nation. Opportunity beckoned, therefore, to men of ambition, who
under normal circumstances might have had difficulty rising to the top
of the system; and Szterenyi rose to the bait. In June, 1905, he entered
the cabinet of Baron Fejérváry as State Secretary for Trade (Deputy Minister), a rank achieved before this by only three Jews in Hungary. [5] As a
result, of course, he found himself in April, 1906, in difficult straits, for
the victorious Coalition was assuaging the bitterness of its *pactum* with
the King by initiating a massive purge of Baron Fejérváry's supporters
Szterényi warded off the danger with bold opportunism. Magicianlike he
produced letters from István Tisza and Ferenc Kossuth, the leaders, respectively, of the centralist and nationalist camps, in which both averred that
his services to Fejérváry had been exclusively "technical." [6] Szterényi also
deployed a connection with Count Gyula Andrássy, a Coalition member
to whose political party he now adhered. [7] And since the Coalition was

---

[4] For the background, see Dolmányos, *A magyar parlamenti ellenzék történetéből*,
p. 19.

[5] The three were Károly Nasch-Csemegi and István Teleszky, the jurists; and Ede
Horn, the economist. Horn was only Deputy State Secretary.

[6] These letters are reproduced in the carefully doctored first chapter of Szterényi's
Régmult idők emlékei. It is reported among historians in Hungary that the real reason
Szterényi was able so successfully to change sides was his wife's position as Ferenc Kos-
suth's mistress.

[7] For the background, see Gratz, *A dualizmus kora*, Vol. II, p. 79ff. Szterényi was a
member of the Constitutional Party, which Andrássy formed when he left the Government Party in 1905.

rich in patriotism but poor in expertise, Szterényi managed to stay in office as State Secretary (and *de facto* Minister) of Trade.

With disaster averted, Szterényi labored diligently for three years to reconcile the Coalition's secret commitment to economic Dualism with its public commitment to economic independence. [8] Then in 1909—1910, when the Coalition fell apart without honor, Szterényi got caught in the tide. He tried to continue his "selfless" service to his nation by making Count Andrássy's party a focus of opposition to Tisza. [9] Andrássy, however, preferred to cross the parliamentary aisle. Arbitrarily he dissolved the party; and Szterenyi for all his efforts received the rank of Privy Councilor and retirement at the ripe age of 48.

The lesson of Szterényi's career was well expressed at about this time by Vilmos Vázsonyi, another Jewish politician:

> [Hungary] has degenerated into a land of political duplicity, of complete lack... of openness, of political adventurism, where no cause is holy. It is not impossible here that men who but yesterday kicked and bit each other, who were so immersed in combat that they fought, not with weapons, but with their bare teeth — it is not impossible that at the next moment, inspired and driven by political interest and adventurism, they should appear arm in arm as partners in the arena. [10]

Nor was the lesson complete. In January, 1918, when the Monarchy was crumbling, Franz Joseph's successor, King Karl, recalled Szterényi, with whom he was acquainted, and, dubbing him Baron, appointed him Minister of Trade. Szterényi promptly made himself a symbol of the regime's determination to gouge its foes. He was responsible at the Bucharest peace-negotiations of that year for Hungary's extortion of a strip of territory from Rumania along the Carpathian frontier. But even so, when in April, 1918, the King proposed him as Prime Minister, political Hungary showed Szterényi its true face. His "friends," Andrássy, Apponyi, Tisza, and Wekerle, all announced he "lacked prestige." [11] In the end it was only Budapest's revolutionaries who acknowledged the "virtues" of Szterényi's career. Early in 1919 he was arrested as a war criminal and blamed for the iniquities of the system.

---

[8] Szterényi and Rudolf Sieghart, the Viennese Jewish banker, were the authors of the revised economic *Ausgleich* in 1908, which proved to be the last.

[9] See Ferenc Pölöskei, *A koalíció felbomlása*, p. 140.

[10] See H. Csergő (ed.), *Vázsonyi Vilmos beszédei és irásai* [Vilmos Vázsonyi's Speeches and Writings] (2 vols.; Budapest: Légrády, 1927), Vol. II, p. 464.

[11] See Szeterényi, *Régmult idők emlékei*, p. 91ff.; and Prince Louis Windischgrätz, *My Memoirs* (London: Allen & Unwin, 1922), p. 165 ff.

* * *

Szterényi's career brings to light not only a corruption which increasingly characterized Hungarian public life after the crisis of 1905, but also a vicarious brutality which the older rulers of the country now increasingly directed against their business-world partners. Out of that crisis a marriage of convenience had arisen. In it, as we have seen in the preceding chapter, the upwardly-mobile business classes obtained for the first time a share of the country's political power. But the price was servile acceptance by these classes of abuse. There was no honor or respect for them in this marriage, even of the sort proverbially common among thieves. In terms of respect the marriage was entirely one-sided.

Prior to 1905—1906 a significant effort was being made to correct such one-sidedness in the relation between the Magyar rulers of Hungary and their urban middle-class allies — a one-sidedness which, after all, was not just a product of the great political crisis, but had to do with the traditional inferior status of urban society in landlord Hungary. In the later 1890's at the Budapest University, for example, certain professors in the faculties of Law and Philology began to question the backbone of the system — the Magyar "constitutional" myths. [12] In 1900, as mentioned in an earlier chapter, these men and others from a variety of walks of life founded a sociological journal, the *Huszadik Század*, with Oszkár Jászi among the editors, to examine the character of Hungarian society in a European light. While this journal was not lacking in respect for the traditions of the Magyar nobility, its express purpose was dissemination in Hungary of new ideas from Western social science that could only challenge the ruling classes. And the following year, to the same end, the *Társadalomtudományi Társaság* [Social Science Society] emerged, an association which contained in its leadership not only Jewish intellectuals but leaders of the German assimilationist movement and of Magyar official Liberalism. [13] Prior to 1905 the leadership of the *Társadalomtudományi Társaság* was in contact with the Social Democratic Party, and in 1905 it was sufficiently detached and clear about the real issues of Hungarian politics to maintain relations with both the Fejérváry Government and the

---

[12] See for the following Zoltán Horváth, *Magyar századforduló*, p. 80ff.

[13] See Horváth, *Magyar századforduló*, p. 117ff.; and Mérei, *Polgári radikalizmus Magyarországon* [Bourgeois Radicalism in Hungary] (Budapest: 1947), Ch. 2, esp. p. 14 where a list of the original *TTT* assembly members is conveniently reproduced.

"gentry" Coalition. [14] This movement, had it been able to develop, might have afforded a base for a general modernization of attitudes within the Magyar-speaking world, and for reduction of the sort of abuse to which the urban classes were subjected.

The peculiarity of the political crisis of 1905—1906 in Hungary, however, was that it crystallized ideological issues while encouraging the ruling classes not to change their ways. Franz Joseph's tactical threat to institute an electoral reform in Hungary made it finally clear that the syllogisms of Magyar liberal nationalism were false. For example, the threat forced men to recognize that the Magyar ethnic nation really had no rational claim to rule all of Greater Hungary, even though the ruling Great-Hungarian noble nation happened to speak Magyar; and even though the expressions for "Greater Hungary" and "Magyar land" were identical in the Magyar tongue. Yet though these Magyar syllogisms were undermined, and *ipso facto* the defenders of the *status quo* were alerted to danger, the outcome was preservation of the *status quo*, and indeed, compulsion on all Magyars to choose immediately between the *status quo* and change.

The consequences of the crisis for the *Társadalomtudományi Társaság* were sufficiently significant to be worth recording. In the middle of 1906, shortly after the Coalition's accession to power, the "establishment" members of the *TTT* [15] felt they should conduct a purge of such "traitors to the Magyar cause" as Oszkár Jászi and his radical colleagues, who had favored working with Baron Fejérváry. [16] The latter, as it happened, were able to foil the purge and to retain control both of the *TTT* and of the *Huszadik Század*. The "establishment" people had to found a new society and a new journal for themselves. But as it turned out it was they alone who had possessed the ear of the Magyar ruling circles. The result of the split was, accordingly, that both sides became inconsequential. Jászi and his friends became an isolated "radical intelligentsia" — to use a Russian expression — wholly lacking political and moral leverage within the exist-

---

[14] For details, see Mérei, *Polgári radikalizmus Magyarországon*, pp. 20—22.

[15] By "establishment members," it is meant persons such as Jenő Rákosi, Gusztáv Gratz, Ambrus Neményi, Károly Szladits, and the historians Gyula Lánczy and E. E. Moravcsik, who were not by reason of their birth in any way committed to the regime, but who through age and experience had grown used to it.

[16] To be precise, the crisis in the *TTT* was precipitated when the radicals impudently elected József Kristóffy, Fejérváry's hated Minister of the Interior, as a *TTT* officer. This was a provocation which Magyar patriots could hardly ignore. But the initiative in actually splitting the *TTT* was taken conspiratorially by Gratz and Lóránt Hegedüs. See Mérei, *Polgári radikalizmus Magyarországon*, p. 23ff.

ing social framework. [17] The "establishment" intellectuals, on the other hand, who might within the original framework of the *TTT* have commanded enough strength to devise a new road for Magyar society, became little more than a helpless appendage of the alerted but unregenerate nationalist nobility.

*   *   *

Factionalization and renewed exposure to the brutality of the ruling class were not the only disagreeable consequences which accrued to the Magyar-speaking urban middle classes as a result of the Coalition crisis. They were married now, generally speaking, to the Government on not disadvantageous terms. But precisely because of that marriage they lost certain political capital. And the case of Lajos Beck shows how debilitating the loss could be.

Beck was born at Budapest in 1876, the son of the eminent judge, Hugó *madarasi* Beck, the nephew of the prominent bankers, Nándor and Miksa Madarasy-Beck, and the cousin of that poet Karl Beck, whom we encountered in an earlier chapter. [18] Young Beck studied law in Budapest and Berlin and early made a name for himself as a legal theorist. Then he opened a law office in Budapest and went into politics. Since the old Liberal Party was at that moment in process of disintegration, Beck joined the victorious Independence Party as the road to the future. In 1906 on the Independence ticket he won a seat in Parliament, and in the following years he went about seeking political reform.

Before he entered the Parliament, Beck had published a political novel, appropriately entitled "Ideals," which mocked the corruption of the Tisza system and called for spiritual regeneration of Hungary's political life. Under the Coalition Government he tried to become more concrete. He published a lengthy study of Hungary's agrarian economy. He investigated

---

[17] On the applicability and non-applicability of the expression "intelligentsia" in turn-of-the-century Hungary, see the interesting distinctions in Süle, *Sozialdemokratie in Ungarn*, pp. 10—11. In mid-nineteenth century Hungary had possessed an "intelligentsia", a small, alienated, self-conscious educated class, entirely similar to those of Poland and Russia. But later in the century the Magyar educated classes found political satisfaction and grew. Magyar Hungary thus lost her intelligentsia until the alienated radicals emerged after 1900. In Poland and Russia, on the other hand, albeit for different reasons, the educated classes remained both discontent and isolated within the population well into the twentieth century. The boundaries between "intelligentsia" as "all the educated classes" and "intelligentsia" as "radical intellectuals" remained consequently much less clear than in Hungary, and there was no interruption of "its" presence.

[18] Extensive biographies of Beck are in various editions of the *Országgyülési Almanach*.

why thousands of good Magyars were emigrating annually to the New World. But nothing, of course, availed. Consequently in 1909, when the Independence Party split over the Coalition's failure to legislate its program, Beck went a step further. He joined the radical nationalist Gyula Justh in founding a new National Radical Party. [19] Yet this step also led nowhere because the Coalition fell. Thereupon Beck became an ardent opponent of István Tisza's return to power; and in 1912 together with Count Mihály Károlyi he helped restore unity to the various Independence Party factions on a program of electoral reform and opposition to Tisza. He led the parliamentary obstruction of 1912—1913. As a follower of Count Károlyi, Beck began towards the middle of the war to resume contacts with the radical intelligentsia with whom his likes had split in the *TTT* in 1906. Then in 1917, after Tisza finally fell, Beck became State Secretary in the Justice Ministry, commissioned to help Vázsonyi work out a new electoral law. In 1918 he published a book on the unequal distribution of the land within Hungary. Yet even now in 1917—1918 Tisza's parliamentary majority prevented Beck from pushing through even the moderate sort of electoral reform with which he felt he could live.

It is customary to suggest that men such as Beck did not really want reform; that they were "gentry," and satisfied with the situation in Hungary. Objectively this may be true, and it is certain that Beck personally styled himself all through his later life as "estate-owner." One may recognize also, however, that even had Beck, born a middle-class member of Budapest society, wanted to reform, the denouement of 1906 left him no possibility of doing so, either in alliance with Tisza, or with the noble opposition. Not until both Tisza and the noble opposition collapsed in the autumn of 1918 was it possible for Magyar-speaking, middle-class "establishment" people such as Beck to guide the country. Through their marriage with the Government in the aftermath of 1906 the middle classes of Budapest lost all political initiative.

They also lost considerable political opportunity. In 1905 both the "gentry" and Government poles of Magyar-speaking Hungary had waved banners of Liberalism which were still attractive to the outside world. Moreover, the Magyars had then faced an "outsider" King who, despite his threats of universal suffrage, was known throughout Europe as a conservative;

---

[19] On the Independence Party in this period, see Ágnes Várkonyi, "Adalékok a Függetlenségi Párt történetéhez" [Contributions to the History of the Independence Party], in *Századok*, no. 1961, p. 360ff.; Gratz, *A dualizmus kora*, Vol. II, p. 197ff.; Pölöskei, *A koalíció felbomlása*, p. 166ff.

and they had faced internal nationality elements which possessed no great organizational power. In that situation Magyar-speaking Hungary had possessed, not only the opportunity (which it chose) of maintaining the *status quo*, but also an opportunity to keep European sympathies while dictating the shape of reform in Greater Hungary. By 1918 Magyar-speaking Hungary had no such opportunities. By then both the great Magyar political parties had, in view of the whole world, dragged the banners of Liberalism in the mud. The external enemy was now a victorious Entente dedicated to the ideal of national self-determination. The internal enemies — the nationalities — were now armed. There was not even an effective army to keep order, and because of the lost war a social revolution had erupted. Magyar-speaking Hungary now had no alternatives save surrender of Saint Stephen's frontiers.

In this situation, to which the denouement of 1906 had condemned them, such urban middle-class leaders as Lajos Beck naturally fled as soon as they could from responsibility. Typically, Beck himself resigned from Count Károlyi's Independence Party even before the revolution of October, 1918, and though he later agreed to represent the Károlyi regime in the negotiations for dissolving the Austro-Hungarian Bank, he withdrew even from that task early in 1919, before the Bolshevik assumption of power. Beck took the initiative only after the Bolsheviks failed. In the chaotic conditions of the late summer and autumn of 1919 he attempted to form an alliance of moderate socialists with a Magyar political "center." And then he, like József Szterényi, felt the brunt of Magyar noble brutality. The counterrevolution brushed him aside, condemning him, on account of his patriotic association with Count Károlyi, for all the misfortunes of the past year.

The lesson of Beck's career is that for middle-class Magyar-speaking Hungarians after 1906 the outlooks were barren. A share in power had been achieved, perhaps; but at a great cost in terms of middle-class dignity, unity, and opportunity. And after the revolutions of 1918—1919, the partition of the Realm, and the political restoration of 1920, they could well look at Hungary and wonder whether they had any future in this narrow land.

The Jewish Magyar Road

For Jewish members of the urban middle class in Hungary after 1905—1906, even more than for middle-class Magyars, the future could have seemed barren. To observe this one need only review the career of Vilmos

Vázsonyi, a lawyer and brilliant orator, who was the leading unconverted Jewish, Magyar-speaking politician of the day. [20]

Vázsonyi was born the son of a teacher named Weiszfeld in 1868 at Sümeg, a small town near Lake Balaton. His family moved to Budapest when he was young, and he was educated there. In the early 1890's, when he was studying Law at the University, he made his political name by throwing himself into the struggle for the "reception" of Judaism as a religion of state, the last episode in the long fight for Jewish emancipation. [21] And in this early period he revealed an essentially optimistic assessment of the situation of the Jews in Hungary.

To highlight this optimism, let us recapitulate briefly what the situation of the Jews there was. Traditionally in Europe until the nineteenth century the Jews had sought security from Christian attacks by clinging to Royal authority. In Hungary they had done so until, in the decades prior to 1848, reformer Jews and liberal Magyars had come together on a platform of common struggle for emancipation. Elsewhere in Europe such alliances between Jews and liberals had not proved lasting after the 1860's, either because they failed in their objectives, as in Poland, and fell apart; or because, as in the Germanies, they succeeded, and the original contracting partners became narrow interest groups, attacked from without by new generations of more radical liberals. In Hungary not so. In Hungary even though the alliance attained its objectives, and both the assimilationist Jews and the Magyar liberals did become distinct interest groups, the narrowness of the political society and the exigencies of Magyar supremacy prevented a split. The Magyar leadership accepted the premise that

---

[20] On Vázsonyi, see Sándor Pethő, *Viharos emberöltő* [Stormy Generation] (Budapest: Stádium, nd.), p. 215ff.; the introduction to Csergő and Balassa (eds.), *Vázsonyi Vilmos beszédei és irásai;* and Mrs. Vázsonyi, *As én uram* [My Husband] (Budapest: 1928).

[21] As may be recalled, the Emancipation Law of 1867 had simply guaranteed Jewish citizens of Hungary civil rights and barred discrimination on account of their religion. It had not placed the Jewish religion on a par with Catholicism, Lutheranism, Calvinism, Unitarianism, and Greek Orthodoxy, which were "received" by the Hungarian State as authorities for supervising births, marriages, and deaths, etc., of citizens. The Jewish Congress of 1868 failed, moreover, to establish such a relation between Judaism and the State. Consequently the Jews were at a considerable disadvantage. In particular, marriage between Jews and Christians remained illegal without the conversion of one partner or the other. Agitation for change began during the anti-Semitic scare in the early 1880's; reached a first climax in 1883—1884, when the House of Lords rejected a civil marriage law; and culminated in 1891—1895 with the passage of such a law and the legal "reception" of the Jewish faith. For details, see Venetianer, *A magyar zsidóság története*, Part III; *MZsL*, "recepció"; and the recent account by Moritz Csaky, *Der Kulturkampf in Ungarn* (Graz: Böhlau Verlag, 1967), pp. 36—39 and p. 94ff.

Judaism was "just a religion," not a nationality. They subdued the political anti-Semitism that broke forth in the 1880's on the model of neighboring Vienna. Nonetheless, from the Jewish point of view danger lurked even in Hungary. In the first place the Jews were utterly disunited, and very many of the Jews, particularly in the provinces, were unassimilated, as distinct in gown and speech from the rest of the population as were the Jews of Poland, and clearly not "just a religious group." The "evidence" existed thus with which anti-Semites could "prove" that the official premises were lies. Further, the Magyar leaders were not, as we have seen, the only Magyars; and when towards the start of the new century political and social antagonisms sharpened, it became less and less probable that what these leaders premised would restrain the entire Magyar nation.

There was reason accordingly for responsible Jewish leaders to show caution in their dealings with authority. Yet Vázsonyi, if we may judge from his actions, showed a feeling that caution was not necessary. His initial political position involved two sorts of operation. On the one hand, in the theatre of Jewish politics he launched something close to a "movement from below" against both the rich secular oligarchs who dominated the Neolog communities, and against the traditionalist rabbinate which governed the Orthodox. [22] On the other hand, in the theatre of Magyar politics he set about organizing, also "from below," a "democratic" reform against the bureaucrats, millionaire capitalists, and aristocrats who backed the *Ausgleich* regime. [23] One can interpret these political offensives in general as an effort to convert the battle for "reception" into a new, long-range common struggle which could bind the Magyars to the Jews. The

---

[22] It is not clear how far Vázsonyi went along the lines of uniting Judaism "from below." But there is no doubt that he violently upset both the Neolog and Orthodox leaderships by appealing from a reform position within the Neolog community to the Orthodox following. Unfortunately, the factionalism in Vázsonyi's generation of Judaism in Hungary was so violent that there is practically no historical literature on the internal Jewish politics of the day. One must reconstruct from the biographies of various individuals what happened. Of these, I have found particularly useful the biography of F. Mezey in the *Egyenlőség*, 9 July, 1927; and an unpublished manuscript entitled "A magyar zsidóság 1930—1941. A Magyarországi Izraeliták Országos Irodájának müködése Stern Sámuel vezetése alatt. . . " [Hungarian Jewry 1930—1941. The National Office of Hungarian Jews under the Leadership of Sámuel Stern). This manuscript is in the possession of Dr. Sándor Scheiber of the Budapest Rabbinical Seminary, who very kindly lent it to me.

[23] In 1894 Vázsonyi organized in Budapest a "Democratic Club." In the following years he agitated with this organization as his base for radical reform in the Budapest city administration. Towards the end of the century he extended his efforts to other towns, and in 1900, the year before he entered the national Parliament, he organized a Democratic Party. See Dolmányos, *A magyar parlamenti ellenzék történetéből*, p. 123ff.

peculiarity of Vázsonyi's offensives was his optimistic willingness to do without powerful alliances, and to rest on the popularity of his cause.

As it happened Vázsonyi did well in his first political efforts. Albeit far from single-handedly, he managed to stir up both a quantity of Jewish emancipationist enthusiasm for the "reception" campaign, [24] and also a good deal of Magyar anticlericalism. The "reception" turned out to be part of a *Kulturkampf* which left Hungary with an array of new religious legislation. And on the basis of this success Vázsonyi got himself elected to the national Parliament in 1901. Even while he was winning his first victories, however, two developments were occurring which were pivotal to Vázsonyi's whole later career. First, in 1896 the Budapest-born Theodore Herzl published in Vienna the book, *Der Judenstaat*, which proved to be the bible of modern Zionism, and in 1897 he organized at Basel the first World Zionist Congress. A first Hungarian Zionist Congress followed in 1903. [25] And meanwhile, as recorded elsewhere, a Social Democratic Party consolidated itself in Hungary. The emergence of Zionism was important — and disastrous — from Vazsonyi's point of view, because that movement boasted that Judaism was a nationality, and not just a religion; whereas the emancipationist Jews in Hungary, among whom Vázsonyi was coming to the lead, claimed that they were Magyars and that Judaism was *only* a religion. Vázsonyi had to dread the emergence of socialism because, while calling himself a "democrat," he was limited in his "democracy" by the nature of his electorate. This consisted of the country's middle- and lower-business strata — people, usually Jewish, often Orthodox, and mostly located in Budapest, who were not accustomed to participate in national political life. [26] Vázsonyi could mobilize these people best by pointing out

---

[24] Vázsonyi's agitation in favor of the reception was more necessary than can be guessed from appearances. It would seem, for example, that in the early 1890's the National Jewish Office, the highest Neolog organization in Hungary, was so anxious to avoid upsetting conservative Magyars that behind the scenes it tried to spike the "reception" campaign, just as in the early 1880's it had sought privately to avoid a public outcry over the Tisza-eszlár Trial. When Vázsonyi's "reception" campaign proved successful, of course, that Office jumped on the band-wagon and claimed the credit. See the account of the reception campaign in the *Egyenlőség* Jubilee number of Jan. 1930, pp. 27—30.

[25] See *MZsL*, "Magyar Cionista Szövetség."

[26] According to most authorities Vázsonyi's Party never claimed much following outside the *Terézváros*, the Budapest VI District, which consistently elected him to the Parliament. It may be mentioned that in the *Lipótváros*, the Budapest V District, a rival middle-class political organization existed. It represented a slightly richer social stratum. Its principal leaders were Mór Mezei, Pál Sándor, and Ferenc Heltai, and it generally stood subserviently behind the Government.

how they were being cheated by "plutocrats" who were richer than they. So long as socialism was an insignificant force, as it was prior to 1903, Vázsonyi did not have to worry about it, and could even on occasion make common cause with it. But after 1903 as trade-unionism became important, it affected the pockets to which Vázsonyi appealed, and either lured Vázsonyi's followers away from him, or drove them into league with the very capitalists against whom he implored them to rally.

Vázsonyi's ultimate response to the double challenge of Zionism and socialism was participation in the Steering Committee of the grand Coalition of 1905 against István Tisza, a move which can seem at first to have been a compromise of his principles. As recently as 1902, Vázsonyi had inflamed a broad range of Magyar nationalists against him by stating that the record of battles and violence which then passed for Hungarian history in Magyar schools was nothing more than *kultúrbestia.* [27] Yet now among his colleagues in the Coalition leadership were the most vocal of those nationalists. Further, the major plank in Vázsonyi's political program was democratic electoral reform. Yet it was the King and Baron Fejérváry (and eventually the SDP) who, in alliance with one another, were threatening to institute electoral reform in 1905, whereas the Coalition leaders, while mouthing appropriate slogans, were notoriously cool to the practical possibility of reform. [28] And one may even perceive what Vázsonyi had to gain from the Coalition which could account for these surprising inconsistencies. He was the humble leader of a "Democratic Party" which had only come into existence on a national scale in 1900 and whose electorate was humble. He therefore needed the prestige which could accrue from acceptance as an equal by the political part of the nobility grouped in the Coalition; and no doubt also his ego was flattered by acceptance.

Vázsonyi's participation in the Coalition did not by any means represent simply a corruption of his principles, however. In this move lay also a new expression of the fundamental confidence which had inspired his politics in the 1890's. There were two ways, for example, in which he could have faced the challenge of Zionism. The one was passive, and involved standing still and hoping that Hungary's Jews would remain assimilationist, and that the Magyars would ignore suggestions that the Jews were a nation-

---

[27] One may intimate the sensation Vázsonyi created from Endre Ady, *A nacionalizmus alkonya* [The Twilight of Nationalism] (Budapest: Kossuth, 1959), p. 33ff.

[28] See Dolmányos, *A magyar parlamenti ellenzék történetéből*, p. 397ff. Of course, when Vázsonyi actually joined the Coalition, late in 1904, the King and the Government had not yet hinted they would back electoral reform, and the Coalition seemed the best horse with which to ride towards that goal.

ality. The other alternative was active search for indications that Zionism, with its denial of the Magyar-Jewish identity, was wrong. This was the alternative Vázsonyi chose when he joined the Coalition. He gambled that it would be possible to elicit evidence from the Magyar nationalist opposition that an alliance of Jews with Magyars was still in the twentieth century the most profitable road for the Jews. Much the same may be judged of his answer to the challenge of socialism. He had the choice of becoming defensively anti-socialist, or of trying to show the poorer voters of Pest that socialism was not worth while. By joining the Coalition, which he did in just such a spirit of outbidding the SDP, [29] Vázsonyi gambled that he could continue to lead both Magyars and Jews "from below" just as he had done earlier in his career. He was still, in a word, optimistic in 1905.

* * *

Vázsonyi, as it happened, gained one major political plum from the Coalition. In the election of 1906, with Coalition backing, Vázsonyi's party won control of the city administration of Budapest, and in the following years he became that city's great reformer, modernizing its administration, developing its public services, encouraging its planned growth, just as Mayor Karl Lueger was doing in nearby Vienna. [30] In the process, however, Vázsonyi drastically changed his political pose. He retreated from the national political arena. He grew vocally and aggressively anti-socialist. He grew rigid and dogmatic in Jewish affairs, protesting still against the authoritarianism of the various sect leaderships, but bluntly pretending that Zionism had no reason for existance, damning it as "un-Magyar." By 1912, while still assailing "plutocrats" as "cowardly Jews" who sacrifice their "masculinity" for a share in the Old Regime's wealth, [31]

---

[29] Again, Vázsonyi's move is only comprehensible in terms of the situation when the Coalition coalesced, late in 1904, before the January, 1905, election victory. The SDP then was also backing the Coalition. It had not yet displayed the signs of independent policy formulation which appeared the following summer. And under the narrow Budapest suffrage of the day the only voters who would be tempted to vote SDP were of a class susceptible also to Vázsonyi's blandishments. Without much risk thus, and with some profit, Vázsonyi could seek to "outbid" the SDP at that time. It was a measure of his success that the SDP afterwards criticized itself for "allowing" its voters to help Vázsonyi win his mandate. See Dolmányos, *A magyar parlamenti ellenzék történetéből*, pp. 407—409.

[30] For Vázsonyi's reform activity in Budapest, see the introduction to Vol. I of Csergő and Balassa (eds.), *Vázsonyi... beszédei és írásai.*

[31] Vázsonyi claimed: "My democracy is not a democracy of eunuchs, nor do I [as they do] guard the sultan's harem in exchange for a share of power and wealth. Ne'er will I sacrifice my masculinity." See Csergő and Balassa (eds.), *Vázsonyi... beszédei és irasai*, Vol. I, p 464.

Vázsonyi was directing his main fire against the young radicals of middle-class Budapest such as Jászi, whom be addressed in wholly materialistic, almost racist terms:

> It was we who sweated in this city to awaken a... civic spirit, it was we who set up and then carried out a municipal [reform] program... and now that the time for clipping the coupons of Democracy has arrived,... these resourceful striplings (who were resourceful also in exchanging their beliefs for petty cash, and began their liberalism by Christianizing), these striplings... (who haven't even spent the ritual thirteen years in politics, and thus are truly babes according to the ritual of their ancestors), they present themselves and claim that they, not we, are entitled to clip the coupons... [32]

At the height of his career Vázsonyi became incapable of seeing that with such attacks he was simply undercutting the petit-bourgeois assimilationist class unity which alone could have brought his own cause to fruition.

In explaining this change in Vázsonyi after 1906 one may recognize first that in the task of reforming Budapest he faced political problems which were sufficient to dull even the most capable men. It was not easy to take on almost singlehanded, as Vázsonyi did, the clique of bankers, lawyers, and wealthy merchants who in collaboration with the National Government controlled both the unreformed Budapest City Administration and the leadership of the Neolog Jews. It was perhaps natural in such a setting that Vázsonyi became narrow and dogmatic in his politics.

A second explanation of the change in Vázsonyi after 1906 has to do with ideology. Had Vázsonyi commanded a towering ideological understanding of the social and political forces which overwhelmed him in Budapest, perhaps despite them, in the fashion of Tomas Masaryk in Prague, he could have overcome. Unfortunately, one must admit his pathetic want of analytical political ideology. Characteristically, when Vázsonyi sought to define what he stood for, he turned not to France, England, or Germany, and certainly not to Prague, but to Vienna: he labelled himself a "liberal Luegerist" in the tradition of Vienna's anti-Semite Mayor. [33] Further, in explaining what this meant he tended to fall back on wholly negative definitions:

---

[32] Csergő and Balassa (eds.), *Vázsonyi... beszédei és irásai*, Vol. I, pp. 466—467.

[33] Vázsonyi compared himself to Lueger, despite their obvious difference in religion, at least twice: once in an essay written in exile in 1919, published in Mrs. Vázsonyi, *Az én uram,* p. 302; and again in an excerpt from his memoirs published in the *Egyenlőség*, 1 Sept., 1923, p. 9.

I learnt from the example of Vienna that if we failed to follow a democratic municipal policy based on liberal principles, others would invade Budapest with a democratic municipal policy based on reactionary principles. [34]

Vázsonyi's ideological disadvantages were particularly serious because even Lueger's formula of religion, demagogic nationalism, and public service was notably weak in comparison to other late nineteenth-century European political ideologies. Further, Vázsonyi's Magyar (and thus implicitly pro-noble) nationalism could not so easily as Lueger's German nationalism be identified with middle-class self-interest. Nor could Vázsonyi rely, as Lueger could, upon a popular Catholicism to fill up his ideological void; and finally, Vázsonyi could not as a Jew either appeal, as Lueger did, to a non-urban following, or safely manipulate middle-class urban passions against the Jews.

The third major reason for the change in Vázsonyi after 1906, however, was the disillusionment he suffered in the Coalition. The agreement of April, 1906, between the Coalition and the King left Vázsonyi, like Szterényi, very much in the lurch. He had counted on the Magyar nationalists to institute electoral reform and thus to reinvigorate the old alliance between the Magyars and the Jews. The King, however, agreed to let the Coalition leaders reform at their own pace; and they lost no time in telling Vazsonyi their unreadiness to move. For a year he had prostituted himself to them, serving as a living proof that they were "really" democratic, despite their "gentry" appearance, and that they were "really" not clerical reactionaries, despite their obvious bigotry. Now, both as a "democrat" and as a Jew, he was simply thrown aside.

And this same treatment was accorded him throughout his later career. After the collapse of the Coalition in 1909—1910, István Tisza reconsolidated his onetime power not only in the national political arena, but also in Budapest, and Vázsonyi found himself badly isolated. Consequently in 1912 he decided to accept an invitation to rejoin the "gentry" opposition. He became a leading figure in the affair of Prime Minister László Lukács, the *Magyar Bank*, and the salt monopoly. In part thanks to Vázsonyi's brilliant oratory, that affair ended in May, 1913, with Lukács' resignation under suspicion of being "Europe's greatest panamaist." [35] For such services Vázsonyi was considered eligible for a cabinet post in 1917, when Tisza fell. He became Minister Without Portfolio and was charged with

---

[34] See the *Egyenlőség*, 1 Sept., 1923, p. 9.
[35] See Béla Fábián, *A Dési-Lukács pör* [The Dési-Lukács Trial] (Budapest: nd.).

drawing up the electoral reform for which he had labored all his political life. But then like Lajos Beck, his State Secretary, he discovered once in office that neither his "gentry" colleagues, nor Tisza's parliamentary majority would have anything to do with the projects he prepared. Again he found himself simply window-dressing on the Magyar noble-supremacist facade.

In the face of such treatment one may hardly blame Vázsonyi for pretending, dogmatically, as he did after 1906, that socialism was "bad," and that the Zionist logic simply contained no substance. [36] The Magyar nationalists had demonstrated that the socialists, who in mid-1905 had taken stand with the "plutocrats" and the King against the Coalition, were "right," while Vázsonyi was "wrong." Because of the denouement of April, 1906, in a sense, Vázsonyi had no logic on his side either against the Socialists or against the Zionists. He had to go on the defensive then.

* * *

By the end of Vázsonyi's career in 1926 the horizons for middle-class Hungarian Jews were, judging by his standards, even more barren than between 1906 and 1918. He had been made an Actual Privy Councilor of the Hungarian Crown — the highest honor bestowed under the Monarchy on an unconverted Jew. But meanwhile disaster had followed disaster. Not only had his ministry been vain, but also it had witnessed the coming together of the two trends, Zionism and Socialism, which he had so long fought. It was followed by their temporary victory, [37] and then their replacement by

---

[36] It is suggestive of the depth of Vázsonyi's position on the Zionist question that not only he, but the entirety of Hungarian assimilationist Jewry, refused to have any official contact with international Jewish organizations prior to 1918, lest they suggest with such contact that all Jews had something in common. Only in November, 1918, when Greater Hungary was being ripped to pieces, did the Neolog Jews finally, in an act they considered wholly revolutionary, decide to address an appeal to the Jews in the Entente lands to save their country. See *Mult és Jövő*, Dec. 1918, p. 459.

[37] My major sources on Zionism during the revolution of 1918 are the account by Patai in *Mult és Jövő*, December, 1918, pp. 459—461; and the *Egyenlőség* for Jan.—April, 1919. See also the charges by Vázsonyi in the *Egyenlőség*, 4 July, 1925, p. 1. It would seem that Zionism underwent a significant growth in Budapest during 1918; that a Zionist Congress lent impetus to this in August of that year; and that after the collapse of the Monarchy there was a pronounced movement, especially among young people, Jewish workers, and Galician refugees to set up Jewish national councils in the provinces, and Jewish trade unions in several districts of Budapest. In the provinces both the Czechoslovak and Rumanian occupation authorities strongly abetted such Jewish national council tendencies in order to split the Magyar speaking population. In Budapest the Zionist movement culminated in an invasion of an assimilationist meeting at the Pest *Vigadó* in November, 1918; a raid on the offices of the *Egyenlőség* on 26 January, 1919; and in a seizure of the *Egyenlőség* when the proletarian dictatorship was proclaimed in March. Between

a political anti-Semitism from which Hungary had all through the *Ausgleich* era been blessedly free. [38] Vázsonyi as minister had struggled against this outcome. Filled with fear, even in 1917 he had advocated police measures against Zionists and Socialists alike. He had actually joined forces then with his old enemies, the "plutocratic" Neolog community leaders, when Oszkár Jászi, a convert Jew, raised the "Jewish Question" in the radical press. [39] He had become, with an epic parliamentary speech early in 1918, Magyar Hungary's first apostle against Russian Bolshevism. Yet nothing had availed. Late in 1918 he had to flee Hungary while Count Károlyi and Oszkár Jászi, whom he abhorred, put an end to the marriage between modern Budapest and the Magyar nobility, gave tolerance to revolutionary Zionism, [40] and then watched helplessly as the nationalities defected from

---

21 March and 12 April, 1919, the *Egyenlőség* appeared as a half-Zionist-half-Bolshevik paper. The Zionists were suppressed without excess of delay by the Bolsheviks. But meanwhile they had greeted the revolution in the following delirious terms:

New Hungary is created! The proletarian dictatorship of the poor and oppressed is born! And who can comprehend and greet it better that the millennially oppressed, the Jews? We are the proletariat of world history. The revolutionary flame which has burned beneath the surface of world history is now blazing up for the first time in a Jewish genius: Leo Trotsky! and it is blazing with a God-like force which shames every earlier revolutionary craving and consciousness.

See the *Egyenlőség*, 29 Mar., 1919, p. 1.

[38] There are few studies on the development of anti-Semitism during the war in Hungary. The most detailed account known to me is by József Patai in *Mult és Jövő*, Vol. VIII (August, 1918), pp. 283—285 (published also in *Österreich. Wochenschrift*). Patai sees anti-Semitism as a phenomenon always latent in the Magyars, which was fanned in the stressing time of war by Catholic agitations (led by Bishop Proháska as well as by conservative Catholic leaders); by popular resentment (particularly in Budapest) of Jewish war-refugees from Galicia and of war-profiteers often (though by no means always) Jewish; by the depressed standard of living of the intellectual and bureaucratic classes, which launched a search for scapegoats; and by the Ágoston-Jászi affair mentioned in an earlier chapter. See also Schickert, *Die Judenfrage in Ungarn*, p. 139ff.

[39] See for details the obituary of F. Mezey in the *Egyenlőség*, 9 July, 1927, pp. 3—5.

[40] Jászi, as Minister of Nationalities in Count Károlyi's Government late in 1918, through silence allowed the public to think he favored Zionism, and on one occasion (26 November) officially authorized the institution of a provincial Jewish national council. After resigning in January, 1919, he denied any sympathy for Zionism and labelled the ust-mentioned authorization a forgery. But one has only to read the Jewish newspapers of the day to realize that his perhaps careless, perhaps malicious silence while in office was an important reason why middle-class Jewry failed to rally to the Károlyi regime. For details see the *Egyenlőség*, 4 Jan. 1919, p. 3; 18 Jan., pp. 4—5; 28 Jan., pp. 1ff; and I Feb., p. 10. I am indebted to Dr. Richard Allen of New York City for confirmation that Jászi's authorization of the Maramaros Jewish National Council is in the Ministerial Archive in Budapest.

from Hungary, as "liberated" peasants, angry nobles, and urban Germans came together on a platform of anti-Semitism; and as Social-Democrats sought to save the country by fostering a Bolshevik republic. By the end of 1919, when circumstance had brought catastrophe even to the Bolsheviks and made a counterrevolution victorious, anti-Semitism was so strong in Hungary that Vázsonyi, from his point of view the most loyal of the Magyars, could not come home. [41]

Vászonyi came home finally in 1920. He lived to see the worst of the anti-Semitism of the counterrevolution toned down and an attempt made to restore the tolerance of prewar days. But until he died the *numerus clausus*, which his beloved Magyar Parliament had placed in 1920 on the education of Jews in Magyar schools, remained on the books. [42] And the memory lived on that in 1920 Vázsonyi's "Jewish" and "democratic" Budapest had been so terrified that it voted for an anti-Semite rightist city administration. [43] Vázsonyi signified his despair over these facts with two new political stands. On the one hand, though remaining formally a "democrat," he became *Habsburgtreu*, advocating the return of the Monarchical authority. Secondly, while remaining rigidly anti-Zionist, he admitted now the necessity of maintaining relations with foreign Jews. [44] Since in 1905 Vázsonyi had clearly considered the Magyar nationalist Coalition forces a better bet than the King, and since until 1918 he, along with all other Hungarian Neolog Jews, had simply denied the validity of any formal links with foreign Jews, these new stands were tacit admission of the end of his optimism and of the bankruptcy of his career.

In Explanation of Hungary's Scientific Geniuses

With these views of the frustration of the Magyar Jewish middle class in modern Hungary in mind, let us probe now in detail why Hungary produced a galaxy of scientific geniuses in the early twentieth century. Hitherto

---

[41] Vázsonyi returned home briefly in the autumn of 1919, but was attacked so bitterly by anti-Semite forces that he had most unhappily to return to exile. See Pethő, *Viharos emberöltő* p. 240ff.

[42] See the detailed account in Pál Bethlen (ed.), *Numerus Clausus* (Budapest: Magyar Zsidóság Almanachja Könyvkiadó, nd.), pp. 91—135.

[43] See the interesting report in *A Textil*, 6 March, 1920, p. 2.

[44] See the *Egyenlőség*, 4 July, 1925, p. 1. Even now Vázsonyi drew back as soon as the Zionists claimed that his words "essentially" supported their position; but he could not deny that now the Hungarian Jews, like the Russian and Rumanian Jews in the past, were sufficiently in danger to require the benevolence of the international Jewish communities. See his *démenti* in the *Egyenlőség*, 29 August, p. 3.

in this book we have attributed this galaxy in part to the fantasia-like atmosphere of turn-of-the-century Budapest, which stimulated the imagination; in
part to the great urbanization movement of the nineteenth century, which
mobilized both men and minds out of traditional cadres; in part to the peculiar patterns of cultural Westernization in Hungary, which led in the nineteenth century to an extravagant and often shallow nationalism among the
Magyars, Germans, and Jews, and which ended towards 1900 in a revul-
sion-like flight into science among the young; and in part to the triumphs
of the economic "take-off" process in Hungary, which generated enormous
optimism in Man's capacity for material accomplishment. We have not yet
inquired, however, whether specific factors such as personal characteristics,
education, or social experience formed the geniuses. Let us do so now with
the help of Theodore von Kármán, the oldest and one of the greatest of
them, who has bequeathed us an extensive intellectual autobiography. [45]

Von Kármán was born in Budapest in 1881, the son of Mór Kármán,
a university professor from Szeged who was one of the great educational
innovators in modern Hungary. Young Todor (Magyar for Theodore) grew
up in the leading circles of the Budapest late nineteenth-century literati,
living in comfortable flats and villas, schooled as a child by private tutors,
meeting everyone who counted even in Vienna, having entrée into aristocratic circles because his father held a court position. [46] This cultured atmosphere, he claims, was the first specific influence on his intellectual development.

The next specific influence was his formal education. Von Kármán as
a child showed a precocious talent in mathematics; for display he could
multiply six-digit numbers in his head. His father, however, firmly believed
that mathematics was too narrow a specialty. Young von Kármán's first
schooling experience, accordingly, was private tutoring in geography, history,
poetry, and in effect everything that might distract him from mathematics.
Then at the age of nine the future genius was sent to the *Minta* or model
Gymnasium, a school which his father had founded as the "gem" of his educational theories. [47] The basic principles of education in this "nursery for

---

[45] See Theodore von Kármán with Lee Edson, *The Wind and Beyond. Theodore von
Kármán. Pioneer in Aviation and Pathfinder in Space* (Boston: Little, Brown & Co., 1967).

[46] Kármán was given responsibility for planning the education of one of the Habsburg archdukes, and it was for this reason he was ennobled in 1909.

[47] In Magyar the school's name is *Tanárképző Intézet Gyakarló Gimnáziuma*, or
Practice Gymnasium of the Teacher-Training Institute. Organized by Kármán in the
seventies, it was run by the State and was supposed to serve as a model *(minta)* for subsequent expansions of the state educational system.

the elite" were social informality between Hungary's best teachers and students; and "learning from experience."

At no time did we memorize rules from a book. Instead we sought to develop them ourselves. I think this is a good system of education, for in my opinion how one learns the elements of reasoning in primary school will determine his later capacity for intellectual pursuit. In my case the *Minta* gave me a thorough grounding in inductive reasoning, that is, deriving general rules from specific examples — an approach that remained with me throughout my life. [48]

Towards the end of his *Minta* career young von Kármán experienced a third educational stimulus. Each year students in the sciences in all Hungary's high schools were encouraged to compete for a prize named after Lóránt Eötvös, the greatest of a line of nineteenth-century Hungarian scientists. Since a victory in the competition was credited not only to the individual student but also to his teacher, promising aspirants were apt to receive very special training. Young von Kármán, who won the prize in 1897, apparently received his initial grounding in the physical sciences precisely in this highly personal fashion.

The later stages of von Kármán's education followed a different pattern. Dissuaded from a career in mathematics by his father, he entered in 1898 the Royal Joseph University of Technology *(Müegyetem)* at Budapest to study engineering, a profession considered profitable in that era of rapidly developing technology and industrialization in Hungary. There, however the teaching in physics was abominable. Kármán recalls one "pleasant old gentleman" who taught on the basis of unreadable notes taken years earlier at the Technical University in Zurich, and who once wrote a long equation on the blackboard and then remarked: "I don't know whether the symbol here is a 2 or a 'z'... but the equation is correct." [49] The teaching in mathematics, however, was excellent. [50] This first phase in Kármán's higher education resulted, thus accidentally, in confirmation of his natural mathematical talents; and a second phase threw him into the wide world.

Young von Kármán himself was content after graduation from the *Müegyetem* to accept a teaching position there, and to work as engineering advisor to the Ganz Electrical Engine Plant in Budapest. In 1906, however, his father forced him to continue his education abroad.

---

[48] See von Kármán and Edson, *Wind and Beyond*, pp. 21—22.

[49] *Ibid.*, p. 26.

[50] Von Kármán mentions in particular the influence of the internationally known mathematician Gyula König.

My father talked to me long into the evenings. He had grown tired and bitter. I remember his saying one day that he had devoted his life to Hungary, but was unappreciated and even tormented by petty university politics. ... He didn't want me to make the same mistake he had made. If I were going to make something of myself as a scientist and an independent thinker, he insisted that I would have a greater chance outside Hungary. [51]

In October, 1906, accordingly, young von Kármán obtained a fellowship from the Hungarian Academy to study at Göttingen. In that mixing pot of international scientific research he rapidly became involved in the then-new science of aviation and became a founder of modern aerodynamics.

* * *

Theodore von Kármán presents his formative experiences as both typical of those of the entire galaxy of Hungarian scientific geniuses to which he belonged, and contributive to their particular prominence among the scientists of other nations of the modern world. In some ways he is evidently correct. In others, however, his explanations seem inadequate. Let us now examine them one by one.

One factor present in von Kármán's own intellectual formation certainly contributed to most of our other scientific geniuses. As a child von Kármán could multiply huge numbers in his head, evidence that the was naturally endowed with mathematical agility. Edward Teller could do the same, [52] as could John von Neumann, one of the founders of modern computer science. [53] It is of course entirely possible that such prodigious biological material was more present in Hungary at the turn of the century than elsewhere in Europe. As von Kármán stresses, however, there is no means available for balancing Hungary's raw material against that of other lands.

It is safer to attempt explanation of the Hungarian geniuses by studying conditions which favored the maturity of prodigiously endowed minds in Hungary. One of these, according to von Kármán and several others of our scientists, was a tradition of respect for intellectual work, and perhaps particularly for scientific work which pervaded both Magyar and Jewish

---

[51] See von Kármán and Edson, *Wind and Beyond*, p. 33.
[52] See Teller and Brown, *Legacy of Hiroshima*, p. 160.
[53] See J. M. Rosenberg, *Computer Prophets* (New York: Macmillan, 1969), p. 155ff. for some interesting anecdotes about von Neumann's extraordinary mathematical capacities.

society there. [54] Perhaps because in Széchenyi's day Hungary had been so little educated, culture became after mid-century a matter of the highest prestige there. Even one of the makers of the *Ausgleich*, Baron József Eötvös, was a professional educator; and although political Hungary buried Eötvös' most special contribution to education, the famous nationalities education legislation of 1868, its society assigned intellectual accomplishment enormous weight. Ármin Vámbéry, who was born crippled, Jewish, and a pauper, but who managed through education to become an orientalist, the explorer of Moslem Central Asia, and a guest at Windsor Castle, was one of the most respected figures in all modern Hungary, and a member of the magnates' *Nemzeti Casino*. [55] Membership in the Academy of Sciences was one of the highest honors to which a Hungarian of the *Ausgleich* Era could aspire, and particularly in Jewish families, where this Magyar respect for education mingled with Jewish traditions, at least one son in every family was usually encouraged to pursue an intellectual career.

This hardly meant, of course, that large numbers of young middle-class boys were encouraged to go into physics. Traditionally, if an oldest son went into the family business, the second went into law, and a third would become a medical doctor, by no means the same as a physicist. Further, the priesthood, the rabbinate, philosophy, literature, journalism, and the study of economics were all considered much more "suitable" — and profitable — "intellectual" professions than the natural sciences. Yet in nineteenth-century Hungary there was a scientific tradition within the general ecouragement of intellectual work. [56] It began with the Bolyais, father and son, who were mathematicians in the Napoleonic and post-Napoleonic era, and eventually became famous all over Europe as founders of modern geometry. [57] This tradition included a significant physicist, Baron Eötvös' son Lóránt, who did work on gravitation which was recognized all over Europe.

---

[54] See, apart from the recital by von Kármán and Edson, Szilard, as quoted by Alice K. Smith, "The Elusive Dr. Szilard," *Harpers*, Vol. 221, no. 1322 (July, 1960), p. 78; and Franz Alexander, *Western Mind in Transition* (New York: Random House, 1960), p. 43.

[55] See Vámbéry's autobiography which was actually written and first published in English, but appears in Hungarian under the title *Küzdelmeim* [My Struggles].

[56] In the following I have been helped by Drs. Gábor Kemény of Michigan State University and Béla Kovaly of the University of Szeged, who both became biophysicists in the educational atmosphere of post-1945 Hungary; and by a long autobiographical letter from Dr. John Schiffer of the Argonne (Ill.) National Laboratory, who studied Physics after his emigration.

[57] There are excellent short essays on the Bolyai family in G. C. Gillespie (ed.), *Dictionary of Scientific Biography* (New York: Scribners, 1970), Vol. I, pp. 268—271.

The most weighty contributions to this Hungarian scientific tradition, however, were in mathematics. Starting with Gyula König and Moritz Réthi in the 1870's, a strong group of distinguished mathematicians became professors at the Hungarian institutes of higher learning, and members of the Academy of Sciences. [58] They included Emanuel Beke, who until 1900 taught at the *Minta* (and whose brother designed two of Budapest's suspension bridges), and Ignác Rados, who taught in the state gymnasia of the *Lipótváros*. In this atmosphere it was not unusual for young men of mathematical talent to become professional scientists, as most of our geniuses did.

In the decades since Theodore von Kármán's day, moreover, the prestige of science has been considerably enhanced in Hungary in a way which can account for a continued outflow of eminent physicists from that country. Von Kármán himself seems to have played a considerable role all through the twenties and thirties in encouraging talented young men of prominent families in Budapest to come into physics. More than one of them regarded him as an adoptive, and very helpful, "uncle," who was willing and able to equip his protégés with personal introductions to the world's foremost scientific teachers, making it easy for them to leap immediately to the frontiers of knowledge. [59] Further, during this same period (and even more in the 1940's and 1950's) various of the traditional educational disciplines, for example the humanities, economics, and law, became discouraging at home, with the result that many (and not only Jewish) young Hungarians came to elect physics as a prestigious, profitable, and non-political profession.

Hungarian intellectual traditions, then, may be seen as contributants to the successful maturity of many scientific minds in that country. But even

[58] Gyula König and Réthi taught at the *Müegyetem* from 1885 and 1886 respectively until after the first World War, and both were several times Rector and Dean. At the Budapest University their peers were Beke, who received a chair in 1900, Ludwig Schlesinger (briefly in 1911), Lipót Fejér after 1911, and Mihály Fekete from 1914. But most of these latter men were forcibly retired after the first World War. It is worth mentioning that Réthi taught also at the University of Kolozsvár (after 1929, Szeged) from 1874—1886, and was succeeded there by Schlesinger from 1902—1911, Fejér from 1905—1911, and by Frigyes Riesz from 1911 and Adolf Haar from 1912. Other well-known mathematicians of this circle (all of whom were Jewish) were Ferenc Wittmann, and Donát Bánki, both of whom taught physics at the *Müegyetem* after 1890; and Ede Mahler, who as an Egyptologist taught at the Budapest University after 1896 and received a chair in 1914. Short biographies of all these men are in *MZsL*.

[59] Letter from Alexander Szalai of the University of Veszprém to WOMc Jr., 3 April, 1969.

in suggesting this we must exercise caution because of hints we receive from individual geniuses. Edward Teller's lawyer father felt towards the end of the first World War that science offered a way out of the Magyar-Jewish morass, and encouraged his son's mathematical talent. [60] Von Kármán's father, however, though a professional educator, did not do so; nor did John von Neumann's father, who as a banker might have seen the uses of mathematics. [61] Furthermore, as Szilard in particular has stressed, Hungary did not offer prior to 1945 any career prospects to serious students of physics apart from high-school teaching. [62] And after 1919 the country in effect barred Jewish students from University positions altogether. [63]

Further, as soon as we attempt to explain in terms of the cultural background why Hungary produced *more* internationally known geniuses than other countries, we encounter great difficulties. It is simply not self-evident that late nineteenth-century Budapest was any more a center of encouragement for intellectual work, scientific or otherwise, than many other of Europe's great capitals. Perhaps von Kármán did as a child meet a large number of eminent Hungarians and was stimulated. But was not the same sort of contact available to the sons of professors in the Vienna which produced Freud and Kurt Gödel, in the Berlin and Göttingen which produced Planck and von Laue, in the Paris of Poincaré, and in the London of Rutherford? These were conditions typical of professorial circles everywhere in European civilization in the nineteenth century. One may easily conclude that in point of cultural stimulus our geniuses were not so different from other middle-class, educated Europeans.

Let us turn to other specific aspects of the education of our scientific geniuses and observe how even here we encounter difficulties in explaining the emergence of such a galaxy. Von Kármán, for example, stresses not just Budapest's cultural tradition, but very specific educational processes for his formation — the *Minta*, the Eötvös Prize, the peculiarities of the *Müegyetem* — and he implies that these are *the* factors which produced all the geniuses. De Hevesy, Szilard, Thomas Balogh, and Nicholas Kaldor, he says, all attended the *Minta*. [64] "More than half of all the famous expatriate

---

[60] See Teller and Brown, *Legacy of Hiroshima*, pp. 160—161.

[61] See von Kármán and Edson, *Wind and Beyond*, pp. 17, 19, 106—107.

[62] See Alice K. Smith, "The Elusive Dr. Szilard," p. 78; Edward Shils, "Leo Szilard, A Memoir," *Encounter*, Vol. 23 (December, 1964), p. 38.

[63] See Tristram Coffin, "Leo Szilard." *Holiday* (February, 1964), p. 66; and the statement by Wigner to Mrs. Fermi in *Illustrious Immigrants*, p. 54.

[64] See von Kármán and Edson, *Wind and Beyond*, p. 2. Kármán errs apparently in espect to Hevesy, who by his own account attended the Piarist Gymnasium in Budapest.

Hungarian scientists," including Edward Teller, Szilard, George Pólya, and John von Neumann, he points out, all won the Eötvös Prize. [65] Tibor Radó, Szilard, Eugene Wigner, and Teller, we may add, all attended the *Müegyetem*. The trouble here is, however, that though there were elements of community in education among various of these men, they simply did not *all* attend the same schools, nor did they *all* have the same teachers. To the contrary, there are several major variants in their educations.

Numerically, by far the most of the future geniuses attended, not von Kármán's *Minta*, but the fashionable Lutheran Gymnasium in Buda. [66] Georg Lukács has taunted they were taught there as much nonsense as intelligence, [67] and although some of the teachers were from the leading ranks of contemporary Magyar "culture," neither the social informality of the *Minta* nor its stress on intuition was reproduced. One may not conclude, therefore, that the geniuses were molded uniquely by the *Minta* training. One may only estimate that several of the Budapest gymnasia of the day, one of them State run, but others religious, inculcated an elitist outlook in their students, and offered a relatively personal training. And this estimate, of course, raises questions about the entire premise that the gymnasia of Budapest somehow favored the emergence of geniuses. [68] Elitist outlook and personal training were characteristic offerings of high schools all over Europe in that day. In England that was the great age of the "public schools" — religiously oriented boarding institutions. In France and Germany, on the other hand, the state-run urban day-pupil gymnasium held sway. In Vienna there was the Benedictine day-pupil *Schottenschule*. All these schools were different. But all produced elites, and some of them even produced scientists. The Budapest gymnasium system, therefore, was not the clear reason why Hungary came forth with her scientific geniuses.

A better case can be made for the annual competitions on which von Kármán lays such stress. Certainly it stands to reason that a nation which annually encourages bright students to compete in one or another intellectual discipline will tend to produce numerous specialists in that discipline.

---

[65] See von Kármán and Edson, *Wind and Beyond*, p. 23.

[66] Not only Georg Lukács, but so far as I can determine virtually all of the Wigner-Neumann generation of physicists attended the Lutheran Gymnasium in Buda, as did a great many of the young scientists who went to school in Budapest between the wars. Michael Polányi, on the other hand, and Franz Alexander seem to have attended a Gymnasium in Pest.

[67] See "Utam a magyar kultúrához", p. 1018.

[68] I am indebted in the following to conversations with my colleague, Prof. P. R. Duggan.

But again, an international perspective tends to reduce the weight of this factor. France and Italy, where the national high-school competitions were as integral a part of the educational system as in Hungary, certainly shone, as did Hungary, in the production of scientific "geniuses" in the nineteenth and twentieth centuries. But England and Germany, which did not have such competitions, were perhaps more even than France, and certainly more than Italy and Hungary, the epicenters of modern scientific exploration. Competition perhaps helped produce Hungary's galaxy of geniuses, but evidently competition does not explain them.

On the college-level of education as on that of the high-schools there was simply no uniformity in the training of Hungary's great scientists. Some of them, as mentioned above, went like von Kármán to the *Müegyetem*. But since Szilard attributed his success to the low level of the teaching of physics there, [69] while von Kármán admits that many of the professors were excellent, there is a question as to whether the good or the bad in the institution was the more influential. More important, many of the Hungarian scientists — de Hevesy, for example, and Pólya, Karl Mannheim, von Békésy, and von Neumann — attended not the *Müegyetem*, but the Budapest University, where the youngest of them encountered a very specific special influence, one of the greatest of Hungary's mathematics teachers, Lipót Fejér. [70] In addition it is evident that several scientists never attended any Hungarian college-level institution. One, in fact, specifically attributes his excellence to the fact that he went directly from his gymnasium to the German universities. [71] This is significant, because from von Kármán right down the line all of Hungary's scientific geniuses received the bulk of their university training and higher education in great schools of the West, such as Vienna, Göttingen, Berlin, Leipzig, Munich, Zurich, and Karlsruhe. [72] Since they were on a par in those schools with students from every other European nation, and since the characteristic of those schools was their internationalism, it is difficult to conclude that Hungary's geniuses were on this level of their training anything but typical Europeans.

---

[69] See the references in notes 62 and 63 above.

[70] See Clay Blair. Jr., "Passing of a Great Mind, John von Neumann," *Life*, 25 Feb., 1957, p. 90. Comp. von Kármán and Edson, *Wind and Beyond*, p. 179.

[71] Alexander Szalai to WOMc Jr., 29 April, 1969.

[72] Mrs. Fermi, after studying some 100 Hungarian emigré intellectuals, claims that most of them studied at Hungarian or Austrian universities, and on this basis tends to reject the thesis that the Hungarians were products of German higher education. Her claim is based, of course, on the premise that Vienna was not a "German" or "foreign" University from the Hungarian point of view — a premise which may be questioned. See *Illustrious Immigrants*, pp. 111—112.

* * *

With this we may proceed to the final factor to which von Kármán attributes his emergence as an international scientific genius — the factor which in our opinion best accounts for the emergence of the whole galaxy to which he belonged — his emigration under special circumstances. [7]

Emigration means that an individual has emerged permanently on one level or another from the local (or in modern terms "national") environment in which he was born. Since emigration can be spiritual as well as physical, the internationally known scientist is in a sense invariably someone who has emigrated. Even if he still lives in his birthland, physically, his knowledge in this century is by definition international, and his education is as often as not in an international school.

But let us make some distinctions in the types of scientific emigration, which will help us pinpoint the peculiarities of our Hungarian geniuses. Let us distinguish in the first place between spiritual emigration, or the temporary physical emigration entailed in leaving one's home to attend a university, on the one hand, and permanent physical emigration — i.e., brain drain — on the other. Further, let us distinguish within this area of brain drain between voluntary emigration and involuntary or violent emigration. Let us suppose that the former is relatively compatible with productive intellectual work, because it presumably involves minimal emotional distraction, whereas the latter — the suddenly forced emigration — is less compatible with intellectual work because of presumable contingent emotional disturbances.

In this framework it becomes evident that spiritual and educational emigration have been universal phenomena in the past century, affecting Americans as well as the inhabitants of all European lands; but that the physical emigration, which von Kármán and most of our other Hungarian scientific geniuses chose, was largely an East European phenomenon until 1933. One may not forget that after 1848 some intellectuals went into exile from France, Italy, and Germany. But these were few indeed in comparison to the massive emigration from Poland after the revolts of 1830 and 1863; or to the great flights from tyranny in Hungary after 1848 and from Russia all through the nineteenth century. In our own century, moreover, the great

---

[73] Since the following pages describe aspects of modern European history which are common knowledge, footnotes seem superfluous. An intelligent and well-documented review of the subject, albeit with emphasis on the emigration to the United States, is in Laura Fermi, *Illustrious Immigrants*, Chs. 2—4.

permanent migration of intellectuals began in 1914 in Eastern Europe, whereas in Germany and the West of Europe and even in Italy it became pronounced only after 1933.

Let us go a step further, and trace the emigration patterns of intellectuals in Eastern Europe since 1900. We can thereupon perceive that in the Far East of Europe — in Russia — the whole educated society was subjected to violent disruption in the years after 1917, which resulted in a substantial violent emigration of scientists, alongside many others. In Eastern Europe proper, on the other hand, though there was considerable violent disruption of society after 1914, and much movement of intellectuals, there was outside of Hungary rather little violent emigration. Moreover, even the Hungarians who like Georg Lukács became refugees after the collapse of the Bolshevik Republic in 1919 had certain advantages over the Russians. They were very few in number, and thus not a glut on the market. When in real need they could rely in many cases on relatives who still had property at home, and who could bring it out. And it is a matter of record that most of the Hungarian intellectuals who, like our scientific geniuses, went abroad after the first World War did so under far more favorable circumstances than Lukács. Von Neumann, for example, used to go home for summer vacations from Princeton as late as 1938, more than a decade after his emigration.

Outside of Russia, thus, the East European emigration of intellectuals prior to 1933 was primarily non-violent, and here we can make another distinction. The movement of intellectuals in Eastern Europe in the 1920's went in two directions. The Magyars, on the whole, like the Russians, went West for, as we have seen earlier in this chapter, the Magyars and particularly the Jews among them had a clear view even before the war that their horizons at home were narrow. They had also lost the war and seen Budapest terribly reduced in status. Austrians, we may note, also went West. But even the Austrians, though they like the Magyars had lost the war and seen their Vienna reduced to the rump capital of a rump state, did not flee massively, if only because they were Germans — and because Germany, unlike Hungary, was still the scientific center of all Europe. For most of the rest of Eastern Europe, moreover, the years immediately after 1918 were years not of emigration for intellectuals but of patriotism.

Most East Europeans had in a sense won the first World War. Poland was recreated. Czechoslovakia, Yugoslavia, and Albania were created for the first time. Rumania was vastly enlarged, as was Greece. Intellectuals of those countries tended thus after 1918 to stay at home; and emigré intellectuals tended to come home. Paderewski is a shining example. And with this observation we can arrive at a first perception of what was special about four Hungarian emigrating scientists. In effect they came from the only country of Eastern Europe whence brain drain was unmistakably advisable, but yet neither forced nor inhibited at the end of the first World War. From 1906 onwards Magyar intellectuals had a clearer and more consistent vision of the bleakness of their future at home than any other intellectuals in Europe; yet they were subjected to none of the pressures to get out which destroyed the Russian educated classes. And while nationalism raged in inter-war Hungary, it was a nationalism of defeat, which after the initial shock exerted none of the pressures to stay at home which inhibited the other East Europeans.

Nor is this the whole of the story, for after 1933 the Hungarian intellectuals enjoyed a very special status in Europe. In Germany after the rise of Hitler all intellectuals were subjected to extreme political pressures. The Jews, on the one hand, were systematically degraded, and eventually they were either forced into penniless exile or were destroyed. Older and well-known scientists among them were able to survive this treatment; but beginners suffered extremely. And on the other hand, "aryan" intellectuals in Hitlerite Germany were subjected to extreme pressure to stay at home, and the bulk of the younger men were trapped and forced to await what the future might bring them at home. The disaster of the German intellectuals was followed by disasters elsewhere. Austrians, for example, whether Jewish or not, were able to feel confident staying at home virtually up till the last minute in March, 1938. Then suddenly they were trapped. The Sigmund Freuds among them were rescued, but the young and less famous were condemned to the war. In Czechoslovakia prior to Munich all the pressures on intellectuals were to stay at home. Then, during a period of less than half a year, the wise, the agile, and the unpatriotic had opportunity both to sense the coming catastrophe and freely to emigrate; whereupon in March, 1939, the trap closed for the Czechs, too. Next in Poland the trap sprang. During the 1930's, no doubt, the Poles could sense their danger. They were ruled by a dictatorship. Anti-Semitism was rife. Many Jewish intellectuals seem to have emigrated to France and Palestine, but in that land where after 1918 the centripetal force of nationalism had operated most strongly to bring intellectuals home, it kept them there just as strongly until September, 1939. Then with lightning speed the country was invaded and partitioned, and its intellectual elite was systematically exterminated. Of all the national educated strata in Europe after 1939, the Poles were among the most brilliant, and among the most sorely wounded by the war.

We need not continue this survey save to note that in Yugoslavia and Greece the pattern was similar to that of Germany and Poland, whereas in

Hungary, Rumania, and Bulgaria alone the patterns were different. In Hungary and in Rumania an unsubtle persecution of Jews began in 1938, and drove many intellectuals into sudden exile or worse. But generally speaking the pressure on Jews in Hungary was much less than 'in Rumania;[74] and it was possible in all three of these countries for non-Jewish intellectuals to make a relatively comfortable emigration virtually until the start of the Russian war in 1941. And here another sort of conditioning enters our considerations. If we judge the size of the intellectual community of an East European country from the size of its main city, the Rumanian intelligentsia was well under half the size of Hungary's, while the Bulgarian group was smaller still by far. This same rule applies to the intelligentsias of Yugoslavia and Greece, which were trapped later than those of Central and Northern Europe. It follows that Hungary was the country of Eastern Europe with a large intelligentsia from which comfortable emigration was possible longest after 1933.

* * *

As one examines the emigration patterns of the Hungarian geniuses with whom we are concerned, one discovers over and again that their emigration was voluntary and comfortable. The experience of the famous physicists is adequately illustrative. The eldest, von Kármán, obtained a teaching position at Aachen in 1912 as a direct offshoot of his Göttingen education.[75] He kept this while retaining his Hungarian citizenship until 1933. Yet mean-

---

[74] In 1938, after the *Anschluss,* conditions for Jews became disagreeable in both Hungary and Rumania. In Hungary a first "Jewish Law" was passed, which limited the percentile of unconverted Jews in schools and economic enterprises. This did not drastically inconvenience the richer middle classes, because there were possibilities of conversion and evasion. But a second "Jewish Law" in May, 1939, defined as "Jewish" anyone who had converted since 1919, and also narrowed the percentile of Jews allowable in enterprise ownership and substituted labor service for military conscription of Jews. This was inconvenient. Nonetheless, it was not until the "Jewish Laws" of 1941 that the Jews of Hungary were systematically subjected to persecution, and they retained until 1944 civic rights which had long since disappeared everywhere else in German-dominated Europe. In Rumania the major anti-Semitic legislation did not appear until June, 1940. Historically, however, Jews had been subject to considerably worse treatment in Rumanian than in Hungary. In 1938 they were subject to extensive terrorism by fascist legions, such as did not occur in Hungary until 1944. Terrorism on a much larger scale occurred in 1940 and 1941. Consequently, though the Jews of Rumania in the end survived those of Hungary, one may estimate that the "trap" closed in Rumania years before it did so in Hungary. A convenient comparative evaluation of these subjects in M. Nagy-Talavera *The Green Shirts and Others* (Stanford: Hoover Institute, 1970), Chs. 4, 5, 10, 11.

[75] For the following, see von Kármán and Edson, p. 140ff.

while he frequently traveled, among other places to Pasadena, California, and from 1926 onwards his friends there were extending him invitations to come permanently to the United States. In 1929, as anti-Semitism began to appear seriously in Germany, he made an arrangement to work part of each year in Pasadena; and consequently it was simple to break his ties with Europe finally in 1933 when Hitler purged the German universities. This emigration, in a word, was hardly different from pursuit of normal career interests, and though he was fifty when he came to America, von Kármán's work experienced none of the interruptions entailed by violent displacement.

Correspondingly, John von Neumann removed from Hungary immediately after receiving his degrees from Budapest and Zurich in 1926, apparently as a result of his dislike for Hungary's counterrevolution. [76] He settled in Berlin and then Hamburg for three years. But then, in the wake of a lecture tour in the United States in 1930, he was invited to join the faculty at Princeton and did so, not because of German anti-Semitism, but because of his computation that his chances of advancement were better at Princeton than in Germany. As in the case of von Kármán, the movement of von Neumann's career was determined by his abilities, and was hardly comparable to the disaster-harried careers of the Germans, Austrians, Poles and others who later on had to flee, without warning or substance, from their homes.

Von Kármán and von Neumann together served as the base for the approach of the other Hungarian physicists to this country. Most of these, and also numbers of the great Hungarian emigré mathematicians, had obtained employment either before or after the war at German universities. Some, for instance Teller, attribute their leaving home originally to the anti-Semitism of the counterrevolution. Others, however (and even Wigner, who confesses to having been physically beaten up by anti-Semites in Hungary)[77], attribute their original emigration simply to the tightness of employment conditions in Hungary, or to the "decadence" and conservatism of Hungarian society. They did not have to leave: they chose to leave. Even before the German catastrophe in 1933 Wigner had followed von Neumann to Princeton. And the others seem to have been far less affected by it than were their German colleagues. Szilard, for example, according to a popular tale left Berlin with a pre-packed suitcase on the "last uninspected train"

---

[76] For the following see the biographical sketches in *Current Biography*, 1955; and *Life*, 25 Feb., 1957, pp. 89—104.

[77] See his explanation to Mrs. Fermi, *Illustrious Immigrants*, p. 54.

after the *Reichstag* fire in 1933. [78] Yet he was in a position in the following years to help organize the rescue mission for the German refugees, and he moved freely from London to America to Zurich and back with his valid Hungarian passport. [79] In 1937 he came to the United States, apparently while still holding a position at Oxford, and then decided to stay, deliberately, though he could have gone back to England. [80] Teller's case was similar. He had to leave Göttingen in 1933; but he was young and brilliant and evidently moved to Copenhagen, London, and Washington, D.C., not as an indigent wanderer, but according to his scholarly interests. [81]

Our general conclusion from this discussion of emigration is that Hungary differed from almost all other East European — and indeed, European — countries in the twentieth century in the sense that the comfortable emigration of her intellectuals became uninhibitedly advisable earlier and remained possible later. This is a sort of broad factor which should appeal to a sociologist seeking to understand such a phenomenon as the emergence of many highly specialized intellectuals from one country onto the world stage. It implies that not biology or any special educational factor in Hungary was responsible for so many emigrations, but simply the fact that the door was long open and the pressures were long there. And because of this factor, we can return now to the thesis which binds this whole book together.

Hungary's capitalists ennobled early in the twentieth century in large numbers, not least of all because of the great political crisis which affected the country after 1900, and because of its peculiar, retrogressive outcome. Now we perceive that the same crisis and the same outcome contributed critically to the emergence of Hungary's internationally known geniuses. A bleakness of middle-class outlook resulted in Hungary from that crisis. This was what made Hungary unique in Eastern Europe in the following thirty-five years as a country from which intellectuals did not have to go abroad, but could find it advisable at their leisure to do so. And perhaps one may add that they were so fertile abroad for the same reason. Perhaps they have seemed to outshine the geniuses of other nations because their careers were consistent. Emigration did not interrupt their life work, as it did for the scientists of most other European lands. The Hungarians came abroad comfortably because of 1906.

---

[78] See the autobiographical fragment in Donald Fleming and Bernard Bailyn (eds.), *The Intellectual Migration*, (Cambridge: Harvard University Press, 1969), pp. 95—96.

[79] See the portrait by Edward Shils, *Encounter*, December, 1964, p. 33ff.

[80] See Shils, *Encounter*, December, 1964, p. 39; and *Current Biography*, 1947, p. 623.

[81] See Fermi, *Illustrious Immigrants*, pp. 177, 179.

CHAPTER IX

EPILOGUE

Let us recapitulate. This book has shown analytically that surprisingly similar factors led to two important phenomena in modern Hungarian history: first to the socio-political collaboration of Hungary's Jewish capitalists with the country's nobiliary old regime; and secondly to the emergence of a galaxy of distinguished Hungarian scientists on the international scene. The book has also had a narrative aspect: it has unrolled the history of Hungary's modern urban non-laboring classes, or bourgeoisie. Now at the end we must pull these aspects together. To do so let us point out that our analysis has left a question begging.

Can we claim here towards the end of the story that the emergence of Hungary's scientific geniuses bears a proven special relationship to the collaboration of the country's bourgeoisie? Perhaps not. We have shown that both phenomena resulted from the overall experience of the bourgeoisie in Hungary, but it is not clear yet whether these two phenomena are the only results of that experience. Nor is it clear whether the one may be considered in some sense a result of the other. This question of the linkage between the two phenomena is important, because from some points of view the emergence of the geniuses from Hungary may not even seem very pertinent to the collaboration of the bourgeoisie. For example, might it not have been more pertinent to link the collaboration of the nineteenth-century Hungarian bourgeoisie to the dilemma of the interwar middle-classes in Hungary, and to the eventual destruction of the Jews there? These were phenomena which, much more recognizably than the emergence of scientific geniuses, resulted from the bourgeois experience we have narrated.

Fortunately, it is not difficult to describe the real connection which binds the two phenomena. To do so let us rehearse very briefly the narrative we have told. The story began when the great urban and industrial revolutions of the past two centuries first affected Hungary and mobilized the country's

223

society out of agrarian lethargy. At the start, until the middle of the nineteenth century, this mobilization was slow, and in a sense quiet, since in
significant part it took the form not of peasants moving into towns but of
wandering Jewish traders moving into Hungary. But then after mid-century
the mobilization accelerated. The twin cities of Pest and Buda in particular
grew by leaps and bounds. Within decades they constituted a great European metropolis in the heart of Pannonia, the nucleus of a modern urban
industrial society. In order to perceive the linkage between the two phenomena described in this book, let us premise that this mobilization released
huge energies, and that our study has really concerned how those enormous energies could be and were spent. So doing, we can perceive that
this has been a tale of deviations.

The new urban classes of Budapest, who were the main vehicles of
this energy, emerged in this land of noble hegemony with no tradition
of urban political power or social dignity to guide them. Indeed, in so
far as they were Jewish they bore the outcast stigma of the medieval ghetto
and from the start tended to subservience in the tradition of the Viennese
court bankers. Further, they could see that the banners of European Liberalism were already waving in the hands of the Magyar-speaking Hungarian
nobility. Consequently, though in economic matters they were purveyors
of the new secular and rationalized values of the European Enlightenment,
the new bourgeoisie of Pest and Buda fell easily, and even insensibly, into
the paths of social and political Liberalism which the nobility had cut for
them. In these directions, thereupon, the exigencies of the Jewish striving
for emancipation and the very forms of Hungary's peculiar economic growth
process pressed them on.

If, accordingly, one may premise that the new energies released by the
great mobilization were "naturally" inclined towards the democratizing
social and political forms we know in the modern West, then one may
see that in Hungarian conditions of the nineteenth century those energies
went astray.

By the end of the nineteenth century and in the first years of the twentieth, as the crisis of European civilization erupted, the energies of the new
urban and industrial Hungary reached an impasse. Externally the mobilization was crowned with success: Budapest was built; factories began to
produce; great wealth became available. But beneath the surface there
was a closing of horizons, an overcentralization of the economy, and a
forced and corrupt political compromise which for the middle classes in
general but particularly for Jews spelled frustation in the future. Hungary
after 1906 was for young men of the urban mobilized society increasingly

a seeming dead-end. Competition was becoming acute for every job in every profession. No one received anything any longer by right, or by simple adventure, as in the past. The economy was too narrow, and the political system was too tight to allow continuation of the exuberant growth of earlier years. Success was obviously possible for Man — this was the lesson of the Hungarian economic take-off; but success was not possible here and now — this was the lesson of the outcome of the turn-of-the-century crisis.

With this we come to the point. The energies of the great mobilization in Hungary were forced on the material level into the collaboration and compromise which have formed one of the prongs of this study. They could escape, in the long run, as energy tends to escape, only through sublimation and emigration — which means with no stretch of the imagination, through the intellectual expressions which have been the other prong of our study. Otherwise put, the collaboration of the bourgeoisie in Hungary and the emergence of the Hungarian geniuses were the two faces of the same coin. They were not the whole faces, perhaps, but they were the main faces.

* * *

Recognition of this functional relation between the ennoblement of Hungary's Jewish capitalists and the emergence of Hungary's great scientists onto the international stage has interesting implications for East European history. Let us recall, to observe this, that the great demographic mobilization of modern times took place in all the vast lands which lie eastward from the Elbe and the Adriatic substantially as it did in Hungary, and decidedly differently from its patterns in the West. *

The newness of Budapest as a city, and of her capitalists as a social group, after 1867 was nothing extraordinary in Eastern Europe, where urban life had in general stood still for 200 years prior to 1800. The two greatest metropoli of the whole region, Berlin and Saint Petersburg, were entirely new cities, as were to a large degree all the Balkan capitals and Lódz (a small village until the final decades of the nineteenth century) and Odessa (founded in 1794 yet blessed with half a million souls in 1900). Besides, even in the older cities of Eastern Europe such as Prague and Warsaw, there seems to have been just as comprehensive a turn-over of the burgher class as there was in Budapest. In the West of course there were

---

* "Western Europe" in the following context includes England, France, the Lowlands, Switzerland, and peripherally Western Germany and Northern Italy — but not Spain and Sweden.

Liverpools, Manchesters, and Essens in great numbers, which were wholly
as new as were the new cities of the East. Yet none were so central to
political power as was Budapest; and in the cities which were politically
important in the West — London, Paris, Amsterdam, and some of the
German towns — there was nothing comparable to the emergence and
commercial domination of entirely new cultural elements such as the Czechs
in Prague and of the Jews in Warsaw and Budapest. In the West the new
people of the cities carried on the traditions and political aspirations of
burghers of the past.

In Eastern Europe as a whole the nineteenth century witnessed not
only a net urban growth, which in individual cases, such as Budapest,
outstripped that of the West, but also a virtual refoundation of the cities.
For such a tremendous release of energies, moreover, there was hardly
anywhere in Eastern Europe, any more than in Hungary, a democratizing
tradition. In the huge band of territory once held by Poland-Lithuania,
moreover, as in the Germanies, the Habsburg dominions and Rumania,
Jews played a sizeable part in the vanguard of the bourgeoisie, and thus
lent it their peculiar heritage of social and political attitudes. And then
Westernization had similar effects all over Eastern Europe to those it had
in Hungary.

In the West the eighteenth-century Enlightenment began in many places,
indigenously, not just around Paris and London, but at Florence and Weimar, Brunswick and Rotterdam; and in the West it blossomed as it were
from below. In the East, even at Berlin and Vienna, and particularly at
Saint Petersburg, it was from the start imported, just as it was in Hungary,
and imposed from above. What is more, the Enlightenment found not
just Hungary, but the whole East of Europe far less developed socially,
politically, and economically, than it found the West; and it found in the
East two important features which were hardly present in the West: the
enserfment of the bulk of the population; and a linguistic fractionalizaton
which in no way corresponded to the existing state frontiers. Generally
speaking, therefore, the Enlightenment, which in the West had stressed
empirical Reason and rationalization, became all over the East of Europe,
as in Hungary, a movement stressing organic Reason and resentment of
things foreign; reflecting the extreme difficulties of effecting political and
social change; and giving voice to linguistic nationalism.

To claim that the patterns of the Hungarian Westernization process
were a precise model for Westernization elsewhere East of the Elbe would
be pretentious. In Poland, to mention one exception, the Enlightenment
began in the mid-eighteenth century in a cultivated, sovereign society such

as a century later Széchenyi's "fallow land," Hungary, could not boast. Yet Poland underwent a terrible reversal of fortunes, losing her sovereignty, enduring awful blood-letting, ripped to pieces by wars and revolutions. After 1830, as a result, Poland entered an "intelligentsia" form of development from which Hungary after 1860 would escape. Comparably profound differences between the cultural development of Hungary, and those of Russia, of the Balkan lands, of Eastern Germany, and even of Austria and Bohemia need not be detailed here to establish our point. There was no single Westernization process in Eastern Europe.

Yet even so there were similarities, which stand out when one compares the Hungarian model of Westernization with that of the West. In Poland and the Danubian Principalities, for example, as in Hungary, one can find that the bearers of the Enlightenment, and particularly of the new ideological nationalism of the nineteenth century, were not burghers, as in the West, but nobles who forced the burghers to collaborate. In the southern Balkan lands as in Hungary one can find new multi-class societies holding together despite tremendous and obvious social and economic imbalances, because of a strong popular nationalism aimed against a "foreign" ruler. In Prussia and in Russia all through the nineteenth century, as in Hungary towards its end, one can find a backward-looking state bureaucracy stealing the wind of a prospectively liberal urban class by deliberately usurping the banners of nationalism. These and many other trends we have observed in Hungary are characteristically East European, and largely absent from the West, where the Enlightenment remained on its original empirical keel, and even from Germany and Italy, where nationalism did play a considerable role.

From Hungary's example we can learn much also that was characteristic of the economic growth process all over Eastern Europe, though again there are obvious irregularities deriving from geography, social complexion and political regime. All these regions, for example, began the nineteenth century with the problem of stagnant, latifundium agrarianism, compounded by legal serfdom. This was as it was in Hungary; and as in Hungary, so elsewhere all over Eastern Europe emancipation of the serfs played an immense role in the process of modernization. Sometimes, as in Prussia, emancipation occurred early in the nineteenth century; elsewhere, as in Russia and Rumania, it occurred only in the 1860's. In some places, as in Serbia, Bohemia, and Bulgaria, it was an effective emancipation once it occurred. In other places, as in Hungary, the peasantry remained landless and burdened by debt. But everywhere, emancipation was the radical step which released the forces of modernization.

Correspondingly, as in Hungary, so from one end of Eastern Europe to the other the salient features of the emergent industrial economy of the later nineteenth century were profoundly similar. These were, first, the importance of agriculture-dependent industries; secondly, the entrepreneurial prominence of banking and finance; thirdly, the critical role of foreign capital and manufactures; and fourthly, the dependence on a political state. The combinations of these elements were various. In Russia, for example, the state for a long time tended to substitute for large financial organizations, and the railroads were built far more through state subsidies than through private finance. In the Balkans, on the other hand, the role of foreign capital and foreign economic personnel was significantly greater than that of native capital and entrepreneurs. In point of time, moreover, the emergence of these features varied greatly. In Prussia industrialization began early in the century; in the Balkans and in parts of provincial Russia it was hardly begun on the eve of the first World War. Yet throughout Eastern Europe in the first years of our own century one could find in one degree or another similar patterns of precocious economic growth, guided by huge, invisible, central financial institutions, backed by state machines, having an overtone of colonialism, which in the ruins of feudal agrarianism in Hungary led to significant political collaboration by the bourgeoisie with the old regime.

Our Hungarian example tells us finally that there were great similarities in the effects of the turn-of-the-century European crisis all over the East of Europe. In England and France the years after 1900 saw the institutions and ennobled classes of the past fall into headlong retreat. In Eastern Europe, on the other hand, as in Hungary, the crisis attested in most places the inability of the urban non-laboring classes to grab political power. Everywhere east of the Rhine, despite the introduction of universal suffrage in Germany and Austria, the outcome of the political struggle between "democracy" and "reaction" remained very much in doubt in 1914 — witness the immense power easily assumed by the military even in Germany the moment the war began. In Russia the forces of "democracy" were bloodily defeated, and autocracy, despite the constitutional *dumas*, ruled on. Nor was this East-West division regarding the outcome of the great crisis after 1900 exclusively a matter of the overwhelming military power of the forces of the past. Frequently, as in Hungary, there was an element of "bourgeois" compromise: it was a Russian, Peter Struve, indeed, who in 1899, wrote:

The farther to the east in Europe, the more politically weak, cowardly, and base the bourgeoisie becomes, and the greater the cultural and political tasks of the proletariat. On its strong shoulders the... working class must and will carry the cause of winning political liberties. Even in the Balkans after 1900, though the trends and tendencies there had a special cast because the states were officially bourgeois and liberal, one could observe a coming-together, on an increasingly corrupt basis, of the urban classes and the state machines against the peasant population.

Exceptions, seeming and real, to this pattern of the great crisis in Eastern Europe, of course, existed. In Bohemia, for example, due to the very special ideological and political directions of the Czech nation, the old classes and the old state were overthrown in 1918, and in the wake of the war practicing democracy emerged. It is very difficult to classify the political regime of interwar Czechoslovakia as a specimen of some sort of collaboratory activity by the bourgeoisie. Yet in Serbia, another seeming exception, the forces of social radicalism which rose to power in 1903 turned out in interwar Yugoslavia to be oligarchical, selfish, and exploitive both of other classes and of other nations. Further, these exceptions cannot conceal the real uniformity revealed by the fate of the bourgeoisies of Eastern Europe after 1917. This is not to suggest that the denouement of 1948 was inevitable; but it is to indicate that behind the dazzling diversity of Eastern Europe's independence between the wars, there existed already dependences and dangers which gave all the independent nations a community of possible fate. Nowhere in Eastern Europe was the future of urban non-laboring society really promising after 1917.

The efflorescence of Hungary's geniuses after 1906 may, thus, have a more than just Hungarian significance. The energies released by the great mobilization of our times in Eastern Europe were everywhere deviated, as in Hungary, though in vastly different forms, and for very different reasons, into material narrows. In all that area, therefore, there existed similar reasons for sublimation of such energies in intellectual work and emigration. We have shown that the Hungarian scientists are numerous on the international scene above all because, by quirk of fate, emigration was clearly advisable for them earlier, and comfortably possible for them later than for other East European intellectuals. Does it not follow that the Hungarian scientific geniuses, their atom bombs, their mathematical breakthroughs, and their psychoanalysis are the obverse, not simply of the collaboration of Hungary's Jewish bourgeoisie, but of the failings of the bourgeoisies all over the East of Europe?

Appendix A

CONTROL GROUPS

In a study such as ours it is necessary somehow to control the conclusions we derive from data about our sample. The problem of control is complicated here by two facts. First in terms of background and profession the Jewish nobility represented the entire disparate Jewish population of Old Hungary; and in terms of wealth and culture they were remarkably diverse. It follows that just one control group will be insufficient to check the entire sample. Secondly, far less information is available about private citizens of Old Hungary who did not obtain nobility than about those who did. This means that the preparation of control groups is considerably more difficult than preparation of the noble group itself.

It has seemed both reasonable and practicable to establish two major control groups. They correspond to Hungary's economic elite at the turn of the twentieth century and between the wars (see tables in Chapter II). These groups comprise 504 and 767 places, respectively. [1] In preparing them, the major problem was determining who was Jewish and who was not, for only the Jews afford a basis for detailed comparison with the members of the Jewish nobility. This problem was complicated by the name-Magyarization which was astoundingly widespread at the upper levels of nineteenth-century Budapest society. On the whole the Pest Israelite Community suffrage lists (mentioned in the bibliographical essay below), together with materials available at Budapest's Jewish Museum and material relative

---

[1] The more important, pre-1918, control group I constructed myself in 1966. The collation of information regarding the second, interwar, control group was largely the work of my assistants in 1969, Edit Mirlay and Márta Tömöry. For details and sources, see Chapter II.

to the Jewish laws of 1938 and 1939, [2] made a satisfactory identification of the Jews in the control groups possible, though there are some doubtful cases. With the help of the extra-archival registers and the Jewish *Lexicon*, it has been possible to accumulate personal and economic data regarding almost all the Jewish members of these central groups.

Several other control groups emerge from the various extra-archival registers (mentioned in the bibliographical essay). Of these the most significant are the Budapest virilist lists, each of which contains 1,200 names with a minimal identification. In recent years a Hungarian scholar, Károly Vörös of the Budapest Historical Museum, has compared several of these lists with other sources and has thus amassed considerable information about many of the people named. [3] Through isolation of those virilists who appear on the Pest Community suffrage lists, it has been possible to achieve a large scale professional profile of pre-1918 Budapest Jewry with which to compare the Jewish nobility. Other less important control groups emerging from the extra-archival records comprise the Jewish directors of companies in various economic fields; Jewish landlords; and Jewish members of Parliament.

Another, more delicate control problem regards the socially collaborative direction of the Jews who acquired nobility. After 1918 the Jewish nobles became rapidly less conspicuous in Hungary's public life. Does this mean, however, that the political and social compromise symbolized before the war by the ennoblement movement ended? Could it not mean simply that since there was no longer a king, there could be no more ennoblements? To resolve the question of precisely when the collaboration

---

[2] Through comparison of the *Compass* volumes for 1938 and 1940, it proved possible to resolve a great many questions regarding who, in the directorships of various banks and industrial enterprises, was considered Jewish. In many doubtful cases, also, Dr. Károly Jenei of the Hungarian National Archive was kind enough to check the Jewish-Law materials in the Archive, which were inaccessible to me personally. For this and other favors I am greatly indebted to Dr. Jenei's profound acquaintance with interwar Hungary's business community.

[3] Vörös has published a paper on the virilists, "Budapest legnagyobb adófizetői, 1903—1917" [Budapest's Highest Taxpayers], *Tanulmányok Budapest multjából*, Vol. XVII (1966), pp. 145—196. Apart from this he has prepared an unpublished book-length study, comparing the lists of 1873 and 1888, entitled *Budapest legnagyobb adófizetői a XIX század utolsó negyedében* [Budapest's Highest Taxpayers in the Last Quarter of the 19th Century]. He has very kindly allowed me to use this in manuscript and to use the personnel cards on which he based his conclusions. It is characteristic of the problems of working on the history of Budapest in the late nineteenth century that Vörös had to derive his information, to a considerable extent, from street address books and address lists of Budapest businesses.

between the Jewish new class and the Hungarian Establishment ended, it seemed desirable to locate an index in the interwar period comparable to the prewar ennoblement movement. Such a measure appeared in Regent Horthy's distribution during the interwar years of the title *"Kormány Főtanácsos,"* or "High Government Councilor," and of membership in the Upper House of Parliament, which was restored in 1927. The collection of Jewish High Government Councilors and Jewish Upper House members makes very clear how long the collaboration which interests us continued. [4]

These large and small control groups notwithstanding, this study depends extensively on the method of control through comparison of individual members of the Jewish nobility with prominent individuals who remained outside it. This method is fallible, but two factors contribute substantially to its utility. The first is that the Jewish noble group in its broadest sense (in other words, including retroactively all male members of each family which received nobility) is extraordinarily comprehensive. So many of the most prominent Jews of nineteenth-century Hungary were in this sense involved in the noble group that the method of control by groups is futile. The second reason why the method of individual comparisons seems valid in this study is that the Jewish *Lexicon* is a very nearly comprehensive catalogue of prominent Hungarian Jews. Insofar as one depends on the outside individuals mentioned in the *Lexicon*, and designated by the *Lexicon* as prominent, one is in effect using an exhaustive control group embracing all Hungarian Jewry in the Dualistic period.

---

[4] The problems of identifying the High Government Councilors are sufficiently similar to those of identifying the Jewish nobles, discussed in Chapter I, as not to require repetition. Suffice it to mention that since the number of Councilors was extremely large, since many were very obscure, and since certainty of identification was not central to my work, I depended extensively on certain rules for eliminating Christians from the list. For example, when an unknown name ended in "y," I presumed him non-Jewish. Correspondingly, I eliminated Italian, French, and Slavic names mechanically in all cases where there was no certainty that a person was Jewish; and I elimi.ated more or less mechanically all unknown provincial bureaucrats. On the other hand, for reasons of expediency, I accepted without documentation the personal recollection of Dr. Jenei that a limited number of High Councilors whom he had known were Jewish.

APPENDIX B

BIBLIOGRAPHICAL ESSAY *

As individuals the Jewish nobles were prominent citizens but usually not great historical personages. Perhaps in most countries it would be difficult today to accumulate consistent information about 346 prominent families of the last century. [1] In Hungary, where wars and revolutions have taken an awful toll of private and public records, and where persecution of Jews and nobles has scattered the descendants of our group, the problems of obtaining information about the Jewish nobility are very great.

A logical source of information about the prominent citizens in the Jewish nobility might seem the Hungarian National Archives in Budapest. [2] In effect, because these prominent citizens took the trouble to acquire nobility, the Archives probably contain more information about them than about most other groups of citizens, much less Jewish citizens, of Old Hungary. There are serious difficulties involved in using the ennoblement records in the Archives, however. For example, three principal Hungarian

---

* The reader may find in the name index below an alphabetical listing of works cited in the footnotes of this book, but not mentioned in this essay.

[1] For discussion of the problems of defining a Jewish noble see Chapter I above.

[2] For the reader's convenience we repeat here that the Archives contain three main sets of dossiers which relate to ennoblement. First are the records of the Hungarian Minister-Attached-to-His-Majesty's-Person, which were sent from Vienna to Budapest under the Treaty of St. Germain. These contain copies of the actual patents of nobility, documentation needed to obtain it, and materials relating to coats of arms. Unfortunately, much of this documentation was not kept, and because of a peculiar filing system the dossiers are often impossible to locate. The second set of dossiers those of the Hungarian Minister of the Interior, are easier to work with. The third set of dossiers, those of the Hungarian Prime Minister, are often the most revealing. But since the Prime Minister concerned himself only with the most important cases, his records are strikingly incomplete.

Ministries were involved in the ennoblement   process; in each of them several administrative departments were concerned, and the *curricula* concerning the candidates' lives and accomplishments are scattered quite unpredictably among the records of these numerous offices. Beyond this, whenever a family wished to acquire a new title, or to confirm an old patent of nobility, the old records were dug out in each ministry and filed under a new number, often without leaving a trace. Many ennoblement dossiers in the Archives are consequently empty. Finally, in many cases in the period of Dualism, which after all was liberal and non-bureaucratic on the whole, a great bulk of the materials submitted in an ennoblement process was returned to the candidate after the royal decision.

It is not only the difficulties of finding the material on the Jewish nobles which makes the Archival records somewhat fruitless for our purposes, however: the information there is also singularly irregular. Testing suggests that full use of the Archive material would produce incomplete data regarding even such matters as birthplace and family origin. In questions of property and of business connections the Archive would simply not provide information satisfying the sociological criterion of uniformity. Even a researcher who had the time and opportunity to examine the Archive fully would in such questions resort to published registers containing standardized economic data. In the preparation of the present study, where time and opportunity were limited, it seemed best to use the Archive as a supplementary rather than as the exclusive source of data.

For social and biographical information about the Jewish nobility the main sources used for this study, outside the Archive, are a number of published digests of the *King's Golden Book*, [3] the Jewish *Lexicon*, [4] and various other genealogical works. [5] Useful also have been the nume-

---

[3] Apart from the original register in the Archive building, there are three aids to use of the Golden Book of the Dualistic Era: Béla Kempelen, *Magyar nemesi almanach* [Hungarian Noble Almanach] (Budapest: 1910); József Gerő, *A királyi könyvek* [The King's Books] (Budapest: Belügyminisztérium, 1941); and József Gerő, *A magyar királyi belügyminiszter által igazolt nemesek*, 1867—1937 [Nobilities Confirmed by the Hungarian Minister of the Interior] (Budapest: Kovács és Szegedi, 1938).

[4] Péter Újváry, *A magyar zsidó lexikon* (Budapest: Pallas Nyomda, 1929).

[5] Kempelen's major work is *Magyar nemes családok* [Hungarian Noble Families] (11 volumes; Budapest: Károly Grill, 1911—1932). This superceded the old authority on the subject, Iván Nagy, *Magyarország családai czímerekkel* [Hungary's Families with Coats of Arms] (12 volumes; Pest: Mór Ráth, 1857—1865). See also Béla Kempelen, *Magyarországi zsidó és zsidóeredetű családok* [Hungary's Jewish and Jewish-Origin Families] (3 volumes; Budapest: Viktoria Nyomda, 1937—1939; and Zoltán Daróczy, *Nemesi Évkönyv* [Nobles Yearbook] (Budapest: May Nyomda Rt., 1923—1935).

rous biographical dictionaries of Hungarian public figures; [6] and newspaper obituaries. [7] An essential aid is a registry of name Magyarizations covering the period up to 1893. [8] A quantity of supplementary data emerges

[6] Apart from the *Országgyűlési almanach* (for variants of which see Chapter I, footnote 15 above), the more useful of these lexicons are József Szinnyei, *A magyar írók élete és munkái* [The Lives and Works of Hungarian Writers] (14 volumes; Budapest: Viktor Hornyánsky, 1891—1914); and the *Révai enciklopédia*, both of which were published in the large under the Monarchy and reflect contemporary views of who was important. Pál Gulyás, *Magyar életrajzi lexikon* [Hungarian Biographical Lexicon] (Budapest: Lántos, 1925—1929); and idem, *Magyar írók élete és munkái. Új sorozat*, are very useful attempts to bring Szinnyei up to date, interrupted unfortunately by the German invasion of Hungary in 1944. The bulk of Gulyás' work is in manuscript form at the Hungarian Academy of Sciences. A number of biographical dictionaries were published in Hungary between the wars. Among the more useful are: *A magyar társadalmi lexikon* [Hungarian Social Lexicon] (Budapest: 1930); *Ki kicsoda?* [Who's Who] (Budapest: Béta, n.d.); and *A magyar nemzetgazdasági enciklopédia* [Hungarian National Economic Encyclopedia] (Budapest: n.d.); Imre Gellért and Elemér Madarász, *Magyarország monográfiája, 1900—1932* [Monograph about Hungary] (Budapest: Europa Irodalmi Rt., 1932). These inter-war publications are of limited utility in connection with Jewish identities, because there was an editorial tendency to minimize the Jewish appearance of Hungarian society by omitting all but the most important Jews. The editorial tendencies of two major post-1945 lexicons likewise limits their utility to us: Marcel Benedek *et al.* (eds.), *Magyar irodalmi lexikon* [Lexicon of Hungarian Literature] (3 volumes; Budapest: Akadémia, 1963—1965); and Ágnes Kenyeres (ed.), *Új magyar életrajzi lexikon* [New Hungarian Biographical Lexicon] (one volume published; Budapest: Akadémia, 1967). Also useful are the volumes edited by Imre Guthi under the title *Fővárosi almanach* [Capital City Almanach] (Budapest: Légrády, 1904, 1910, 1916). Each of these contains identifications, which sometimes amount to biographies, of all 220 members of the Budapest elective Administrative Council. A comparable interwar collection is Endre György (ed.), *Amíg városatya lettem* [While I Became City Father] (Budapest: Biró Miklós, 1930). Four non-Hungarian encyclopedic efforts have been useful enough to bear mention: S. Winniger, *Grosse Jüdische National-Biographie* (5 volumes, published; Czernowitz: Arte, 1925—1931]; *Encyclopaedia Judaica* (10 volumes, published; Berlin: Eschkol, 1928—1934); *Österreichisches biographisches Lexikon* (5 volumes, published; Graz: Böhlau, 1957—1969); *Allgemeine-Deutsche Biographie* (56 volumes; Leipzig: Duncker & Humblot, 1875—1912).

[7] I have checked the obituaries in the major Jewish weekly the *Egyenlőség* between 1883 and 1896, and between 1917 and 1936. I have also read through the important financial weekly the *Pesti Tözsde* [Pest Stock Exchange] between 1919 and 1942. In other respects I have not had time to use this important sort of source material. There exists an obituary file in the National Széchenyi Library; but to use it one must know the day on which an individual died. This has been beyond my capacities. Another source I was unable to use is the records of the principal Jewish cemeteries in Budapest.

[8] A Magyar Heraldikai és Genealógiai Társaság, *Századunk névváltozásai* [Our Century's Name Changes] (Budapest: Viktor Hornyánsky, 1895). The period of mass name-changing came after 1895, however, and if one cannot find out about the change in one or another secondary record, one must rely on biennial reports issued by the Minister of the Interior, which are clumsy to use.

from such Jewish periodicals as the *Egyenlőség* [Equality] and the *Magyar Zsidó Szemle* [Hungarian Jewish Review], publications connected with the Pest Israelite Community; and from the Yearbooks of the Hungarian Jewish Literary Association. [9] The greatest difficulty in accumulating this sort of information regards religious affiliations. The Jewish Communities all over Hungary, and the Jewish Museum in Budapest, were stripped of their records on such matters by the Germans and Fascists in 1944. [10] Further, even before that they had dropped records on individuals who left Judaism. The best sources remaining about the religious affiliation of our noble families are four lists, published by the Neolog Jewish Community in Pest in the 1890's and in 1913, of those of its members who had the suffrage in community elections. [11] This was the largest and socially most fashionable community in Hungary. Absence from these lists is reasonably presumptive evidence, at least in the case of wealthy Budapest residents, of pre-1918 conversion out of Judaism.

For economic information this study relies principally on four sorts of extra-archival register. The first are lists which the Hungarian Government published in 1893, 1911, 1925, and 1935 of all the larger estates in the country, together with their size, economic character, and the names of their owners and renters. [12] The second are the business registers of

---

[9] These yearbooks bear the title *IMIT Évkönyv*.

[10] The Jewish Museum has immensely valuable records for the study of all Hungarian Jewry up to the middle of the nineteenth century, but nothing for the Dualistic Era. The Budapest Israelite Community has valuable raw materials for the inter-war period, but so far as I could learn, virtually everything from the Dualistic Era and from 1919—1920, the years of massive conversion, has been lost. The Jewish Rabbinical Seminary in Budapest has a rich library, but whatever raw materials it contains regarding late nineteenth-century Budapest Jewry are uncatalogued. I am indebted to Dr. Sándor Scheiber of the Seminary, and to Drs. Seifert, Imre and Ilona Benesovsky, and Apfel of the Budapest Community for help and advice in searching these institutions.

[11] These are catalogued in the Budapest collection of the Szabó Ervin Fővárosi Könyvtár in Budapest under the title: *A Pesti Chevra Kadisa Izraelita Szent Egylet tagok névsora* [List of Members of the Pest Israelite Chevra Kadisa] (Budapest: no publ., n.d. [1892?, 1896?, 1901?]; Pesti Chevra Kadisa, *A Pesti Chevra Kadisa választóképes tagjainak névjegyzéke, 1914* [The Roll of Ensuffraged Members of the Pest Chevra Kadisa] (Budapest: Pesti Lloyd Társasag Nyomda, 1914).

[12] Gyula Rubinek (ed.), *A magyar korona országainak... gazdacímtára* [Estate Directory of the Lands of the Hungarian Crown] (1st ed.; Budapest: Pesti Könyvny, 1897; 2nd ed., 1911); and *Magyarország földbirtokosai és földbérlői: Gazdacímtár* [Hungary's Landlords and Land Renters: Estate Directory] (Budapest: Statisztikai Hivatel, 1926, 1937). These registers list only a simple name and a town of residence; in cases of common names, this leads to confusion. Also when title was registered in a lady's name, or in the name of a junior member of a family, it is difficult to achieve exact identification.

Austria-Hungary and Hungary, the *Compass*, which listed annually from 1873 on the management and the financial standing of all the publicly-owned stock-companies and banks. [13] The third are the lists of 1,200 *virilists* or highest taxpayers, published annually prior to 1918 by the Budapest City Administration, [14] and lists, published by Dezső Zentai in 1936, 1941, and 1943, of interwar Hungary's highest taxpayers. [15] Finally, there are the annual lists published by the Hungarian Government of public office holders. [16] These, from the 1890's on, contain the names of the leaders of the Stock-Exchange, of the Hungarian Association of Manufacturers, and of other important economic organizations. Through circumspective use of these records, one may arrive at adequate and uniform definitions of the principal forms of wealth and economic power in Old Hungary: land, stocks, Budapest real-estate, and institutional prominence. [17]

The Jewish nobility contained an important contingent of cultural figures. For information about them there exists a very extensive bibliography; [18] an encyclopedic biographical dictionary; [19] and three major

[13] There were two *Compasses*. The first, which began publication in 1867 under the editorship of Gustav Leonhardt, and continued later under Rudolph Henel, was published annually under variations of the title: *Compass. Financielles Jahrbuch für Oesterreich-Ungarn* in Vienna. The 1913 and 1937 volumes are particularly useful, because of their name indices. The second *Compass* began under the editorship of Sándor Mihók in the early 1870's, and goes by the title *Mihók-féle Magyar Compasz*. This also was annual, although slightly irregular. Both continued in slightly varied form after 1918.

[14] Only two of these received wide publication. The first appeared in J. Lajos Máté (ed.), *Magyar almanach* (Budapest: A. Mezei, 1888); the second appeared in Imre Guthi (ed.), *Fővárosi almanach* [The Capital City's Almanac] (Budapest: Légrády, 1904). I have used the lists for the years 1908—1917 in a limited administrative edition available at the Museum of the History of Budapest. For description of these lists and evaluation of them as a record of real property holdings, see Károly Vörös, "Budapest legnagyobb adófizetői, 1903—1917" [Budapest's Highest Taxpayers], *Tanulmányok Budapest múltából*, Vol. XVII (1966), pp. 145—196, esp. footnote 6.

[15] Dezső Zentai, *Beszélő számok* [Telling Numbers] (12 volumes; Budapest: various presses, 1933—1943), Vols. IV, IX, and XII.

[16] The general title of these yearbooks is *Magyarország cím és névtára* [Hungary's Title and Name Register].

[17] This convention is accepted by economic historians of Hungary today.

[18] A comprehensive, though anti-Semitic, bibliography of Hungarian Jewry is in Mihály Kolozsváry-Borcsa, *A zsidó kérdés Magyarországi irodalma. A zsidóság szerepe a magyar szellemi életban. A zsidó származású írók névsorával* [The Hungarian Literature of the Jewish Question. The Role of the Jews in Hungarian Intellectual Life with a List of Names of Writers of Jewish Origin] (Budapest: Stádium, 194(1)).

[19] See above, footnote 6.

multi-volume literary histories. [20] The major problem of research in this area is the glut of available, but often useless or incorrect, information.

The origins and the ultimate fate of the Jewish noble families are far more difficult to discover than their identities, their public works, or their wealth. Uniform information about where the families came from is, indeed, simply unavailable. Exceptionally, one comes upon a register of family ancestors; but this occurs almost exclusively in cases where the ancestors were distinguished, and where the family came to Hungary in the eighteenth century or earlier. In only two cases in the entire Jewish nobility is it documented that the family came from Poland, where, as is known, the great bulk of European Jewry dwelt. To fill in this gap in our knowledge we are reduced to charting whether the families are first heard of in the West of Hungary near the Leitha frontier, or in the South, or near the Carpathian passes (see the tables in Chapter III).

Comparably, the Jewish noble families tend to disappear from the historical stage after 1918, and it is only exceptionally that we can tell precisely what happened to them during and after the second World War. The fault here is in part the relative inaccessibility of the Hungarian National Archive to American researchers of the inter-war period. [21] Equally contributive, however, is the fact that after 1918 the Jews who had acquired nobility began rapidly to die out. In very many cases there were no children, or the children were less talented and less ambitious than their fathers, decided not to enter public life, and as a result left no records. Coincidentally, in 1919 and 1920 there was a massive wave of conversions out of Judaism among wealthy families. Contingent on this was a great deal of name changing and deliberate expunging of the past, trends which are difficult to follow in public records. [22] Meanwhile, political and economic develop-

---

[20] The more important lengthy prewar literary histories are Jenő Pintér, *Pintér Jenő magyar irodalom története* [Pinter's History of Hungarian Literature] (8 volumes; Budapest: Stephaneum, 1930—1941]; and a series by Gyula Farkas, of which the most important for our purposes are *A "Fiatal Magyarország" kora* [The "Young Hungary" Era] (Budapest: Magyar Szemle Társaság, 1932); and *Az asszimiláció kora* [The Assimilation Era] (Budapest: Franklin, 193—). In the past decade the Hungarian academy has published a massive new literary history, *Magyar irodalom története* (6 volumes; Budapest: Akadémia, 1960—1967).

[21] This is not to suggest that Americans cannot obtain access to the interwar Archives. Some have, and more will. But the problems of access have hitherto been considerable.

[22] There is some evidence that the Jews themselves lost track of their renegades in 1919 and 1920, when conversions were permitted without registration at the Jewish Communities. I have, for example, seen the names of György Lukács and Lajos Hatvany in a massive register of the Pest Chevra Kadisa for the year 1923!

ments took their toll. The noble families who lived in the lands Hungary lost at Trianon are on the whole difficult to follow without visits to Czechoslovakia, Rumania, Yugoslavia, and Austria. The families which went bankrupt and those which emigrated, likewise, have disappeared from the records available in Budapest. And, finally, no record was kept at Auschwitz. [23] In determining the fate of the Jewish nobles, therefore, we are dependent on some published lists of people who were arrested in 1944; [24] on some selective lists of people who survived the catastrophe; [25] on some interesting lexicons of Hungarians who live today in America; [26] and on a quantity of miscellaneous information.

---

[23] There exists at the Budapest Israelite Community a huge typewritten list of all the Jews who remained in Hungary at the end of the war. Because of name changes, the postwar abolition of noble titles, and the overwhelming changes in residence, however, it seemed impractical to try and locate in it the members of noble families. The nearest estimate I have found of how terrible the losses were in the Jewish nobility is a report on the losses in the *Lipótvárosi Casino* to which many Jewish nobles traditionally belonged. In 1941 there were 1800 members. By 1946 1125 were dead. This record probably affords a conservative picture of the losses among Jews at this social level, because there was a strong contingent of non-Jews in the casino. See the report by István Lengyel in *Képes Figyelő* [Pictorial Observer], 1947, no. 6, p. 19.

[24] Some of these are published in Elek Karsai and Ilona Benesovsky (eds.), *Vádirat a nácizmus ellen* [Indictment Against Nazism] (3 volumes; Budapest: M. Izr. Orsz. Képviselete, 1958, 1960, 1967); Jenő Lévai, *Zsidósors Magyarországon* [The Fate of he Jews in Hungary] (Budapest: Magyar Téka, 1948); and Randolph L. Braham (ed.), *The Destruction of Hungarian Jewry* (2 volumes; New York: World Federation of Hungarian Jews, 1963).

[25] For example, Gyula Turcsányi (ed.), *Kivel mi történt* [What Happened to Whom] (Budapest: Légrády, 194—).

[26] See Tibor Szy, *Hungarians in America* (New York: Hungarian University Association, 1963); and Sándor Incze (ed.), *Magyar album* (Elmhurst, Ill.: American Studies Foundation, 1956).

SUBJECT INDEX

Academy of Sciences, 77, 80, 212.

Anti-Semitism, German, 91, 100, 129, 203—205, 219—220; in Hungary, 19, 36, 64—65, 91, 102, 105, 129, 164, 185, 199—200, 207—208, 220—221.

Archival Sources, 18, 21, 238—241.

Army: as political factor, 124, 127, 170; share in ennoblement, 130; supplying as source of wealth, 59, 122, 127, 131—132, 148, 187—188.

Assimilation. See Germanization, Magyarization, Magyars.

Ausgleich, Austro-Hungarian, 33, 120, 124—125, 170—174; economic, 128, 146, 193.

Austria: political development of, 124—128, 171, 175.

Balkans: trade with, 54ff, 59ff, 145, 153, 157, 188.

Bank aristocracy, 41—43.

Banks, Viennese, 53—54, 116—117, 119, 138, 149—152, 154—157; Hungarian, 26—27, 42—43, 61, 116, 147, 148—158, 183, 188; as entrepreneurs, 150.

Bohemia-Moravia: Jews from, 55—56, 61, 63—65, 82, 89, 134, 148, 154.

Bourgeoisie, Hungarian: development of, 91, 118—120, 182—186; problems facing, 59—61, 65—67, 84—85, 180ff, 191ff; burgher spirit in, 88—89, 140—142, 151—152, 179; feudalization of, 17, 36—37, 43—44, 60—61, 186, 228—229.

Brain drain, 217.

Budapest: economy in mid-century, 115—116, 143; sudden growth of, 31, 66—67, 114, 138, 140—141, 157—158, 183; Jews in, 30, 39, 130; reform in, 200, 201, 203ff. See also Young Budapest.

Coalition, 171ff, 202—203; social forces behind, 184.

Cabinet of Ministers: Jews in, 179—180, 192.

Congress, Jewish, 88, 92—94, 132.

Economy, Hungarian: pre-1848, 53—58; mid-century, 114—118; role of state in, 121, 131—133, 146—147, 189—190; role of foreign capital in, 117—118, 133, 157; role of agriculture in, 116—117, 132—142; crash of 1873, 134, 144; war-economy, 189—190. See also Balkan trade, Banks, Budapest, Grain trade, Industries, Railroads, Stock-exchange, "Take-off."

Emigration, 217—222.

Ennoblement: in Austria, 20, 123—125; in Hungary: process, 33, ftn. 21, 38, ftn. 35, 178; as Magyar nationalism, 75—80; chronology of, 122ff; relation to politics, 124—135, 172—180; Jewish part in, 130.

Estate acquisition by Jews, 53, 60, 118—119, 133—135, 184—186.

Galilei Circle, 73, 108.

Genius: definition of, 22—23.

"Gentry" idea, 100—103.

Germanization, 89—91, 95, 191.

243

NAME INDEX *

Adelsberg-Nemeshegyi, 143, 148.
Ady, Endre, 44—45, 71, 107—108; *Nacionalismus alkonya*, 202.
Ágoston, Péter, 105, 207; *Zsidók útja*, 105.
Alexander, Bernát, 161; Franz, 15, 160—165, 215; *Western Mind*, 161.
Allen, Dr. Richard, 207.
Altmann-Hahn, *czacsai*, 177.
Ambrus, Zoltán, *Berzsenyi Báró*, 36.
Andics, Erzsébet, *M. nacionalizmus*, 76.
Andrássy, Count Gyula, Sr., 77, 95, 96; Gyula, Jr., 46, 176, 192, 193.
Apponyi, Count Albert, 77, 96, 176, 193.
Arányi-Losteiner, Lajos György, 20.
Arató, Endre, *Nemzetiségi kérdés*, 82.
Arnstein, Freiherr von, 53.

Bachruch, *királykúti*, 178.
Back, *bégavári*, 173, 177.
Bailyn, Bernard, *Intellectual Migration* 222.
Balassa, Imre, "Nagy kalmárok," 119; "Elek Pál," 153.
Balázs, *verőczei*, 129.
Balla, Vilmos, *Vadember*, 134.
Ballagi-Bloch, Mór, 80—83, 84, 96.
Balogh, Thomas, 214.
Bandholz, Harry, *Undiplomatic Diary*, 16.
Bánki, Donát, 213.
Barany, George, "Hungarian Nationalism," 76.
Barea, Ilse, *Vienna*, 53.
Baronyi, *csángóhétfalusi*, 122.
Barta, Stefan, *Judenfrage*, 36.

Bartha, Miklós, 64; *Kazár földön*, 65.
Bartók, Béla, 23.
Baruch, *felsőványi*, 122.
Basch family, 140.
Basch-Földváry, *kisrédei*, 35.
Beck, Karl, 83—85.
Beck, *madarasi*, Barons, 83; Hugó, 196; Lajos, 179, 196—198, 206; Miksa, 196; Nándor, 173.
Behrmann, S., "Ferenc Molnár," 72.
Beke, Emanuel, 213.
Békésy, George von, 23, 216.
Beksics, Gusztáv, 97.
Belatiny-Braun family, 19, 35.
Benedek, Marcel, *M. Irodalmi Lexikon*, 70.
Benedikt, Heinrich, *Wirtschaftliche Entwicklung*, 113; "Schey," 123.
Benesovsky, Ilona, 238; *Vádirat*, 241; Dr. Imre, 238.
Berend, T. Iván, *M. gyáripara — 1944*, 16; *M. gyáripara — 1914*, 31; *Középkelet Európa*, gazdasági fejlödése, 113; "Economic Factors," 182; *Csepel*, 187.
Bernstein, Béla, *1848 m. szabadságharc*, 75.
Bethlen, Pál, *Numerus Clausus*, 208.
Bettelheim, Samu, "Lackó," 38.
Bibó, István, "Zsidókérdés," 35.
Biedermann family, 36, 56—57, 122, 172; Gustav von, 57; Hersch Freistädtler, 56; Michel Lazar, 56—57; Baron Rudolf, 172; Baron Simon, 57.

---

* Includes reference to the main entry of all works cited in footnotes.